*Racial* TRANSFORMATIONS

# *Racial* TRANSFORMATIONS

*Latinos and Asians*
*Remaking the United States*

Edited by Nicholas De Genova

Duke University Press
Durham and London 2006

© 2006 Duke University Press

All rights reserved

Printed in the United States of America
on acid-free paper ∞

Designed by Heather Hensley

Typeset in Bembo by Keystone
Typesetting, Inc.

Library of Congress Cataloging-in-
Publication Data appear on the last
printed page of this book.

# Contents

# Acknowledgments

Some intellectual dialogues can be realized only at the intersections of research and arguments that have previously been effectively segregated into their respectively concealed corners of mutual unfamiliarity. Yet, in the wake of such an encounter, it becomes frankly incomprehensible to fathom how such a dialogue could ever have been so elusive, how such palpable comparisons and pertinent analogies could have been so sorely neglected, and how such fields of scholarly inquiry and exchange could ever have been so thoroughly obstructed and, by all appearances, systematically partitioned. It has been my precious opportunity and rare privilege to be able to facilitate the advancement of such a seemingly counterintuitive but desperately needed intersection—that between Latino and Asian American studies. The scholars whose work I have been fortunate to coordinate here are contributing in fundamental ways, through their boldly creative research and conceptual *practice*, to the larger ongoing project of subverting the veritable balkanization of the various ethnic studies fields that together have played such vital but often disjointed, if not divergent, roles in problematizing and critiquing the centrality of white supremacy in the historical and contemporary constitution of the United States as a nation-state and social formation.

Like many other edited collections, this one is a result of the intellectual excitement and synergy originally generated by an academic conference. This book grew out of the conference of roughly the same title that took place on 1–2 March 2002, which I organized for the Center for the Study of Ethnicity and Race at Columbia University, with the cosponsorship of the Asian/Pacific/American Institute at New York University and the Centro de Estudios Puertorriqueños/Center for Puerto Rican Studies, Latin American and Caribbean Studies Program, and Asian American Studies Program at Hunter College of the City University of New York. Gary Okihiro, the director of the Center at Columbia, deserves a special note of appreciation for having originally suggested the thematic focus for the gathering and for having thus entrusted me with the responsibility for making the event happen. The actual conference that eventually ensued was incredibly memorable, owing to the impressive originality and intelligence of everyone who presented papers (including six of those included as chapters of this book) as well as the passionate engagement of those who served as panel facilitators or participated from the audience in the relatively long discussions following the formal presentations.

In the intervening three years, despite a variety of quite extraordinary and unanticipated difficulties followed by rather more mundane but inevitable obstacles and delays, my contributors' constant and unwavering confidence in the merit of this project has been a source of tremendous gratification. I am acutely aware of how very fortunate I have been to enjoy the enduring commitment and resolve of everyone whose work has enriched this volume. Collaborating with them has been its own unique reward.

A special note of my deepest gratitude is owed to James Warren, who originally sought to publish this collection with Columbia University Press, for his remarkable integrity and support. Ultimately, however, this book found a rather more felicitous home with a publisher notably distinguished for its admirable lists in American studies, ethnic studies, Latino and Latin American studies, and Asian American studies as well. My contributors and I are proud to see our contributions in this collection appear alongside the works of so many fine scholars who have published with Duke University Press.

I am confident that I speak for all the contributors to this book in expressing my sincere appreciation to Ken Wissoker and genuine delight that he was prepared to move with such determination to usher this collection into print and that we have enjoyed the exceptionally good fortune of seeing the project come to fruition with Duke. In his energy and enthusiasm for this project, Ken exhibited all the characteristic and extraordinary acumen for which he is deservedly renowned as an editor. Likewise, in her capacity as Ken's editorial assistant, Anitra Sumaya Grisales displayed a veritable devotion to her work—indubitably yet another blessing in the genesis of this collection.

Finally, I and all the contributors to this volume are honored to share these pages with the late Toni Robinson (1942–2002), whose participation in the original "Racial (Trans)Formations" conference was among her last public acts as a scholar. Toni's coauthored chapter in this book is among the first academic publications to emerge from an ambitious intellectual agenda that she was cultivating at the end of her life, an agenda based on her practical knowledge of the law and her enduring commitment to the struggle for social justice. Her work and her example remain a vital inspiration for us all.

# INTRODUCTION

*Latino and Asian Racial Formations*
*at the Frontiers of U.S. Nationalism*

Nicholas De Genova

Next to the case of the black race within our bosom, that of the red on our borders is the problem most baffling to the policy of our country.

—JAMES MADISON TO THOMAS L. MCKENNEY (1826)

As the color of our skin began to confuse the color line drawn tyrannically between blacks and whites in the United States—segregated in the respective corners of their misplaced confidence about their races—we Asians and Latinos, Arabs, Turks, Africans, Iranians, Armenians, Kurds, Afghans and South Asians were instantly brought together beyond the uncommon denominator of our origin and towards the solidarity of our emerging purpose.

—HAMID DABASHI, "THE MOMENT OF MYTH" (2003)

There is a key to unlocking the hegemonic polarity of whiteness and Blackness that has so enduringly distinguished the racial order of the United States, especially as that tyrannically drawn binary has defined the decisive parameters for the racializations of "Latinos" and "Asians" and all other groups historically racialized as neither white nor Black. That key is to be found in the history of the U.S. nation-state's subjugation of Native Americans.

From his vantage point as a "founding father" and the fourth president of the United States, James Madison's formulation about the vexations presented for "the policy of *our* country" by the "black" and "red" races recalls to mind, not simply that white supremacy supplied the bedrock of U.S. nation-state formation, but moreover that the foundations of racism were devised not singularly around the enslavement of Africans and the denigration of racial Blackness but also by the genocidal dispossession and colonization of American Indians. Madison's elegant turn of phrase invites us to revisit the precise meaning of his implicit but self-consciously white U.S. nationalism and its two-sided formulation of the racial "problem" as one that was posed with respect to both its "bosom" and its "borders," in relation to both an "inside" and an "outside." This originary triangulation of whiteness with the subordination of *both*

Blacks and Indians demands a reconsideration of how it has been possible historically for this racial triangle to be so thoroughly and effectively reduced to a mere binary.

In the effort to resolve this puzzle, it is, of course, insufficient to seek dubious comfort in the reassurance that the ideological disappearance of the Native American third term was nothing more than an inevitable consequence of the real annihilation of indigenous humanity. Such a proposition, after all, could only be an unwitting endorsement of the "fantasies of the master race," to borrow a phrase from Ward Churchill, inasmuch as it would be tantamount to maintaining that genocide simply settled the matter, as if mass slaughter ever accomplished the end of absolute extermination and extinction.[1] Contrary to that most central ambition of what Herman Melville memorably called "the metaphysics of Indian-hating," even centuries of relentless warfare and colonization were nonetheless inadequate to the murderous task of genuinely eliminating Native Americans altogether.[2] Furthermore, such an awkward complicity with the literal as well as ideological "removal" of the Indians likewise signals an analogous collusion with that distinctive historical amnesia that William Appleman Williams has incisively identified as "one of the central themes of American historiography . . . that there is no American Empire."[3] If it became tenable historically to conveniently forget the extermination of the indigenous peoples, doing so likewise reinforced the myth that the North American continent had really been empty all along and was, in effect, the rightful and preordained inheritance of the U.S. "nation"—its purported Manifest Destiny. Indeed, if the restlessly imperial character of the U.S. nation-state is abundantly manifest and indisputable in the face of the history of American Indian displacement and colonization, then the ideological hegemony of a Black-white racial binary is exposed as an *effect* of precisely this double erasure.

Madison's remark is instructive, furthermore, in that it reminds us that the U.S. social order of white supremacy may have been always premised on racial Blackness as its own utterly degraded bottom, indeed, its absolute antithesis, but in a manner that was strictly *internal* to the ongoing constitution of an "American" national society. Forged through chattel slavery, whereby African Americans were denied any semblance of juridical personhood or collective representation and were generally compelled to exist as the mere property of white men, racial Blackness could be figured as a wholly owned subsidiary, possessed by, subjected to, and fully encompassed *within* an "American" social

NICHOLAS DE GENOVA

order of white power and prestige. Throughout the nineteenth century, however, that presumed inside, which was systematically elaborated along this defining white-Black axis of racialized dominance and subjugation, was always already coupled with an equally defining and highly articulated awareness of its own inexorable expansiveness and the ever-advancing frontier beyond which it always confronted an outside. That outside, of course, was preeminently identified with Indian "savages" and, thus, taken to be racially "alien," culturally inferior, intrinsically hostile, menacing, and ripe for conquest. Rather than the despicable bottom of white "American" society, however, Native Americans were despised as its inimical and incorrigible outsiders who could never be incorporated into white "civilization" and so were condemned to extinction. In his discussion of race in *Democracy in America* (1835/1840), uncritically embracing the common sense of the U.S. whites whom he otherwise seeks to scrutinize, Alexis de Tocqueville declares baldly: "I think that the Indian race is doomed to perish, and I cannot prevent myself from thinking that on the day when the Europeans shall be established on the coasts of the Pacific Ocean, it will cease to exist." In contrast, Tocqueville affirms: "[T]he fate of the Negroes is in a sense linked with that of the Europeans. The two races are bound one to the other without mingling."[4] The long-standing common sense about the U.S. racial order as one wholly or primarily apprehensible in Black and white has, therefore, always been inherently confined to the premises of U.S. nationalism's own hegemonic self-understanding about its putative inside and outside. Upholding one of the most cherished conceits of U.S. imperialism itself, the one-sidedness of such an angle of vision on U.S. racism also serves to obscure the racialization of all manner of nonwhiteness that has come to be variously figured as "foreign" and identified with the alien wilderness beyond the borders of "American" nationhood.

The ideological contrast between African American slavery as a type of abject domestication and American Indian "savagery" as an irreducible "foreign"-ness intrinsically relegated to a space beyond the frontier and essentially inimical to white "civilization" and capitalist "modernity" likewise has profound ramifications. If Indians were presumed to be an endangered species of humanity, irrevocably slated for extinction in the face of white civilization owing to their irremediably anachronistic savage cultures, the integration of enslaved Blacks into that same white-supremacist social order, albeit only on terms of complete subordination, was premised on the supposition that every last vestige of their own cultural specificities, any shred of Africanity, had been effectively obliterated. Thus, in his landmark *Slavery and Social Death*, Orlando Patterson identifies "natal alienation" as the definitive centerpiece of slavery's cultural politics of authority, by which the social death of slaves is distinguished by "the loss of ties of birth in both ascending and descending generations" and "a loss of native status . . . deracination." Slaves could be reduced to "the ultimate human tool" for their master, Patterson continues, only if they were systematically alienated not only "from all formal, legally enforceable ties of 'blood,' " but also "from any attachment to groups or localities other than those chosen for [them] by the master."[5]

Again, Tocqueville is revealing in the extent to which he captures and recapitulates the racist common sense of the era:

> In one blow oppression has deprived the descendants of the Africans of almost all the privileges of humanity. The United States Negro has lost even the memory of his homeland; he no longer understands the language his fathers spoke; he has abjured their religion and forgotten their mores. Ceasing to belong to Africa, he has acquired no right to the blessings of Europe; he is left in suspense between two societies and isolated between two peoples, sold by one and repudiated by the other; in the whole world there is nothing but his master's hearth to provide him with some semblance of a homeland.[6]

Blacks might be construed as racially inferior, in a "natural" and immutable condition that was alternately cast as indelibly "childish" or "savage," but anything that might connote the cultural integrity of a specifically *African* savagery was widely considered to have been successfully eradicated.[7] Tocqueville repeatedly underscores the apparent bifurcation between the respective predicaments of African Americans and Indians, and the distinction is especially pronounced around precisely this question of "cultural"-ness: "In contrast the pretended nobility of his origins fills the whole imagination of the Indian. . . . Far from wishing to adapt his mores to ours, he regards barbarism as the distinctive emblem of his race. . . . The North American native preserves his opinions and even the slightest details of his customs with an inflexibility otherwise unknown throughout history."[8] While indubitably homogenized as a generically contemptible racial type (*Indians*), Native Americans, for as long as their colonization remained an ongoing project yet to be achieved, were, nevertheless, also consistently sorted and ranked according to their particulari-

NICHOLAS DE GENOVA

ties as discrete "tribes" with distinct forms of social and political organization.[9] Whereas the subordination of African Americans involved rendering racial Blackness bereft of any cultural specificity or integrity, the racialization of Indians could, therefore, be internally differentiated and refracted according to their diverse nationalities.[10] In short, the alterity of Native Americans was always saturated with an excess of "culture," figured as an inscrutable foreignness impervious, if not actively hostile, to any prospect of "assimilation."[11] When the assimilation of Native Americans later became an avowed aim of U.S. policy following the General Allotment (Dawes) Act of 1887, notably, such putative assimilation was quite explicitly equated with the annihilation of Indians *as Indians* and was conjoined to a project whose purpose was the effective decimation of tribal sovereignty as such by extending U.S. citizenship to Native Americans as individuals on the basis of their status as the virtual owners of a kind of pseudoprivate property in Indian land on reservations.[12]

Despite the desire of former British colonists and their inheritors to boldly assert their "American"-ness in defiance of their European patrimony and as an emblem of their national independence and republican self-government, U.S. nationalism's very appropriation for itself of "American"-ness as its exclusive "national" identity could never be other than a European settler-state's imperial gesture of usurpation. U.S. "American"-ness was the expression of a white nationalism, first with respect to the indigenous nations of the North American continent, whom it disparaged as mere tribes and expelled to a condition of utter marginalization, and then in relation to all the societies of Latin America and the Caribbean.[13] Indeed, already as early as 1823, the Monroe Doctrine had declared that all the newly independent nations of the Americas would thenceforth be presumptively considered by the U.S. nation-state to constitute its own exclusive sphere of influence and interest, such that any intervention by European imperial powers anywhere in the Western Hemisphere would be taken as "an unfriendly disposition toward the United States" and its own "rights," "peace," "happiness," "safety," and "defense."[14] Not long thereafter, when the United States instigated a war of conquest against Mexico in 1846, leading to the colonization of roughly half its national territory and the subjugation of the newly conquered land's resident population, the palpable salience of the Indian wars for the U.S. military's orientation to its frontiers led ineffably to the racialization of Mexicans as "savage," "barbarous," or, at best, little more than "half-civilized" Indians and degraded racial "mongrels."[15]

Indeed, the U.S. Senate had debated the annexation of the entirety of Mexico and the "removal" of the majority of the population (those deemed not to be white) to Indian reservations, but the prospect of becoming ensnared in a protracted guerrilla war in the effort to colonize the more densely populated portion of the country commanded a somewhat less ambitious conquest.[16]

Once the superintendent of the U.S. Bureau of the Census announced in 1891 that a "frontier line" between areas of white settlement and Native American wilderness, as measured by population density within the territory of the continental United States, had effectively vanished and that the "internal" frontier was, thus, officially closed,[17] the presumed Manifest Destiny that had inexorably driven the U.S. settler-state west across the North American continent to the Pacific Ocean left it similarly poised for still more conquests in Asia and Latin America. In the years immediately following that momentous pronouncement, U.S. political intrigues and military interventions in Nicaragua, Colombia/Panama, Honduras, Samoa, and Wake, military intervention in Hawaii leading to its subsequent annexation, and the Spanish-American War of 1898—culminating in the invasion and occupation of Cuba, the colonization of Puerto Rico and Guam, and the brutal subjugation of the national liberation movement in the Philippines and these islands' subsequent colonization—all bolstered the triumphalism of the United States as an ascendant global power. Following the U.S. defeat of Spain and the acquisition of new colonies in Latin America and Asia, Albert Beveridge, in his first speech as a U.S. senator from Indiana in 1900, became a national sensation when he affirmed that the colonial question transcended all political and legal considerations because it was a matter of preordained Anglo-Saxon "racial" vocation: "God . . . has made us the master organizers of the world to establish system where chaos reigns . . . that we may administer government among savage and senile peoples. . . . And of all our race He has marked the American people as His chosen nation to finally lead in the regeneration of the world."[18] In recognition of his boldly racist and ambitiously colonialist millenarian vision, Beveridge was assigned his proper place on the senatorial committee that would oversee the colonization of Puerto Rico and the Philippines. Similarly, the Wall Street banker and U.S. senator Chauncey Depew declared the Pacific Ocean to have been reduced to "an American lake" and confidently proclaimed: "The world is ours."[19] So began what would later be dubbed "the American Century."[20]

NICHOLAS DE GENOVA

These imperial adventures would be readily, almost seamlessly, apprehensible in the same racialized political idiom that had served to rationalize Native American colonization. "All along, the obverse of Indian-hating had been the metaphysics of empire-building," Richard Drinnon has argued. "If the West was at bottom a form of society . . . then on our round earth, Winning the West amounted to no less than winning the world."[21] Indeed, Drinnon convincingly demonstrates that U.S. wars in Asia over the course of the twentieth century—beginning with the ruthless war against the independence struggle of the Philippines and culminating with that conflict's ghastly reincarnation in Vietnam—persistently had recourse to the full battery of ideological weapons as well as practical military strategies and tactics that had first been devised in the genocidal dispossession and racial oppression of the American Indians. The U.S. nation-state's invasions and occupations, perpetrated variously against Mexico, Cuba, Puerto Rico, Haiti, the Dominican Republic, and Panama, as well as the diverse assortment of imperial exploits, military interventions, and covert operations throughout Latin America during both the nineteenth and the twentieth centuries, necessarily relied on that same arsenal. In many of these instances, even the personnel were the same. This is not to pretend that the histories of Latinos' and Asians' relations to the U.S. nation-state and its imperialist expansion have been distinguished by the same singular and monumental fact of genocide that has been such a defining feature of the Native American experience (although, in some episodes, such as the atrocity-ridden suppression of Filipino national aspirations, there was, indeed, an uncanny resemblance).[22] But it is, nonetheless, to insist on the central significance and enduring meaningfulness for Latinos and Asians of imperialist warfare, conquest, and colonization as the elementary means by which the U.S. nation-state has so commonly sought to dominate the "savage" and "barbarous" "alien races" that it confronted on its ever-expansive and increasingly virtual frontiers. The proverbial "red" race on the borders that so baffled the policy of Madison's United States inevitably supplied the paragon and the paradigm for how the U.S. nation-state and its military would contend with intractable "natives" wherever they presented an obstruction to the progress of U.S. prerogatives. Hence, that red race likewise necessarily provides a critical conceptual key that unlocks a variegated spectrum of "browns" and "yellows."

While it is certainly necessary to attend to the respectively irreducible particularities of the specific historical experiences of all the groups that have come to be crudely homogenized under the generic racial umbrellas *Native Americans*, *Latinos*, and *Asians*, it is, nevertheless, productive to emphasize the broad analogies that reveal compelling continuities among these experiences because such comparisons facilitate theorizing the social relations that historically conjoin them despite their apparent divergences. If it seems somewhat far-fetched to press these analogies, one need only be reminded of the challenge of producing an analysis that could account for the following examples. In 1854, in the legal case *People v. Hall*, the California Supreme Court upheld the appeal of a white defendant who challenged his conviction for murder on the grounds that the case had relied exclusively on the testimony of a Chinese witness and that such testimony ought to have been impermissible because an 1850 statute had established that "no Black, or Mulatto person, or Indian shall be allowed to give evidence in favor of, or against a White man." The court ruled that *Black* was a sufficiently capacious term that it could encompass all nonwhites in any event. Specifically, however, the court reasoned that Indians originally had migrated to the New World from Asia and that, in effect, all Asians were, therefore, conversely Indians.[23] Such simpleminded racist reasoning was, of course, not the exclusive purview of U.S. jurisprudence. As early as the sixteenth and seventeenth centuries, speculative theories concerning the origins of the indigenous peoples of the Americas became inextricably interwoven with a great variety of competing raciological claims as to the "Asiatic" character of the aboriginal Americans. Across the convoluted terrain extending from biblical anthropological notions of human monogenesis and racial degeneration, through scientific racism's assertions of polygenesis and the immutable stability of a more or less restricted number of discrete and identifiable biological "races" and philology's confabulations of circuitous racial genealogies evidenced in linguistic resemblances, to the nineteenth- and twentieth-century physical anthropological syntheses distinguished by muddled concepts of the dispersion and diffusion not only of human cultural and linguistic but also of *biological* "traits" (see Jew, chapter 3 in this volume), one or another theory of the Asian origins of American Indians has persistently contended for primacy in the dreary but incessant efforts to produce expressly raciological catalogs of humankind.[24]

Within these same racial inventories, Latin Americans came to be pervasively racialized as the characteristically "hybrid" products of centuries of "miscegenation" under Spanish and Portuguese colonial rule (see Jew, chapter

3, and Okihiro, chapter 1 in this volume). Thus, Latinos were identified with a racial condition intrinsically anathema to the entrenched and obsessive segregationist prohibitions in the United States against racial "mixing" and intermarriage. In the case of Mexicans and many other Latinos, the despised figure of the Indian savage was routinely foregrounded as a crucial resource for their distinctive denigration as racial mongrels, the worst common denominator that remained as the debased refuse of their constituent parts.[25] Thus, one encounters a revealing corollary to the nineteenth-century case of *People v. Hall* in the infamous "Sleepy Lagoon" trial in Los Angeles in 1942, in which twenty-two U.S.-born Mexican youths were alleged to be members of a "gang" and collectively accused of criminal conspiracy to commit murder (see Jew, chapter 3, and Robinson and Robinson, chapter 4 in this volume). A special committee of the grand jury accepted an "expert" report prepared by the "*Foreign Relations*" Bureau of the county sheriff's department concerning Mexican criminality. The chief of the bureau, Captain Ed Ayres, himself partly of Mexican heritage, was officially designated the author of the report. "When engaged in fighting," the report asserted, ". . . [the Mexican's] desire is to kill, or at least let blood. That is why it is difficult for the Anglo-Saxon to understand the psychology of the Indian or even the Latin." This bloodthirsty impulse attributed to Mexicans, thus figured as simultaneously Latino and Native American, was depicted as an "inborn characteristic that has come down through the ages."[26] Such innate criminality and cruelty in Mexicans could be traced, the report contended, to the Aztecs' reputed proclivities for human sacrifice.[27] Indeed, the report asserted not only that Mexicans were really mere Indians at heart but furthermore that, as Indians, they were essentially "Orientals" and, thus, were distinguished by an incorrigible disregard for human life.[28]

These pronouncements were, after all, generated in the context of the U.S. race war against Japan over imperial primacy in the Pacific and in the aftermath of the Pearl Harbor suicide bombings.[29] Later, when the fascist propaganda outlets Radio Berlin and Radio Tokyo cited the Ayres Report as evidence that the United States actually upheld the same sort of racial doctrines as Hitler, the enigmatic response of Captain Ayres was to make allegations that the southern California Japanese—prior to being evacuated for summary incarceration ("internment") in wartime concentration camps (see Robinson and Robinson, chapter 4 in this volume)—had actually incited Mexicans to violence.[30] Thus, the figure of the Indian provided the pivotal link in the lethal nexus of racialized associations that made it possible to mobilize the patriotic conceits of U.S. imperialism's warfare in Asia for the oppression of Latinos within the United States and, likewise, to insinuate phantasmagoric racial conspiracies between Latinos and Asians in the United States as nonwhite "aliens" in the service of a foreign enemy (cf. Levine, chapter 6, and Parikh, chapter 7 in this volume).[31]

To discern the critical significance of Native American racialization as a decisive ideological template in the material and practical subordination of Latinos and Asians is not, however, to deny or trivialize the very salient analogies that could, likewise, be drawn between African American experiences of enslavement and subsequently reconstructed servitude and the colonial migration systems that subordinated the labor of Asians (especially Chinese, then Japanese and Koreans, and later Filipinos and South Asians) and Latinos (especially Mexicans, Cubans, and Puerto Ricans) in the era prior to the 1965 reconfiguration of the U.S. immigration and naturalization regime (see Jew, chapter 3, and Robinson and Robinson, chapter 4 in this volume). Both prior to and after the abolition of African American slavery, the "free labor" ideology persistently celebrated the republican virtues of white workingmen by projecting "slavishness" and "servility" on all those racialized as something other than white, who were then perniciously judged incapable of self-control, "unfit" for self-government, and systematically subjected to the most merciless exploitation.[32] In this context, there were also sometimes substantial analogies between the racialization of Asians or Latinos and that of African American Blackness, including the facility with which the term *nigger* could be deployed, for example, to disparage such disparate racial targets as Chinese migrant workers in California and Filipino natives during the U.S. invasion (see Okihiro, chapter 1 in this volume).[33] Indeed, in contradistinction to so many overtly racist justifications for U.S. colonial expansion, one of the explicit white-supremacist articulations of "*anti*-imperialism"—predictably most vocal among some Southern segregationists during debates over the annexation of the entirety of Mexico or the colonization of Cuba, Puerto Rico, Guam, and the Philippines—was, simply enough, in the blunt words of Major General John Dickman while stationed in U.S.-occupied Cuba, that the United States "has too many niggers already."[34] While the analogies between the Latino or Asian experience of racial oppression in the United States and that of African Americans are compelling and instructive, there is a danger nonetheless that

NICHOLAS DE GENOVA

such recourse serves to reinstate Blackness as a singular template for comprehending the workings of white supremacy in the United States and, thereby, inadvertently to recapitulate precisely the timeworn Black-white binary as well as the "American exceptionalist" elision of U.S. imperialism with which it is entangled, which I have sought to problematize. If it is indisputably true that white supremacy in the United States has long relegated Latinos and Asians to a racial terrain of nonwhiteness that they inevitably share with African Americans and that, thus, positions them in a complex, contradictory, but still substantial relation to Blackness, it is likewise the case that they are situated in a comparably complicated but meaningful relation to that other antithesis of whiteness—the "red" racial borderland of Native Americans.

Precisely because of the profound differences and divergences historically between the racial predicaments of American Indians and those of Blacks, Madison's proverbial "border" and "bosom," the Native American analogy is indispensable in theorizing Latino and Asian racial formations. Whether as racialized labor migrations or colonized subject populations, Latinos and Asians have long played crucial roles in the social production of "America" and "American"-ness. Both Latin America and Asia, as well as Latinos and Asians within the United States, have been central to the consolidation of historical projects of U.S. nation-state formation and empire-building. Yet, insofar as they have largely been rendered racially legible either as the natives of foreign lands or as immigrant and alien border-crossers, their respective racialized conditions of nonwhiteness have been constructed, like that of Native Americans, to be essentially not "American" at all. Like American Indians, therefore, and in marked contradistinction to African Americans, Latinos and Asians have each served as a constitutive outside against which the white supremacy of the U.S. nation-state could imagine its own coherence and wholeness.

Against an "American" national identity historically produced to be synonymous with racial whiteness and pervasively identified as such by many migrant communities of color, and in the face of a hegemonic denigration of the Blackness that has been reserved as the distinctive and degraded racial condition of African Americans, Latinos and Asians have long found that their own *national* origins come to be refashioned in the United States as *racialized* (or reracialized) identities inimical to the "American"-ness of white supremacy. Thus, the meaning of "Chinese"-ness, for instance, was reconfigured for nineteenth-century Chinese migrants as their pronouncedly and irreducibly racialized station within the U.S. social hierarchy. Similarly, the very word *Mexican* became a derogatory epithet of racist contempt. And so on and on. The ever-proliferating assortment of Latin American and Asian colonial subjects and labor migrants repeatedly experienced the process by which white supremacy's lurid alchemy readily transmuted their distinct nationalities into new racialized categories of social distinction and discrimination. To be Latino or Asian within the space of the U.S. nation-state or its imperial projects has, therefore, nearly always meant having one's specific national origins as well as cultural, religious, and linguistic particularities—in short, the convoluted amalgam of one's foreign or alien status—rendered virtually indistinguishable from a conclusively racial condition of nonwhiteness. The additive elaboration of racial categories derived from terms that refer to, or may be associated with, supranational global regions—*Asian*, *Latino*—abides by the same fundamental logic that racializes people in terms of their presumed affiliation with foreign *places*. Thus, as Lisa Lowe has incisively argued, as an effect of this particular dynamic of racialization, and in spite of U.S. citizenship and having been born in the United States or descended from prior U.S.-born generations, "the Asian is always seen as an immigrant, as the 'foreigner-within'" and "remains the symbolic 'alien'" (see Molina, chapter 2, Jew, chapter 3, Levine, chapter 6, and Parikh, chapter 7 in this volume).[35] Contending with a strikingly parallel problematic in Chicano studies, Francisco Balderrama and Raymond Rodríguez have discussed the "once a Mexican, always a Mexican" racist premise that was a fundamental condition of possibility for the mass deportation and repatriation during the 1930s, not only of migrants but also of their children who were U.S. citizens by birth (see Jew, chapter 3 in this volume).[36] Addressing the broader implications of the characteristically racial nativism of the 1990s, furthermore, Rodolfo Acuña has argued that this new racism "does not distinguish one Brown person from another, citizen from immigrant, recent immigrant from second generation," that it categorizes all people of color, in effect, as immigrants, "sees *all* immigrants of color as 'illegal aliens,' regardless of their actual legal status," and, thus, stigmatizes them "as welfare recipients, criminals, or other morally inferior creatures"—in short, disqualifies them from any conceivable credibility as "real Americans" (cf. Jew, chapter 3, and Levine, chapter 6 in this volume).[37]

The racialized equation of Latinos and Asians with foreignness and their figuration as inassimilable aliens and permanent virtual immigrants were the ideological preconditions that have galvanized a heightened and increasingly pronounced public awareness of the pertinence of Latinos and Asians for the ongoing transformation of the U.S. social fabric that has arisen largely in the wake of the monumental reformulation of the U.S. immigration law in 1965 (see Saito, chapter 5, Levine, chapter 6, and Parikh, chapter 7 in this volume). With Latinos and Asians together constituting the vast majority of contemporary migrants to the United States, the intensified interest in these social groups is rather evidently animated by questions of racial formation and transformation. In spite of the long historical legacies of their diverse but agonistic trajectories of racially subordinated incorporation within the U.S. social order, however, Latinos and Asians frequently blur into one as they assume the appearance in public discourse of a more generic and enigmatic *question* about *immigration*. Not only does the *immigration* rubric generate a euphemistic ruse for what is, in fact, *racial* discourse; it also elides crucial distinctions by conflating Latin American and Asian migrations with earlier migrations from Europe that came to be racialized as white.[38] Elusively shared between the xenophobic nativism of immigration restrictionists and the xenophilic liberal celebration of an "immigrant America," the transhistorical and teleological figure of "immigration" as such is exposed as a symbolically charged, ideologically overburdened fetish of U.S. nationalism itself.[39] Likewise, homogenized discourses of "immigration" dilute the irreducible historical specificities of distinct migrations, and the substantive inequalities among them, *within* and *between* Latino and Asian racial formations (see esp. Molina, chapter 2, and Parikh, chapter 7 in this volume).

Conversely, a critical scrutiny of the legal economies of immigration, naturalization, and citizenship becomes utterly indispensable for understanding Latino and Asian racial formations. Recent migrations, and the role of the law in hierarchically evaluating, ranking, mobilizing, and regulating them, are simply incomprehensible without an appreciation of the tenacious centrality of white supremacy for U.S. immigration and citizenship law, historically, especially as these have been deployed in divergent but complementary ways against Latinos and Asians in particular. In what was the first legislative determination of access to U.S. citizenship and, in effect, the first official definition of U.S. nationality, the First Congress of the United States mandated in the Naturalization Act of 1790 that a person who was to become a naturalized citizen of the United States must be "white."[40] What is perhaps most remarkable, however, is that this whites-only policy for migrant access to U.S. citizenship remained in effect until 1952.[41] Among the first actual U.S. immigration laws, furthermore, was none other than the Chinese Exclusion Act of 1882, which prohibited any further Chinese migration.[42] Not only was citizenship explicitly barred on the basis of race, but now began an era of unprecedented immigration regulation that would increasingly seek to exclude whole groups even from entry into the country, solely on the basis of race or racialized nationality. Chinese exclusion was followed not long thereafter by prohibitions against Japanese and Korean labor migration by diplomatic accord and, finally, with the passage of the Immigration Act of 1917 (primarily in order to exclude migration from British colonial India), the establishment of an "All-Asia Barred Zone" proscribing migrations from Afghanistan to the Pacific.[43] Thus, the formulation of *Asiatic* and *Asian* as overtly racialized categories became institutionalized by law and ensconced in U.S. immigration policy.[44] Notably, the staggeringly expansive and rigid restrictions against Asian migrations were coupled with a stunningly absolute omission of Latin American migrations from any specific national-origins or hemispheric stipulations or regulations, leaving the robust and enthusiastic importation of Mexican migration in particular simultaneously unhindered by any all-encompassing exclusions and sufficiently flexible to be rendered "illegal" and conveniently subjected to mass deportations as a routine technique of labor subordination and discipline.[45] Hence, the operations of U.S. laws of citizenship and immigration reveal decisive features of how the variously racialized identities of Latinos and Asians have, indeed, been profoundly shaped in historically specific relation to the U.S. state (see esp. Molina, chapter 2, Jew, chapter 3, Robinson and Robinson, chapter 4, Saito, chapter 5, Levine, chapter 6, and Parikh, chapter 7 in this volume). Such intimate entanglements between racial formations and the state thus remind us that all racial identities are always preeminently *political* identities and, moreover, reveal U.S. nationalism itself to be a racial formation.

Social categories such as *Latino* (or *Hispanic* as well as such precursors as *Spanish speaking*, *Spanish surname*, or *Spanish American*) and *Asian* (or *Asian American* as well as precursors such as *Asiatic*, *Oriental*, or *Mongolian*) are, of course, notorious for the ambiguities and incongruities that they entail for efforts in the United States to identify and name diverse groups of people with origins in these vast regions of the globe. Nonetheless, these hotly contested labels have become pervasive and increasingly salient, both for hegemonic projects that homogenize these groups as "minority" populations, political constituencies, or market segments and for efforts that seek to produce community and build strategic coalitions for self-representation (see Robinson and Robinson, chapter 4, and Saito, chapter 5, in this volume). How do competing projects reveal themselves in the social and political struggles over these racialized labels? Indeed, how are these struggles often manifested precisely as struggles to fix the meaning of these categories, to reify them and impose a homogenizing coherence that may be exclusionary or, on the other hand, spuriously inclusive? The intrinsic incoherence of such social categories, combined with their persistent meaningfulness, is a telltale indicator of the ongoing reconfiguration of Latinos and Asians as precisely *racial* formations in the United States. If we repudiate the preposterous absurdity of essentialist claims concerning a putative cultural basis for Latino or Asian identities and likewise dispense with *ethnicity* as an analytic category that merely muddles notions of *culture* and *race* (understood anachronistically in narrowly biological terms) precisely when it is presumed to bridge them, then our critical attention may be focused sharply on the dynamic and relational historical processes through which "Latinos" and "Asians" have been *produced* as such—*as groups*, subordinated within a sociopolitical order of white supremacy.[46]

Suspended in more or less excruciating conditions of indefinitely deferred exception as the U.S. nation-state's seemingly permanent outsiders whose alien racial status insinuates an effect of irredeemable foreignness, Latinos and Asians continue to confront the stubborn intransigence of an "American" racial order defined in Black and white. What are the wider processes of racialization that mediate constructions of both nationally specific and more broadly inclusive Latino and Asian identities—in relation to one another as well as in relation to the hegemonic polarity of whiteness and Blackness? What are the implicit or explicit ways that whiteness and Blackness might figure in the formulation of these identities? What might be the ways that particular Latino or Asian groups discern crucial differences, and, perhaps, sustain racialized distinctions, between and also within these same broad labels, among various nationally identified groups? What, in short, are the incipient racial formations and emergent racialized transformations at stake in how these groups relate to one another and the broader U.S. social formation in ways that reveal critical new issues in the ongoing remaking of the racial order of the U.S. nation-state? How are these transformations linked to multiple transnational social formations, such as migrations, international and civil wars, refugee crises, the mobility of labor and capital, and U.S. imperial projects in the past as well as the present? How do Latino and Asian racial formations in the United States demonstrate the necessity for transnational perspectives in American studies more generally? Likewise, how do the perspectives that emerge from research on Latino and Asian racial formations enable a critique of the U.S. nationalist conceits and presuppositions that have conventionally undergirded much of the scholarship in American and (U.S.) ethnic studies? The essays in this collection have been framed by these vital questions and gesture toward an audacious and still emergent research agenda.

This collection contributes to a much-needed density of critical dialogue in the study of the United States through a concentrated focus on research that examines diverse social relations and substantive intersections *between* Latinos and Asians, or scholarship that otherwise interrogates the sociopolitical processes that have served to reify their mutual separation or exacerbate their apparent divisions. The essays that it contains emphasize the wider processes of racialization that mediate constructions of both nationally specific and more all-encompassing Latino and Asian identities in the United States—in relation to one another as well as in relation to the hegemonic polarity of whiteness and Blackness. While the contributors have foregrounded the salience of Latino and Asian *racial* formations, however, it is likewise crucial that these processes of racialization have not been artificially divorced from their articulation within wider conjunctures of gendered, sexualized, and class-specific axes of differentiation and inequality. Indeed, one of the central concerns of this book is precisely to examine some of the ways that Latinos and Asians do not exist in isolation, within the narrow, hermetically sealed segregation of their officially designated respective corners, but rather, together, are dynamically implicated in historical as well as ongoing transnationalized reconfigurations of the broader social formation of the U.S. nation-state itself.

Finally, this book arises in the midst of U.S. imperialism's so-called War on Terrorism—a militaristic frenzy without limits, definitions, or boundaries against an amorphous but undeniably racialized "Arab" and "Muslim" enemy, a global campaign of "preemptive" invasions and military occupations, immediately manifest as a new outbreak of U.S. wars in Asia—and the imposition of a draconian "Homeland Security" regime chiefly distinguished by an onslaught of mass detentions and deportations of Asian and also Latino migrants and the suppression of political dissent and elementary civil liberties among U.S. citizens. How are Latino or Asian identities posited in relation to, and potentially in contradistinction to, some notion of "American"-ness? Rather than presuppose that what is automatically at stake in such a question is a presumably obligatory positive affirmation of each group's putative membership and proper belonging in the U.S. polity, however, this book poses this question as a genuinely open-ended one. If, indeed, hegemonic formulations of the national identity of "American"-ness have always been profoundly entangled with the racial formation of whiteness as well as various other dominant configurations of "middle-class" status, masculinity, and heteronormativity, then one of our critical tasks is to illuminate the ways that racially oppressed people do and do not make claims on "American"-ness. Do they disrupt, repudiate, subvert, recapitulate, or endorse the hegemonic U.S. social formation? Do their very efforts to challenge their subjugation by white supremacy become captive to its grinding machinations and even enlisted in the service of sustaining the efficacy and reenergizing the resilience of their own and others' oppression? These questions must necessarily be among the more urgent and most dire concerns of any responsible and engaged scholarship that critically investigates the workings of racism in the United States. For we must have the political courage to soberly assess not only the heroism of our organized mobilizations but also the mundane struggles of our alienated everyday life; not only the elements of antagonism within our estranged compliance but also the accommodation within our resistance; not only the integrity and vision of our movements but also their fragmentation and blind spots; not only the urgency of our insurgencies, therefore, but also the patience required to move beyond the uncommon denominator of our accidental origins and ossified identities, toward the vital solidarity of our inherently incomplete and still-emerging purpose.

## Notes

The first epigraph is taken from James Madison to Thomas L. McKenney, 10 February 1826, Library of Congress, Madison Papers, "Vol. 75: Feb. 4, 1826" (I am grateful to Philip Bigler, director of the James Madison Center, James Madison University, for his gracious assistance in identifying the original source of this much-cited quotation and to my research assistant, Kimberly Seibel, for her admirable and unfaltering diligence in pursuing this question until it was finally resolved). The second epigraph is taken from Hamid Dabashi's "The Moment of Myth: Edward Said (1935–2003)," published by AsiaSource, an online resource of the Asia Society (http://www.asiasource.org).

1. Churchill, *Fantasies of the Master Race*.

2. For considerations of this phrase from Melville, see Drinnon, *Facing West*; cf. Takaki, *Iron Cages*, 80–107.

3. Williams, "Frontier Thesis"; cf. Williams, *Empire as a Way of Life*.

4. Tocqueville, *Democracy in America*, 326, 340.

5. Patterson, *Slavery and Social Death*, 7.

6. Tocqueville, *Democracy in America*, 317.

7. Even during the earliest era of African enslavement in the British colonies in North America, Winthrop Jordan has suggested, the "heathenism" and "savagery" of Africans tended to be given relatively minor emphasis—in contradistinction to such characteristics in the Indians—and, generally, treated as secondary to their skin color (*White over Black*, 20–28).

8. Tocqueville, *Democracy in America*, 319 and 319 n. 1.

9. For an important consideration of the persistence and perpetuation of *Indian* as a generic category in spite of an always increasing ability on the part of whites to differentiate among distinct Native American tribes, see Berkhofer, *White Man's Indian*.

10. Analogously, Winthrop Jordan has argued that, for Europeans on both sides of the Atlantic, "the Indian and the Negro remained . . . distinctly different intellectual problems": Indians raised a question as to their *origins*, whereas Blacks presented a puzzle concerning their *color* (*White over Black*, 239–40).

11. Here, it is important to note that I am not using *foreign* in any strict geopolitical sense. The enduring modern foundations of federal Indian law, based principally on U.S. Supreme Court Chief Justice John Marshall's decisions in *Cherokee Nation v. Georgia* (1831) (30 U.S. 1 [1831]) and *Worcester v. Georgia* (31 U.S. 515 [1832]), figured the legal status of Indian tribal sovereignty as precisely *not* that of foreign nations but rather that of "domestic dependent nations."

12. See Ruppel, "Nations Undivided," chaps. 3–4; cf. Deloria and Wilkins, *Constitutional Tribulations*; Hoxie, *Final Promise*; and Smith, *Civic Ideals*.

13. I adopt the term *white nationalism* from Takaki (*Iron Cages*, 15) as well as Wahneema Lubiano's incisive remark: "The perspective of black nationalism permits the realization that . . . the dominant discourse of U.S. history has been some form or other of white American nationalism" ("Black Common Sense," 235).

14. James Monroe, "Message to Congress, December 2, 1823," in Hofstadter, ed., *Great Issues in American History*, 244–47.

15. See esp. Horsman, *Race and Manifest Destiny*; but also Acuña, *Occupied America*; and Hietala, *Manifest Design*.

16. Hietala, *Manifest Design*, 152–66.

17. Nobles, *American Frontiers*, 241.

18. Beveridge quoted in Smith, *Civic Ideals*, 430–31; cf. Jacobson, *Barbarian Virtues*, 226–27.

19. Depew quoted in Foner, *Spanish-Cuban-American War*, 2:672.

20. So called by Henry Luce, the conservative millionaire publisher of *Time*, *Life*, and *Fortune* magazines and a vocal isolationist through the 1930s, in the essay "The American Century," which appeared in the 17 February 1941 issue of *Life*, ten months *prior* to the bombing of Pearl Harbor. For an insightful discussion of Luce's geopolitics, see Smith, *American Empire*, 1–28.

21. Drinnon, *Facing West*, 464–65.

22. Jacobson notes: "Historically constant casualty-to-kill ratios were dramatically reversed in the Philippines, with the Filipino dead outnumbering the wounded by fifteen to one. . . . By 1902, General [Jacob] Smith had ordered the summary death, not of actual Filipino combatants, but of 'all persons . . . *who are capable of bearing arms*. . . .' When asked by a marine commander where the line should be drawn between mere children and potential combatants, Smith replied, 'ten years of age' " (*Barbarian Virtues*, 244).

23. *People v. Hall*, 4 Cal. 399 (1854). This example is borrowed from Haney López, *White by Law*, 51–52; cf. Okihiro, *Margins and Mainstreams*, 50–51.

24. See generally Smedley, *Race in North America*.

25. See, e.g., Horsman, *Race and Manifest Destiny*, 208–48.

26. Edward Duran Ayres Report (1942), Sleepy Lagoon Commission Papers, in *Readings on La Raza: The Twentieth Century*, ed. Matt S. Meier and Feliciano Rivera (New York: Hill and Wang, 1974), 131.

27. Ibid., 129.

28. Ibid., 128.

29. For an analysis of the U.S. war against Japan as a race war, see Dower, *War without Mercy*.

30. This example is discussed in McWilliams, *North from Mexico*, 233–35; cf. Acuña, *Occupied America*, 268–69.

31. Notably, soon thereafter, during the 1943 "zoot-suit riots," when white sailors and soldiers stationed or on furlough in Los Angeles, augmented by civilian white mobs and the police, rampaged in the streets against Mexican youths as an alien and criminal menace, African Americans and Filipinos were likewise targeted.

32. See Almaguer, *Racial Fault Lines*; Roediger, *Wages of Whiteness*; Takaki, *Iron Cages*; and Saxton, *White Republic*; cf. Saxton, *Indispensable Enemy*.

33. Modified adaptations—such as *timber niggers*, used for Chippewa Indians in northern Wisconsin, or *sand niggers*, used for Arabs, especially during and since the first U.S. war against Iraq in 1991—are also noteworthy. For parallel examples of how the racist epithet *gook* was deployed not only against the Asian targets of U.S. military aggression in the Philippines, Korea, and Vietnam but also against a variety of other nonwhite natives, including Haitians, Nicaraguans, Arabs, and Hawaiians, see Roediger, *Abolition of Whiteness*, 117–20.

34. Dickman quoted in Jacobson, *Barbarian Virtues*, 233.

35. Lowe, *Immigrant Acts*, 5–6.

36. Balderrama and Rodríguez, *Decade of Betrayal*, 218; cf. Guerin-Gonzales, *American Dreams*; and Hoffman, *Unwanted Mexican Americans*.

37. Acuña, *Anything but Mexican*, ix–x.

38. Compare, e.g., the respective critical discussions of "the immigrant analogy," "the ethnic myth," or "ethnicity-based theories of race" in Blauner, *Racial Oppression*; Steinberg, *Ethnic Myth*; and Omi and Winant, *Racial Formation*.

39. For a more extended critique of the essentialized figure of *the immigrant* as an object of U.S. nationalism and nativism, see De Genova, *Working the Boundaries*; cf. Honig, "Immigrant America?" and *Democracy and the Foreigner*, 73–106.

40. Act of 26 March 1790 (*Statutes at Large of the USA* 1 [1845]: 103). For a more extensive discussion, see Haney-López, *White by Law*.

41. Immigration and Nationalities Act of 1952 (Public Law 82-414; *U.S. Statutes at Large* 66 [1952]: 163), also known as the McCarran-Walter Act.

42. *U.S. Statutes at Large* 22 (1882): 58.

43. Act of 5 February 1917 (*U.S. Statutes at Large* 39 [1917]: 874). Filipinos, notably, having been designated as U.S. nationals owing to their colonized status following the U.S. occupation that began with the Spanish-American War in 1898, were an important exception to the all-Asian exclusion (see Ngai, "Undesirable Alien"; cf. Ngai, *Impossible Subjects*, 96–126).

44. For more extensive discussion, see Ancheta, *Asian American Experience*; Chang, *Disoriented*; Haney-López, *White by Law*; Hing, *Making and Remaking*; Kim, *Legal History*; and Salyer, *Laws Harsh as Tigers*.

45. For a more detailed account, see De Genova, "Production of Mexican/Migrant 'Illegality'"; and Ngai, *Impossible Subjects*. For a more general critical consideration of migrant "illegality," see De Genova, "Migrant 'Illegality' and Deportability."

46. For a related and more extended discussion of Latino racial formations, see De Genova and Ramos-Zayas, "Latino Racial Formations."

*Part One*  RACIAL SCIENCE,
SOCIAL CONTROL

# COLONIAL VISION, RACIAL VISIBILITY

*Racializations in Puerto Rico and the Philippines during the Initial Period of U.S. Colonization*

Gary Y. Okihiro

Racialization changes over space and time and the differential locations of subjectivities, of self and other. Racialization, thus, is clearly a historical process of social construction. Both Puerto Ricans and Filipina/os were racialized differently under the successive colonial regimes of Spain and the United States, even as Filipina/os and Puerto Ricans held distinctive racialized ideas of themselves during those historical periods. Those variations emanated from, among other things, the ethnic, class, and gender positions of Puerto Ricans and Filipina/os and the subject positions of business, military, government, and intellectual Spanish and U.S. elites.

In this essay, I survey the racializations (and their apparent absence and transparent presence) among the colonizers of the colonized during the first few years of the U.S. occupations of Puerto Rico and the Philippines. I do not consider the racializations that occurred during the war of conquest, which might suggest differential treatments of the U.S. enemy. In Puerto Rico, the United States fought a nineteen-day campaign—which some called a "picnic"—in which three Americans died and the troops were allegedly bombarded with cigars and bananas, whereas, in the Philippines, the United States waged a bloody four-year war of attrition that involved 200,000 U.S. troops and resulted in 4,300 American and more than 50,000 Filipina/o deaths.

What seems obvious from this review is the comparative lack of interest on the part of the U.S. colonizers in Puerto Rico's peoples as contrasted with their prodigious fascination with the peoples of the Philippines.[1] Perhaps Sidney Mintz's insight about anthropology's neglect of Caribbean peoples generally and globally is operative here in the particular case of Puerto Rico. Mintz astutely observed anthropology's valuation of the native and the exotic and its consequent neglect of the migrant and the familiar. The indigenous peoples of the Caribbean, perceived as vanished, and their cultures, seen as Westernized and as transplantations, have, thus, carried scant cachet within the discipline.[2] Similarly, it seems, Puerto Ricans in the United States have been simultaneously racialized as a visible other and rendered invisible within the U.S. social formation, as pointed out by the linguist Bonnie Urciuoli. "For decades," writes Urciuoli, "research, media, and public entertainment have either ignored Puerto Ricans or portrayed them as a social problem," despite the fact that they have lived in U.S. cities since at least the 1890s.[3] Another part of that erasure has been the divergent racialization of darker-skinned Puerto Ricans as blacks and lighter-skinned Puerto Ricans as whites within the dominant U.S. binary of color.

## Contexts of Empire

Those narratives of peoples, women, and workers of the new possessions carried special significance for many whites in the United States. The late nineteenth century, the years of this discussion, was a troubling period in U.S. history. The 1890 U.S. Census declared an end to the frontier, the manifest outlet for continental expansion and mythical ground for democracy and rugged individualism. Frederick Jackson Turner, the historian of the frontier, summed up the implication of the Census report. "This, then, is the real situation: a people composed of heterogeneous materials, with diverse and conflicting ideals and social interests, having passed from the task of filling up the vacant spaces of the continent, is now thrown back upon itself, and is seeking an equilibrium," he wrote in 1896. "The diverse elements are being fused into national unity. The forces of reorganization are turbulent and the nation seems like a witch's kettle."[4]

Among those "diverse elements" were the 25 million immigrants, or more than four times the total of the previous fifty years, who streamed to the eastern and western shores of the United States between 1865 and 1915 and who originated, not from familiar Britain or Northern Europe, but from Italy, Greece, Poland, and Russia in the Northeast and from China, Japan, Korea, India, and the Philippines in the West. They flocked to the U.S. Northeast and West, where captains of industry, in cities and fields, accumulated fortunes by monopolizing land, resources, and capital. Racial, ethnic, and class conflicts boiled and bubbled in this "witch's kettle." In 1882, Congress passed the Chinese Exclusion Act because, in the framers' words, "the coming of Chinese laborers to this country endangers the good order of certain localities within the territory thereof."[5] In 1886, police killed four strikers in Chicago, and the next day a bomb killed seven police officers and injured sixty-seven other people.

GARY Y. OKIHIRO

The Haymarket Square bombing came to symbolize to many Americans the alien menace posed by Southern and Eastern Europeans, immigrants, radicals, and anarchists. "These people are not American," a Chicago newspaper reported of the Haymarket strikers, "but the very scum and offal of Europe."[6]

In a letter dated 14 May 1892, the editor and writer Thomas Bailey Aldrich explained the circumstances surrounding the writing of his poem "Unguarded Gates" (1895), which warned against the alien tide. "I went home and wrote a misanthropic poem called 'Unguarded Gates' . . . in which I mildly protest against America becoming the cesspool of Europe. I'm much too late, however," he lamented. "I looked in on an anarchist meeting the other night . . . and heard such things spoken by our 'feller citizens' as made my cheek burn. . . . I believe in America for the Americans; I believe in the widest freedom and the narrowest license, and I hold that jailbirds, professional murderers, and amateur lepers . . . and human gorillas generally should be closely questioned at our Gates." Aldrich closed his lamentation on criminality, contagion, and evolution with an endorsement of the writer Rudyard Kipling's acid observation that New York City had become "a despotism of the alien, by the alien, tempered with occasional insurrections of decent folk!" In "Unguarded Gates," Aldrich raised the alarm against "a wild motley throng" pressing through America's wide-open gates, bringing with them "unknown gods and rites," "strange tongues," and "accents of menace alien to our air."[7]

The acquisition, thus, of colonies with their "motley throngs" and "accents of menace" added more ingredients to the seething brew. Advocates of the new possessions countered that rhetoric of race by sublimating racializations within discourses of gender and class, even as those who refused to embrace the new possessions engaged in race mongering. Of course, promoters of the new possessions deployed the language of social uplift and the social gospel, popular at the time among white reformers and progressives, and some saw U.S. overseas expansion as the salubrious extension of the generative frontier. The U.S. president, William McKinley, who took up "the white man's burden," explained his decision to colonize the Philippines.[8] After ruling out giving the islands back to Spain, turning them over to commercial rivals France and Germany, and granting them independence, McKinley concluded: "There was nothing left for us to do but to take them all, and to educate the Filipinos, and uplift and civilize and Christianize them and by God's grace do the very best we could by them, as our fellow men, for whom Christ also died."[9] And McKinley's secretary of state, John Hay, the architect of the U.S. open door China policy, observed that the Far East had become the United States's "Far West," a reference to the reopening of the symbol-laden frontier.[10]

Other anxieties troubled some white, middle-class men. Domestic spaces were facing challenges from the "New Woman," who sought to remake herself and her society. Middle-class privileges allowed women to pursue higher education, albeit attenuated by degree and career constraints, and to engage in a variety of causes of social uplift. Under the banner of progressivism, these women sought to cure some of society's ills associated with urbanization and industrialization. The settlement house movement, represented famously by Jane Addams's Hull House in Chicago, was an example of that attempt to improve the lot of immigrants by teaching them the middle-class values and lifestyles deemed necessary for their success in the United States. White women played key roles in that movement and the field and profession it helped institute—social work. And economic growth drew working-class women out of the home and into the factory, and the distance between private and public spheres lessened. The New Woman sought to enhance her opportunities and reduce her dependence on men, she participated in the public arena formerly occupied by men only, and she rallied for woman suffrage, one of the largest reform movements in U.S. history.

These erosions of what were formerly the preserves of white, middle-class men prompted a crisis of masculinity and privilege. "Between 1880 and 1910," the historian Gail Bederman summarized, "middle-class men were especially interested in manhood. Economic changes were undermining Victorian ideals of self-restrained manliness. Working-class and immigrant men, as well as middle-class women, were challenging white middle-class men's beliefs that they were the ones who should control the nation's destiny. Medical authorities were warning of the fragility of men's bodies. . . . All this activity suggests that men were actively, even enthusiastically, engaging in the process of remaking manhood."[11] Imperial expansion was a means by which to reconstitute whiteness and manliness, as in "the white man's burden," and a way to integrate the diverse nation, which involved for some white, middle-class men domestic order both within the home and homeland and abroad in the empire.[12]

*Racializing Puerto Ricans*

Among the gleanings of U.S. racializations of Puerto Ricans about the turn of the century are brief commentaries by politicians and businessmen who deployed the race card to advance their particular ends. Whitelaw Reid, a member of the U.S. delegation that shaped the Treaty of Paris, which ended the Spanish-American War in 1898, and the owner of the *New York Tribune*, warned of the dire consequences of admitting the peoples of the newly acquired territories into the Union. "Their people," Reid declared of the new possessions, "come from all religions, all races—black, yellow, white, and their mixtures—all conditions, from pagan ignorance and the verge of cannibalism to the best products of centuries of civilization, education, and self-government." And, speaking to members of the Massachusetts Club, Reid raised the alarm that "the enemy is at the gates . . . [and] may gain the citadel." "The enemy," explained Reid, was Puerto Rico's "mixed population, a little more than half colonial Spanish, the rest negro and half-breed, illiterate, alien in language, alien in ideas of right, interests, and government." Their absorption, he predicted, employing the language of eugenics, would lead to the "degeneration and degradation of the homogeneous, continental Republic of our pride."[13] Thus racialized by Reid, the newly acquired peoples in general and Puerto Rico's "mixed population" in particular served to advance his white-supremacist and anti-annexationist ends.

Henry K. Carroll, unlike Reid, advocated greater interaction between the United States and Puerto Rico, especially for the purpose of commerce. Carroll was sent by (and reported to) the U.S. Treasury secretary as his special commissioner to Puerto Rico in 1898 after the signing of the armistice. Race, in Carroll's report, disappears almost entirely as a category and is, instead, embedded within a discourse of class. According to the report, Puerto Rico is densely populated, most of its people are poor, and because of their poverty, resort to crime and sink to immorality. "Porto Ricans are not bad people," assures the U.S. consul, Philip C. Hanna, whom Carroll quotes, in advocating free trade between Puerto Rico and the United States. "Remove from them the terrible temptation produced by enforced hunger and nakedness; give to these people an opportunity to earn an honest living; teach them that toil is honorable; build for them factories instead of forts . . . and we shall produce upon them a moral effect which the Spaniards failed to produce, and make of them a people whom we shall not be ashamed to recognize as fellow-citizens of our grand Republic."[14] In the promotion of U.S. business opportunities in Puerto Rico, race was apparently absent, yet folded within the description of the Puerto Rican working class was race, insofar as dense populations, poverty, crime, and immorality signified nonwhites and denizens of U.S. urban centers and of the tropics.[15]

Not surprisingly, this narrative of race, class, and morality was gendered. Work, asserted a group of businessmen from the district of Ponce whom Carroll quoted, eliminated poverty and allowed women to "take the fruit of their labor to their homes, thanks to the factory, which has saved them from the wages of sin." Wage labor, it is explained, "especially elevates and dignifies woman, to whom it opens a wider field than that of ordinary labor as a domestic, and enables her to turn away from the inducements offered by houses of ill fame." In short, labor was presumed to both provide for material wants and elevate morals.[16] Even as class position signified race within the colonial context, where workers conjured nonwhites and employers whites, women figured morality. Capitalism or the factory signified whiteness, manliness, and productivity in this racialized, gendered, and classed discourse, which rescues both the nonwhite poor, elevating them from poverty to plenty, and the nonwhite woman, directing her assets homeward and away from immorality.

Puerto Rican working-class men were feminized by those promoting the colony's economic potential and, thereby, represented as ideal laborers, as best exploited. Amos K. Fiske, the influential business writer for the *New York Times*, urged the annexation of Puerto Rico for U.S. economic gain. Describing the Puerto Rican labor force, Fiske wrote: "There are many blacks, possibly a third of all the people, and much mixed blood, but the population is not ignorant or indolent or in any way degraded. It is not turbulent or intractable, and there is every reason to believe that under encouraging conditions it would become industrious, thrifty and prosperous."[17] William Dinwiddie's widely read *Puerto Rico: Its Conditions and Possibilities*, published in 1899, described the Puerto Rican man and laborer: "The Puertoriqueño is not an anarchist or an insurrectionist, for he knows no other life and does not starve or grow cold, while the burdens of oppression are his birthright, handed down for centuries. He is, then, in spite of his wretchedness, dirt, and poverty, as we see it, a fairly-contented man. . . . [H]e is docile, obliging, appreciative of favors, and, best of all, possesses an inbred courtesy and politeness, and an equability of temperament, which permit him to readily absorb new ideas."[18] As docile, obliging, and appreciative of favors, feminized Puerto Rican working-class men were ideal laborers and bore racialized and gendered features of nonwhites generally, albeit sublimated within a discourse of class and economic uplift.

Less inclined to bury race under the debris of class was the U.S. military, which saw its role in the colony as that of a police force and was skeptical about

GARY Y. OKIHIRO

the prospects for labor in the racial advancement of the Puerto Rican working class. Although the common belief among Americans was that Puerto Ricans were white, the military governor reported in 1900 that "the so-called white race have a decided color—a reddish brown not unlike the color of those persons in the United States who have more or less Indian blood." Puerto Ricans, however, were not Indians, nor were they "negritic." Instead, they had Asiatic features, and their brown skin color was probably due to "Moorish" influences, speculated the report, that is, "the intermixture of the Spanish and Moors over a thousand years ago." Besides those "whites," there were many "Negroes and mulattoes" among Puerto Rico's peoples who were descendants of slaves.

Ignorance and indigence were the hallmarks of Puerto Rico's working class, the military governor asserted. Their vacuity was "beyond American comprehension," and they faced "slow starvation" and anemia owing to their diet, which was "less nourishing than that of convicts in our most severe penitentiaries." Coupled with mental incapacity and material poverty was immorality, as in Carroll's report, just as class was coupled with gender. Men and women simply lived together without having first married, the military governor noted, because they did not have the money required for a civil or church wedding. And the Puerto Rican working class was feminized as "a gentle, patient, uncomplaining lot, living in ignorance and penury, generally polite, and willing to work in a plodding, undemonstrative way." Those conditions favored capitalism, the governor was quick to point out. And, like women, and without contradiction, the report concluded, "the natives are lazy and dirty, but are very sharp and cunning."[19]

Puerto Ricans were racialized, gendered, and sexualized in Frederick A. Ober's 1898 travel account of the island. The Spanish colonizers, wrote Ober, did not share "the aversion felt by the Teutons and Anglo-Saxons for the races that have complexions more deeply dyed than theirs" and, thus, mixed freely with the indigenous Indians and transported Africans to produce "half-breeds" or "a brood of semi-savage children." Sexuality was unbridled, perhaps, Ober offered, because of the tropical climate, wherein "children may disport themselves in the garb invented and worn by the sartorial artists of Eden, crave no greater excitement than a cock-fight and no greater variety of food than a raw banana or boiled yam." In other words: "[T]he tendency is toward Nature's way!" The writer's language is surely choice, and his appeal to "Nature's way" is self-evident and purifying. "Making love, of course," Ober disclosed know-ingly, "goes on all the time, for the creole nature is soft and languishing, complaisant, easily tickled by compliment, and prone to hanker after the 'for-bidden fruit.'"

Ober waxed eloquent over Puerto Rican women: "Those of gentle birth and breeding are sweet and flower-like, with a bright alertness peculiar to the Latin woman transplanted in American soil and climate. Their glances are swift and meaning, their great black eyes capable of seeming quite full of expression; their features are not always classically regular, but usually attractive. They are petite of form and have small hands and feet . . . in a word, are thoroughly feminine. It is this charm of femininity that makes the creole, whether French or Spanish, so potent with man." And, as if to overdetermine Puerto Rican femininity, Ober invoked the commonplace trope of Oriental sensuality by noting that the island's Spanish architecture of courtyards, fountains, and high stone walls hid interiors that were "steeped in an air of mystery as deep as that enveloping the harem of any Turk of Cairo or Constantinople."[20] The Puerto Rican man vanishes in Ober's guide to the island's "resources," Spanish men act on diminutive, "thoroughly feminine" subjects, and Puerto Rican women wait for their masters in harem-like havens, exude "potent" charms, and pine for cockfights, raw bananas, and boiled yams.[21]

## Racializing Filipina / os

While Puerto Rico's ethnography might have been left to the imaginings of travel writers like Ober, the peoples of the Philippines were mapped, mea-sured, and cataloged by scores of social scientists from the Spaniards to the Germans to the Americans. The Germans were perhaps the most assiduous in this project of Philippine studies, and their treatises, especially those of Ferdi-nand Blumentritt, a geography professor in Bohemia, were influential in shap-ing an American school of Philippine anthropology. Blumentritt, appropri-ately, was an armchair ethnographer who never set foot in the Philippines yet was considered by his peers the foremost authority on Philippine ethnology. Such was the conceit of European science. Besides compiling and systematiz-ing the body of information collected by others, Blumentritt created a typol-ogy of ethnic groups in the Philippines that included the Negritos and two strains of Malays descended from separate waves of migration.[22]

When the Americans began their colonial rule, they were, nonetheless, evidently ignorant of that considerable body of scholarship on the Philippines and, instead, saw their new territory as unmapped and peopled by unclassified "races." The University of California professor David P. Barrows wrote of that terra incognita in 1901: "[W]e note that . . . the pagan and Mohammedan tribes of the Philippines are estimated at from a million to a million and a half souls. Furthermore, they form not a single homogeneous race . . . but an unknown number of tribes and peoples belonging to no less than three or four races and to various mixtures thereof. Added difficulty as well as interest is given to this work by the fact that the country inhabited by these tribes is largely unknown. The Cordilleras of Northern Luzon, the mountains of Mindoro, Palauan and Mindanao are not only unmapped and unexplored but have hardly been penetrated by white men."[23] The scientific task outlined by Barrows was a veritable colonizing mission—a penetration and apprehension by white men—and, hence, a recouping of race, manliness, and citizenship both at home in the United States and abroad.[24]

Surely a paragon of that white, manly conquest and achievement was Dean C. Worcester, a scientist and colonial administrator and a physician's son and descendant of bedrock, old-stock New England clergymen and missionaries. Worcester entered the University of Michigan, majored in biology, and, in 1887, accompanied his professor, Joseph Beal Steere, on a specimen-collecting expedition to the Philippines. Three years later, with funds from a private donor, Worcester returned to the Philippines to resume his study of the islands and their biotic communities: plants, animals, and peoples. In 1895, Worcester gained an appointment at his alma mater as an assistant professor of zoology, and, in 1899, shortly after the United States acquired the Philippines in 1898, he was invited, as an authority on the colony, to join the First Philippine Commission, headed by Cornell University's president, Jacob Gould Schurman. By dint of his assumed expertise and persistent personality, Worcester dominated the commission and supervised the writing of its massive final report. He was a member of the Second Philippine Commission in 1900, and a year later became secretary of the interior in the Philippine insular government.[25]

In those capacities, Worcester saw anthropology as a means by which to manage his subjects. In truth, the commissioners had been instructed by the president that their task was to prescribe a form of administrative government that would, like British colonial indirect rule, maintain "the happiness, peace and prosperity" of the Philippines through measures that conformed to the customs, habits, and prejudices of the people to the extent possible. As interior secretary, Worcester created agencies to collect information on the natural and human resources of the colony, and he himself undertook ethnographic research among "several wild and savage tribes inhabiting the more remote and inaccessible portions of the archipelago." To Worcester, the task of his applied anthropology was to inform legislation for the paternal "control and uplifting" of Filipina/os, especially the non-Christian ethnic groups.[26]

In his 1898 *The Philippine Islands and Their People*, Worcester scored his contemporaries for lumping "the whole population of the Philippines as barbarians and savages" and proceeded to distinguish, like a scientist, among the estimated 8–10 million inhabitants of the colony. There were the Negritos "at the bottom of the scale," wrote Worcester of his evolutionary schema of human types in the islands, Mohammedan and pagan Malays in the middle, and Christian or civilized Malays at the top. The Negritos, he determined, were "weaklings of low stature, with black skin, closely-curling hair, flat nose, thick lips, and large, clumsy feet. In the matter of intelligence they stand at or near the bottom of the human series, and they are believed to be incapable of any considerable degree of civilization or advancement." The pagan Malays were varied. Some were "harmless and docile," while others were "naturally warlike and intractable." And the Christian Malays were, on the whole, "fairly intelligent" and eager to learn, but they were also "inveterate liars," with "no sense of moral guilt," and, hence, needed to be disciplined by white masters because "too much kindness" would very likely "spoil" them. The civilized Malay was also a happy native. "He loves to sing, dance, and make merry," Worcester declared, recuperating a caricature of enslaved Africans in the U.S. South. "He is a born musician, and considering the sort of instruments at his disposal, and especially the limited advantages which he has for perfecting himself in their use, his performances on them are often very remarkable." Yet, despite their "amiable qualities," even those civilized natives were, in Worcester's estimation, "utterly unfit for self-government" and, thus, required the firm hand of U.S. benevolence.[27]

In addition to his ample writings, Worcester produced visual representations of Filipina/os, some forty-seven hundred still photographs and six movie reels that were systematically collected to facilitate U.S. rule and to familiarize Americans back home with their new colonial subjects.[28] Those and similar

GARY Y. OKIHIRO

representations by Worcester and other U.S. anthropologists helped formulate a science of race and rule in the Philippines and, as commodities of mass circulation in the United States, shaped images of whiteness and citizenship, on the one hand, and nonwhiteness and alienness, on the other.[29] The fall 1900 Sears catalog featured a drawing of Filipino Igorots clutching spears in its advertisement for stereoscopic slides, and a 1903 *National Geographic* revealed photographs of bare-breasted Tagbuana and Negrito women.[30] Indeed, those peoples and objects of empire were, like their photographs, brought home to the colonizing metropole through the circuses and world's fairs that were important sites of mass distribution and consumption in the United States about the turn of the century. For the Philippine colonial government, the 1904 Louisiana Purchase Exposition in St. Louis provided such a venue for displaying Filipina/os.

The exposition's anthropology department was the most extensive of any world's fair, and its directors promised to offer "a comprehensive anthropological exhibition, constituting a Congress of Races, and exhibiting particularly the barbarous and semi-barbarous peoples of the world, as nearly as possible in their ordinary and native environments."[31] Among that assembly were representatives of the nation's expansionist past, American Indians, and its imperial future, Filipina/os. In truth, the federal and colonial governments saw the 1904 exposition as a means by which to advance the U.S. imperial project in the Philippines. "Filipino participation would be a very great influence in completing pacification and in bringing Filipinos to improve their condition," declared William Howard Taft, then civil governor of the Philippines, and President Theodore Roosevelt endorsed Taft's efforts to organize an exhibit of the resources and products, along with the human populations, of the controversial and contested acquisition. There were still pockets of resistance to the U.S. occupation of the Philippines, and anti-expansionist sentiment at home remained strong.[32] Consequently, "the white man's burden," borne for the uplift of America's "little brown brothers," and the material and ideological gains of empire were to be prominently exhibited at the St. Louis fair.

Taft appointed a Philippine Exposition Board to mount the St. Louis display. The end result was the Philippine Reservation, which spread out over forty-seven acres and housed nearly twelve hundred Filipina/os living in villages that depicted a variety of Filipina/o types, including Visayans, deemed "the high and more intelligent class of natives"; Moros, the "fierce followers of Mohammed"; Bagobo "savages"; and "monkey-like" Negritos.[33] But, of all the displays in the reservation, the most popular by far was that of the "picturesque" Igorots, who riveted the attention of fairgoers and the nation in an unprecedented fashion. The attraction was surely the supposed savagery of the Igorots—a savagery exemplified in their racialized bodies, their gender inversions of cigar-smoking and tattooed women, and their alleged culinary penchant for dog meat (a kind of cannibalism of man's proverbial best friend)—but also their nakedness and imagined, unbridled sexuality as children of nature. Although part of the intention of the reservation's organizers was to show the primitive state of the human condition in the Philippines, thereby demonstrating the necessity for the U.S. mission of benevolent assimilation, Filipina/o barbarism might also suggest the inability of the colonized peoples to evolve and progress and reveal them as unfit and undesirable for membership in the U.S. body politic.

President Theodore Roosevelt, anticipating a Democratic anti-imperialist field day over unassimilable dog eaters in the upcoming 1904 elections, conveyed his thoughts on the Filipina/o exhibit through his secretary of war, William Howard Taft, the former Philippine governor and architect of the Philippine Reservation. "The President has heard severe criticism of the Igorrotes and wild tribe exhibit on the ground that it verges toward the indecent," wired Taft to Clarence Edwards, the War Department's man in charge of matters concerning the Philippines. "He believes either the Igorrotes and wild tribes should be sent home or that they should be more fully clad. He thinks scouts and the constabulary [U.S.-trained and -outfitted Filipina/os] should be given more prominence and that everything possible should be done to avoid any possible impression that the Philippine Government is seeking to make prominent the savageness and barbarism of the wild tribes either for show purposes or to depreciate the popular estimate of the general civilization of the Islands."[34] Edwards confirmed the president's fear. The Negritos, he reported, "were until recently dressed up like plantation nigger[s], whom they diminutively represent, [however,] recently . . . [the] men have discarded these clothes and put on their native loin cloth."[35] In response, Roosevelt instructed: "President still thinks that where the Igorrote has a mere G string that it might be well to add a short trunk to cover the buttocks and the front." And, for good measure, he repeated: "Please look into the feasibility of putting short trunks on the Igorrotes."[36]

GARY Y. OKIHIRO

When made public, the government-inspired cover-up drew a hoot of protest from a nature-loving public. "Dog-Eaters in Pants" announced a newspaper editorial. "The putting of pants on the Igorrote imputes a decided want of culture to the War Department of this, our glorious Empire," the editorial opined. "It is doubtful art, to say the least. . . . Draping Venus is as nothing to the crime of creating a scarecrow out of a beautiful live savage. . . . Putting pants on the Igorrote is cruelly incasing him in a capsule to render him less unpalatable." A cartoon in the *St. Louis Post-Dispatch* showed a pants-wielding Taft chasing a G-string-clad Igorot, and the paper's editor asked: "What do we all go out to the World's Fair for to see? The frank savagery of unaccommodated manhood or the symbol of shamefaced civilization?"[37] Within twenty-four hours of the announcement that the pants-on policy would soon take effect, the public overwhelmingly sided with "frank savagery," paid admissions to Igorot Village reportedly doubling from five to ten thousand in a rush to see the exhibition while the Igorots were still scantily clad.[38] And, in the end, the barrage of letters and the newspaper glee over the government cover-up forced the administration to relent, and loincloth prevailed over pants.

The triumph of ethnographic authenticity correlated unsurprisingly with the drawn line between savagery and civilization, nonwhite and white, woman and man. U.S. benevolence notwithstanding, a native dressed in the garb of Western culture was still a native. When St. Louis's white female schoolteachers invited men of the Philippine scout and constabulary, the finished products of U.S. tutorials, to accompany them on wanderings around the fairgrounds and the city, whites taunted the Filipina/os as "niggers." And, when those walking tours continued, despite the harassment, U.S. marines and the exposition's guards threatened to arrest the white women and expel their Filipina/o escorts from the fairgrounds. A group of marines charged the Filipina/o camp as if on a lynching party, shooting their revolvers in the air, and shouting: "Come on boys! Let's clean the Gu-Gus off the earth!"[39] The racial border patrol, generally white men intent on preserving their raced and gendered privileges, enforced the distinctions that defined whiteness or self in opposition to nonwhiteness or the other, manliness in opposition to womanliness, and citizenship or civility in opposition to alienness or barbarism. And, because the border-crossers—white women and Filipino men[40]—threatened the subjectivities and accompanying powers of the lynch mob, they had to be arrested or expelled.

## Comparative Racializations

The contrasting racializations of Puerto Ricans and Filipina/os appear affirmed by the U.S. Immigration Commission's *Dictionary of Races or Peoples*, published in 1911 and used to determine the race and, thereby, the qualification of peoples for entry into the nation-state. In that reference work, the term *Puerto Rican* inspires scant notice when compared with the treatment of *Filipino*. The *Dictionary* classes *Puerto Rican* as "any citizen of Porto Rico regardless of race" and directs the reader to the cognate terms *Spanish American, Cuban,* and *Negro.* In contrast, *Filipina/o* triggers an extended discussion of "a geographical rather than an ethnographical term, meaning any native of the Philippine Islands." For immigration purposes, the *Dictionary* notes, Filipina/os are covered under the terms *East Indian* and *Mongolic Division,* and they are divided into Malays and Negritos. Malays include Christians and non-Christians such as the Christian Tagalogs, Muslim Moros, and non-Christian Igorots, who are "the best-known representatives of the Primitive Malayan stock, still head-hunters." The Negrito, or "dwarf Negro stock," is dwindling in numbers, according to this reference work, and is "a disappearing remnant of one of the earliest and lowest races of mankind." Mestizos of Filipina/o-Spanish and Filipina/o-Chinese ancestry are another group in the Philippines, along with the pure Chinese, who constitute an important segment of the urban population. Like Puerto Ricans, the *Dictionary* directs, Filipina/os are not counted as immigrants, but Chinese from the Philippines are subject to "the usual restrictions," that is, the Chinese exclusion laws.[41] Instead, Filipina/os were, as colonial subjects, U.S. "nationals" and escaped, for a time, the exclusion laws that targeted Asians.

Appearances, however, can deceive, and racializations can occur under various guises.[42] As the historian Eileen J. Suárez Findlay observes: "Discourses about race became interwoven with those of gender and class—often deflecting and refracting off them, but never completely buried."[43] When racialized, Puerto Ricans were a "mixed population," half-breeds, and coloreds. Hybrids, the products of miscegenation in the racialized language of the late nineteenth century, were invariably of an inferior stock and of lower intelligence than "pure" whites, according to a standard text of the period.[44] Thus racialized, Puerto Rico's "mixed population," emphatically declared Whitelaw Reid, was the "enemy" at the U.S. gates because, I hold, multiracials defy the logic of white supremacy by embodying the falsity and perversity of racial categories and boundaries, especially the binary of black and white.[45] To U.S. capitalists,

Puerto Rico's peoples were racialized in class and gender terms as constituting dense populations of poverty, crime, and immorality (workers and unemployed women) but also as populations that were docile, obliging, and appreciative of favors (women and feminized male workers).[46] To white, heterosexual men on the prowl for the erotic exotic, Puerto Rican women exuded a potent sensuality that derived from their petite bodies, their air of mystery, and their hankering after the forbidden fruit. That sexuality, of course, was simultaneously a racialization and a gendering and contradicts the commonplace renderings of Puerto Ricans as invisible, racialized subjects. In truth, that very representation of invisible yet racialized (and gendered, classed, and sexualized) subjects serves the purposes of colonization and exploitation in Puerto Rico and on the U.S. continent.[47]

Likewise, Filipina/o racializations, gender inversions, and hypersexualities were images deployed by the state to advance its colonial interests in the Philippines. Science itself—ethnographies and photographs that mapped and named peoples—was part and parcel of that colonizing mission to reconstitute whiteness, manliness, and the nation-state in the face of nonwhiteness, womanliness, and the inchoate assembly of natives utterly unfit for self-government. Those reconstitutions came at a crucial moment in the nation's history, one involving the frontier's end, immigration, the New Woman, and the rise of urbanization and industrial capitalism. Filipino, like Puerto Rican, men were rendered feminine in their barbarism or condition of stunted intellectual development (as in children and women) and in the manliness of their women. The distinction between men and women of the "lower" races, a famous ethnographer advanced, was less than that between men and women of the "higher" races because men of the former group were less manly in size and muscular development.[48] Racialization thereby also involved a gendering. And, like the invisible racialization of Puerto Ricans, the very visible racialization (and gendering and sexualizing) of Filipina/os underwrote the U.S. colonial project in the Philippines and its domestic agenda of white supremacy, patriarchy, and nationalism.

## Notes

1. See, e.g., Worcester, *Philippine Islands*; Brinton, "Peoples of the Philippines"; Foreman, *The Philippine Islands*; Kroeber, "Measurements of Igorotes"; Bean, "Types of Negritos," "Philippine Types," and *Racial Anatomy*; and Barrows, "The Negrito and Allied Types."

2. Mintz, "North American Anthropological Contributions." I am grateful to my colleague Viranjini Munasinghe for this reference. On the absence (the self) and excess (the other) of culture, see Rosaldo, *Culture and Truth*, 196–217.

3. Urciuoli, *Exposing Prejudice*, 51.

4. Turner, *Frontier in American History*, 220–21.

5. Wu, ed., *"Chink!"* 70.

6. Quoted in Brinkley, *American History*, 511.

7. Quoted in Parrington, *Main Currents in American Thought*, 58–59.

8. Rudyard Kipling's poem "The White Man's Burden" was written expressly to prod the United States into assuming the responsibilities of colonialism in the Philippines (*Rudyard Kipling's Verse*, 373–74).

9. From a report of an interview with William McKinley at the White House on 21 November 1899, originally published in the *Christian Advocate*, 22 January 1903, and re-printed in Bailey and Kennedy, eds., *American Spirit*, 2:579–80. History contradicts McKinley's version, as pointed out in Drinnon, *Facing West*, 279–80.

10. Quoted in Drinnon, *Facing West*, 278.

11. Bederman, *Manliness and Civilization*, 15.

12. Empire abroad and social reform at home provided white, middle-class women with opportunities for their own uplift, especially when confronting racialized inferiors (see e.g., Holt, *Colonizing Filipinas*, 60–80; and Pascoe, *Relations of Rescue*).

13. Reid, *Problems of Expansion*, 13–14, 205, 208–9.

14. Carroll, *Report*, 77.

15. On the criminalizing of the rural poor, see Santiago-Valles, *"Subject People."*

16. Carroll, *Report*, 22–23. For an insightful study of Ponce and the intersections of race, gender, sexuality, and class, see Suárez Findlay, *Imposing Decency*.

17. *New York Times*, 11 July 1898.

18. Dinwiddie, *Puerto Rico*, 166.

19. War Department, *Puerto Rico*, 43, 44, 47. See also Dinwiddie, *Puerto Rico*, 162, 166.

20. Ober, *Puerto Rico*, 162–63, 163–64, 168, 169–70, 170.

21. A popular source of racialized and gendered imagery was William S. Bryan's *Our Islands and Their People as Seen with Camera and Pencil* (2 vols. [St. Louis: N. D. Thompson, 1899]). For an insightful close reading of Bryan's representations of Puerto Rico, see Thompson, *Nuestra isla*. For a review of Bryan's *Our Islands* and its representations of Filipinas, see Holt, *Colonizing Filipinas*, 98–119.

22. Hutterer, "Philippine Anthropology."

23. Quoted in ibid., 129–30.

24. See, e.g., Bederman, *Manliness and Civilization*; and Hoganson, *Fighting for American Manhood*.

25. Drinnon, *Facing West*, 279–306. Drinnon points out that Worcester's principal contribution was to insist on the "native" and "tribal" nature of the Philippines, thereby denying the inhabitants "peoplehood" and, hence, the possibility of self-rule. For another connection between empire, Native Americans, and the Philippines, see Williams, "Philippine Annexation." On U.S. colonialism's mission to mold "a people" in the Philippines, see Rafael, "White Love."

26. Hutterer, "Philippine Anthropology," 132, 133.

27. Worcester, *Philippine Islands*, 472, 473–82; Hutterer, "Philippine Anthropology," 138.

28. On the colonial cataloging of races for their management, see Cohn, *Anthropologist among the Historians*.

29. See Vergara, *Displaying Filipinos*; Hutterer, "Philippine Anthropology," 139–42; Edwards, ed., *Anthropology and Photography*; and Holt, *Colonizing Filipinas*, 98–119.

30. Vaughan, "Ogling Igorots," 220, 221. See also Worcester, "Non-Christian Peoples."

31. Rydell, *All the World's a Fair*, 160.

32. On the continuing war in the Philippines, see Miller, *"Benevolent Assimilation."* On the antiwar movement in the United States, see Beisner, *Twelve against Empire*.

33. Rydell, *All the World's a Fair*, 167, 171.

34. Vaughan, "Ogling Igorots," 224–25.

35. Rydell, *All the World's a Fair*, 172.

36. Vaughan, "Ogling Igorots," 225.

37. Rydell, *All the World's a Fair*, 174; and Vaughan, "Ogling Igorots," 225.

38. Vaughan, "Ogling Igorots," 226.

39. Rydell, *All the World's a Fair*, 176–77. On the career and possible origin of the epithets *goo-goo* and *gook*, see Roediger, *Abolition of Whiteness*, 117–20.

40. There would arise later occasions in the United States when Filipino men threatened white manly privilege in their intimacies with white women (see, e.g., Quinsaat, ed., *Letters in Exile*, 63–71; and Cressey, *Taxi-Dance Hall*, 145–74).

41. *Dictionary of Races or Peoples*, Reports of the Immigration Commission, U.S. Senate, 61st Cong., 3rd sess., 1911, S. Doc. 622. 106, 57–58. Chinese exclusion laws included the 1875 Page Law, which was used to bar Asian women, and the immigration acts of 1882, 1892, and 1902, which excluded Chinese laborers.

42. Lanny Thompson has correctly pointed out that it is insufficient to label the new U.S. possessions as an undifferentiated other, given the differential means of incorporation of Hawaii, as a territory, and of Puerto Rico, the Philippines, and Guam, as unincorporated territories (see Thompson, "Imperial Republic"; cf. Jacobson, *Barbarian Virtues*, 221–59; and Cabán, *Constructing a Colonial People*, 87–88).

43. Suárez Findlay, *Imposing Decency*, 7. Suárez Findlay's main concern is not the representations by the colonizers of the colonized but the regulation of practices and Puerto Rican self-representations around the axes of race, gender, sexuality, and class.

44. Brinton, *Races and Peoples*, 287.

45. See Okihiro, *Common Ground*, 28–54; and Nakashima, "Invisible Monster."

46. On the racialization of class, see Martínez-Alier, *Marriage, Class, and Colour*; and Santiago-Valles, *"Subject People,"* 43–48. On the racialization of gender (as docile and childlike), see Fernandez, *Disenchanted Island*, 12–15.

47. See, e.g., Thompson, "Representation and Rule."

48. Brinton, *Races and Peoples*, 37–38.

## 2   INVERTING RACIAL LOGIC

*How Public Health Discourse and Standards Racialized the*
*Meanings of Japanese and Mexican in Los Angeles, 1910–1924*

Natalia Molina

In the late nineteenth century and the early twentieth, the health inspectors on Ellis Island represented one of the most familiar examples of public officials empowered to decide who was fit to be a member of U.S. society. There, public health officials examined newly arrived immigrants to try to assess whether they would be productive workers or were likely to become public charges owing to poor health. These officials based their assessments on practices ranging from cursory physical inspections, such as flipping immigrants' eyelids with a buttonhook instrument to check for conjunctivitis, to visual evaluation of how immigrants carried their luggage and whether their posture hinted at any possible afflictions.[1] By means of such ostensibly scientific practices, public health workers were some of the first professionals to decide whether immigrants had the makings of good citizens.

But public health officers' roles in assessing the potential worthiness of immigrants did not stop at the nation's points of entry. This essay demonstrates how, through various discourses and programs, public health professionals could help define who was considered an acceptable member of U.S. society. Policymakers considered public health an important component of the Americanization agenda, along with learning English and adopting American customs and diets. Health professionals were vested with the power to declare some groups "inassimilable." Other groups were marked as culturally inferior yet, under the proper guidance, capable of adopting U.S. customs and standards. For immigrants deemed necessary for the body politic, such as greatly needed manual laborers, public health standards and discourses could serve as normalizing agents, making them more acceptable to the general public. For immigrants considered to be a threat to the social order, such as those who transcended their role as laborers to become entrepreneurs, for example, public health standards and discourses could mark their bodies as threats to the well-being of the nation.[2]

In order to define some immigrant groups as more "assimilable" than others, public health officials ascribed "objective" characteristics and differences to each ethnic and racial group. Public health officials were, therefore, instrumental with regard to the infusion of meaning into racial categories. Two ways that public health officials contributed to understandings of racial categories were by expanding definitions of racial categories and by reinforcing racial hierarchies. According to Michael Omi and Howard Winant, racialization constitutes a "sociohistorical process by which racial categories are created, inhabited, transformed, and destroyed."[3] This essay examines how public health professionals in the United States expanded understandings of Japanese and Mexicans from 1910 to 1924, establishing not only the means but also the justification for disparate treatment of immigrant groups. For example, Los Angeles health officials added a medicalized dimension to the notion of the Yellow Peril, further perpetuating an anti-Asian sentiment that defined all Asians as infinitely foreign and threatening to white Americans. At the same time, health officials offered a public health component to the Americanization efforts extended to Mexicans, one designed to assist this group's acceptance into society.[4] Just as the meaning of racial categories varied across groups, so did those groups' position in the U.S. racial hierarchy, some being valued more highly than others. The political scientist Claire Kim refers to this process as *racial ordering*.[5] Public health created discourses of inclusion and exclusion and, thus, actively participated in this racial ordering. In so doing, it served as a key institution in regulating these different racialized groups' positions within the social order.

Concepts of race were also gendered. Many health programs were extended (or denied) to men and women differently in accordance with their racial and ethnic backgrounds. For example, those opposed to Japanese immigration singled out Japanese women as transgressing domestic boundaries by working in the fields of family-owned and -operated farms, thus competing against white farmers. Mexican women, however, worked as low-paid laborers alongside their male relatives in agricultural fields or lived with them in railroad camps. Moreover, their domestic and social reproduction work supported low-paid Mexican men. Thus, Mexican women, unlike Japanese women, did not threaten existing racial hierarchies. Therefore, health officials extended programs to Mexican women that would help normalize their position as immigrant women in U.S. society while not disrupting their acceptably low social position. They denied such programs to Japanese women and, instead, singled them out in perpetuation of nativist discourse.

Both Japanese and Mexicans readily resisted both negative cultural depictions of their communities and the structurally disadvantaged positions that their groups occupied within the U.S. racial hierarchy. One example of this resistance is the strategies employed by Japanese immigrants in response to the Alien Land Acts. In 1913, and again in 1920, based on the belief that Japanese farmers were gaining an economic foothold in the United States, and encouraged by medicalized racializations of Japanese farmers as dirty (see below), California passed the Alien Land Acts, which prevented those ineligible for citizenship from owning land or even leasing land for more than three years. Japanese—who were, indeed, ineligible for citizenship—circumvented these laws to ensure their economic livelihoods by placing land titles in the names of their Nisei children, who were American citizens.[6] In urban areas such as Los Angeles, Japanese formed community groups, like the Japanese Association of Southern California, which was part of the umbrella group the Japanese Association of America. The historian John Modell characterizes the Japanese Association of America and its offshoots as organizations that embraced Americanization and sought social acceptance through accommodation, not resistance.[7] They worked with local and state health departments and taught health, hygiene, and child care to their members in hopes that they would "cultivate the taste of American social life."[8] Other members of the Japanese community challenged the medicalized representations of Japanese head-on. In the 1920s, when Senator James Phelan went on a statewide tour to garner support for his Japanese exclusion movement, Professor K. S. Inui of the University of Southern California challenged him in community forums throughout Los Angeles.[9] As the second-generation Japanese community, the Nisei, increased and grew older, strategies of resistance changed as well. The historian Lon Kurashige skillfully demonstrates how the Japanese community, both first-generation Issei and second-generation Nisei, created a community-based festival, Nisei Week, in order to engage in a process of racial rearticulation, in which they reclaimed and re-created popular cultural constructions of their community.[10]

Like the Japanese, Mexicans also combated their disenfranchised position within the U.S. racial hierarchy. Mexican laborers were the main sources of labor in the railroad and agricultural fields, which is where health officials established some of their very first programs directed at Mexicans. Mexicans fought their poor (unsafe and unclean) working conditions through unions.[11] As a largely immigrant population, they sought assistance, not from American

NATALIA MOLINA

institutions, but from the Mexican consulate.[12] Mexicans were most likely to seek help from the consulate when seeking redress against employers who fired them or burdened them with hospital bills after they had been injured on the job. In many cases, it was the laborers' families who contacted the consulate for help when family members had been killed on the job and the clearly at-fault employers refused to provide any form of compensation.[13] As the population began to be dominated by second-generation Mexican Americans during the 1930s, the Mexican community, like the Japanese community, formed activist groups, community groups, and unions that embraced strategies of racial rearticulation.[14]

Los Angeles is a particularly rich site to examine with regard to the construction of racial categories during the early twentieth century because of the specific attention paid there to particular immigrant groups. While in other parts of the country citizenship and race were often equated with whiteness and blackness, within the multiethnic setting of Los Angeles government leaders across institutions directed their attention to Mexican and Japanese residents of the county.[15] In the late nineteenth century and the early twentieth, Los Angeles boosters (promoters) publicized the city to Midwest and East Coast whites in hopes of attracting them to the city as investors and as residents. In their promotions, boosters erased the presence of ethnic communities, preferring to depict Los Angeles as a white, homogeneous city.[16] This cultural representation of the city extended far beyond boosterism. Ethnic communities were marginalized, not just for promotional purposes, but in actuality, through local ordinances and policies.[17] Public health programs both took their cue from and reinforced the racial politics of the city and of the nation.

Racializing Japanese and Mexicans as nonwhite held particular significance in Los Angeles, a city promoted as racially pure. In a 1935 historical account of Los Angeles, one writer reminisced: "Seen from a distance, Los Angeles is a white city."[18] Since Japanese and Mexicans were racialized as nonwhite, they were by extension considered second-class residents of the city. By attributing specific problems, such as disease and deviance, to these communities, these inadequacies could be separated from the city and considered a result only of the cultural deficiencies of immigrant groups, not of wider, systematic inadequacies in the developing city. There was, therefore, a clear stake involved in defining Japanese and Mexicans as nonwhite.

An influential body of literature has demonstrated the ways in which European immigrant groups in the Midwest and on the East Coast that are now considered white were once racialized others and subjected to discrimination.[19] Likewise in the West, Mexicans and Japanese were the racialized other.[20] While Mexicans occupied a higher position than Japanese within the racial hierarchy, they were, nonetheless, racialized as nonwhite, limiting their access to power.[21] While some groups, such as the Irish and the Italians, were accepted into society and became white, Japanese were deemed ineligible for citizenship, while Mexicans were suspended in the process of becoming American.

The experience of Mexicans and Japanese illustrates the origins of the category *nonwhite* in Los Angeles. While the two groups were racialized very differently, they shared a neocolonial relationship to the United States. Although Japanese were eventually barred from the United States, they left behind a legacy of expanding the category *nonwhite*. Mexicans, who were a *mestizaje* (mixture) of Spanish, Indian, and African ancestry, also helped expand the category *nonwhite* far beyond the notion of blackness.

This essay relies mainly on the Los Angeles County Health Department's records, which include reports, memos, press releases, and public speeches. The records, which are sparse at times, mainly provide an overview of department programs. Through an examination of the health department in its first few years of development, one can trace the progression of an institutional culture shaped by the contemporary racial politics of the day, a racial politics that would have long-lasting effects. This essay does not apply twenty-first-century standards to judge whether public health officials practiced good or bad science. Instead, it examines the programs that public health officials developed in order to help understand the prevailing racial discourses of the day.

Japanese began emigrating to the United States in large numbers after 1882 in response to the labor demand that resulted after the Chinese Exclusion Act limited the number of Chinese laborers available for hire. In the aftermath of the Chinese Exclusion Act, Japanese bore the brunt of residual anti-Chinese sentiment. Such racism continued into the twentieth century as the Japanese population continued to grow. In 1890, the Issei population in California numbered just over 1,000. In just ten years, this number grew to over 10,000. Although these figures represent the Japanese population for the entire state, Japanese concentrated mainly in San Francisco and the San Joaquin Valley until 1900. As the agricultural industry grew in southern California, more Japanese settled in Los Angeles. By 1910, the Japanese population there at 8,641 rivaled that of San

Francisco.[22] Two decades later, Japanese residents in Los Angeles would number 35,000, with Japanese Americans constituting half this population.[23]

Japanese made significant inroads in California's agricultural industry. They were most highly represented in the sugar-beet industry, where they constituted 85 percent of the labor force, but they were to be found across the agricultural spectrum. Despite their notable contribution to the agricultural industry (or because of it), Japanese came to be seen as a threat because of their significant numbers and because they often underbid competitors. According to Tomás Almaguer, Japanese were often successful in organizing labor and demanding and receiving higher wages once established in a given area.[24] In addition, they began to purchase and lease their own farmland and to sell the produce at market stands and out of their trucks. In Los Angeles County, it was estimated that Japanese operated 85 percent of the vegetable truck businesses.[25]

Dominant views to the effect that Japanese represented a racial and economic threat to the United States constituted one strain of the Yellow Peril. Politicians and civic leaders popularized this belief, portraying Japanese independent farmers as threats to white livelihoods. Legislators considered Japanese such an economic threat that, as we have seen, they passed the Alien Land Acts of 1913 and 1920. But the threat that they perceived went far beyond the issue of ownership of land to encompass the high Japanese birthrates, which they evoked as more evidence of a Japanese takeover. Slogans such as "Keep California White" were used to rally people to support the 1920 act.[26]

Through public speeches, municipal forums, and policy formation, public health officials also clearly aligned themselves with opponents of the Japanese, thus adding medical authority to such nativist campaigns. Thanks to the medicalized racializations of Japanese farmers as dirty, mentioned earlier, public health officials had an excuse to monitor Japanese-farmed produce, which, they claimed, was cultivated under unsanitary conditions and could therefore spread disease, particularly intestinal diseases, to which "the Japanese nation [was] subject."[27] In the process, the perceived threat of the Japanese overtaking all American farmland was repositioned as a more immediate concern. In addition, public health officials in Los Angeles began keeping track of Japanese birthrates, adding scientific legitimacy to otherwise unsubstantiated claims by politicians that Japanese immigrants were going to overtake the city.[28] In Los Angeles, health officials were essentially the only government employees coming into contact with the Japanese in the county. Their numbers, reports, and interpretations therefore became the official narrative on the Japanese, highlighting the power of public health in legitimizing and perpetuating the threat of the Yellow Peril.

Just as public health officials could add a medicalized dimension to anxieties concerning the Yellow Peril, conversely, they also had the capability to assuage people's fears of Mexican immigration. Public health officials did not disagree with immigration restrictionists that Mexicans were culturally deficient as compared to white Americans. They did assert, however, that they could redeem Mexicans through "supervision and temporary aid only," teaching them how to conduct themselves in a proper American manner.[29]

Such assurances were deemed necessary as a response to alarm expressed by whites over the increasing Mexican presence in the Southwest. The Mexican population in the United States in the early twentieth century increased for a variety of reasons. Since the 1890s, Mexicans had grown dissatisfied with Mexican President Porfirio Diaz's land policies, which left many landless and with few economic options. In Mexico, people who lived in rural areas migrated to cities in search of employment and opportunities. The Mexican Revolution, which began in 1910, encouraged further emigration to the United States. The establishment and connection of railroad lines facilitated transportation for Mexicans who sought employment in the United States, many of whom had migrated from central Mexico. While El Paso was the main port of entry into the United States, many Mexicans eventually migrated and settled in Los Angeles. That city's Mexican population grew rapidly in the first few decades of the twentieth century—from five thousand in 1910, to thirty thousand in 1920, to ninety-seven thousand by 1930.[30]

Public health officials represented one of the professions that would help to both supervise and sanitize this population. Big business leaders lobbied on behalf of Mexicans, countering images of them as having poor health and hygiene and being culturally backward.[31] Health officials stressed that, through their programs, Mexicans could adopt American practices and become better workers. Like other Americanization programs of the time, these public health programs strove to teach American standards to immigrants, thereby reducing the more troubling aspects of ethnic differences. Adoption of American standards, however, did not translate into socioeconomic mobility for Mexicans, as it did for many European groups, nor did it guarantee acceptance into the U.S. body politic.[32]

NATALIA MOLINA

As government institutions shaped popular perceptions of immigrants, so too would immigrants' racial position in the United States be shaped by their encounters with these institutions. The everyday health issues faced by Mexican and Japanese residents in Los Angeles—communicable diseases, birthing concerns, access to safe water—all came under the jurisdiction of the newly established Los Angeles County Health Department. Prior to 1915, the health department had existed as a one-person office, and the health officer's duties mainly involved dealing with quarantines and conducting sanitation inspections of such industries as hog farms and slaughterhouses. Only in the case of an epidemic had the health officer focused on providing health services to the residents of the county. By examining the development of the new health department programs, one can clearly see how they were shaped by the dominant racial attitudes of the time.

Dr. John Larabee Pomeroy headed the Los Angeles County Health Department from its inception in 1915, and he set forth an anti-Asian agenda that he maintained for the twenty-six years he was in office. Like many other prominent leaders in Los Angeles who were transplants to the city, Pomeroy hailed from a region of the country where race was conceived of in black-white terms. Born in 1883, Pomeroy grew up in Louisville, Kentucky. After receiving his medical degree, he moved to New York. While working for the New York City Health Department, he trained under one of the national leaders in public health, Dr. Herman Briggs. After serving a few years as an assistant surgeon in the U.S. Army in Spokane, Washington, Pomeroy accepted a position as a resident physician in Monrovia, California, and soon opened his own private practice. In 1912, he became Monrovia's health officer, and, in 1915, he became the newly established Los Angeles County Health Department's first full-time health officer. In his position as the head of the health department, Pomeroy dealt with ethnic groups that did not readily fit in his black-white notion of race but were, nonetheless, familiar to him through national discourses of the Yellow Peril and Manifest Destiny.[33]

As the department developed and began to focus more on communities within Los Angeles County, health officials often discussed Japanese and Mexicans as obstacles to their progress and modernization efforts. Of the 120,000 estimated residents who lived in the county's rural areas in the late 1910s, health officials estimated that 7,500 of those residents were Japanese and 10,000 Mexican. Because African Americans lived mainly within the city limits, they did not come to the attention of county health officials as readily. Health officials often referred to Japanese and Mexicans as communities that had "difficulties peculiar to their ignorance and lack of understanding English."[34] Although there were other ethnic groups (e.g., Russians, Syrians, and Italians) living in the county, health officials expressed no concerns over them. While Progressive-era reformers in other parts of the country focused their programs on these European ethnic groups, in Los Angeles the need to Americanize such groups appears to have been less pressing in comparison to the need to deal with Mexicans or Japanese.[35]

Birthrates were one of the main issues that focused the attention of health officers on Japanese and Mexicans. Health officials expressed concern over the birthrates of both, but more so over those of the Japanese, many equating the increase in the Japanese population with the development of an economic stronghold. Such concerns likely increased with the establishment of the Gentleman's Agreement of 1907–8 between the United States and Japan, under the terms of which Japan prohibited the emigration of men seeking jobs as laborers, but not that of women as wives or prospective wives, whose fertility was therefore considered a particular threat. Prior to this time, the ratio of men to women in the Japanese community was eight or nine to one. By 1920, this ratio had declined to two or three to one.[36] Because renewed Mexican emigration to the United States had begun only in the 1910s, the public expressed concern mainly over an increase in the Mexican population through immigration, not so much birthrates.

The language of overpopulation was not new, but it was now linked to eugenics. In the early years of the twentieth century, eugenics was an emerging practice and discourse with the stated purpose of improving society. Eugenicists embraced hereditarian beliefs that advocated reproduction only for the superior races. Both race-suicide and race-betterment discourses, interdependent theories, stressed that white women's birthrates were dropping while immigrant women's were rising. The proponents of race betterment, a positive form of eugenics, worked toward the end of increasing birthrates among white women, thereby strengthening the nation's racial stock. The proponents of race suicide, a negative form of eugenics, worked toward the end of decreasing birthrates among immigrants and African Americans.

Eugenics gained widespread currency through the work of such figures as Lothrop Stoddard (e.g., *The Rising Tide of Color*), Madison Grant (e.g., *The*

NATALIA MOLINA

*Passing of the Great Race*), and Oswald Spengler (e.g., *The Decline of the West*). These authors were concerned primarily with Southern and Eastern European immigrants, only occasionally mentioning Asians and Mexicans. But, in the American Southwest, their ideas were appropriated and applied to Japanese and Mexicans.

The majority of public health officials distanced themselves from the most extreme of eugenicist policies. But, just as the foundation of eugenics rested on a belief in a racial hierarchy, many public health programs targeting immigrants in the early twentieth century were based on a theory of racial hierarchy.[37] Nationwide, medical and public health professionals, as well as social reformers, heralded a growing concern over high immigrant birthrates, which, they contended, threatened to equal or even surpass white birthrates. This essay demonstrates how race-betterment and race-suicide discourses influenced public health practices and shaped how (and why) the Los Angeles County Health Department offered disparate public health programs to Mexicans and Japanese.

Within an overall context of concern about the rapidly increasing immigrant population in general, health officials primarily focused on Mexicans and Japanese as specific examples of rapidly growing immigrant groups. Through departmental reports and memos issued to the public throughout the 1910s, health officials kept track of the birthrates of both these groups. The public, however, expressed more concern about the recent increase in the Mexican population through immigration than about birthrates among the Mexicans. Nevertheless, health officials used terms such as *enormous* and *rapidly growing* to describe the birthrates of Japanese and, to a lesser extent, Mexicans. They compared the number of Japanese and Mexican births directly to the number of white births in order to position Japanese and Mexicans as growing racial threats. In a memorandum to the *Los Angeles Tribune*, health officials informed the public: "Of 1,725 births last year, 25 percent were Japanese, 12 percent Mexicans, and only 62.5 percent white. . . . The Japanese are rapidly increasing throughout the rural districts."[38] The memorandum, however, does not make clear that these figures refer only to the rural areas of the county. Japanese and Mexicans were known to concentrate more heavily in rural areas because, there, they could find farmland to lease and more affordable rents. For example, the title of the chart in the 1917 annual health report from which the figures in the memo are taken clearly reads: "Births: In Rural Territory, outside of Incorporated Cities."[39] Because only birthrates for the rural areas of the county have been provided, the ratio of Mexican and Japanese births to white births appears higher than it would had birthrates for the entire county been provided. In fact, the percentage of native-born whites in the entire county remained consistently between 77.7 and 80.1 percent from 1900 to 1930, but highlighting the white births in the rural areas of the county at 62.5 percent makes it appear as if birthrates had dropped dramatically.[40]

These numbers were particularly dangerous as they were reported as fact and then circulated by civic and political leaders. For example, Senator James Phelan adopted them as he toured southern California to rally support for his anti-Japanese campaign. He argued that white Americans had a duty to do something about the birthrate in rural Los Angeles County, "where for every three births one is Japanese." Appropriating the language popularized by the eugenics literature, Phelan warned that "[w]e must stop this yellow tide and regain the soil for our own people," again highlighting how public health statistics, in this case birthrates, could be used for political ends.[41]

Health officials not only produced statistics but also led a charge against Japanese (but not Mexicans). An examination of the health department's programs, or lack thereof, demonstrates how racial discourses affected local practices. Dr. Pomeroy launched a series of attacks against the Los Angeles Japanese community that portrayed it as both a racial and a financial threat. In a speech entitled "The Japanese Evil in California," presented to the congregation of the San Dimas Church and later published in the California magazine *The Grizzly Bear*, Pomeroy warned Californians that the Japanese were successful farmers and that their achievements could undermine American farmers' prosperity, although he acknowledged that, "due to the shortage in labor," employers often needed to hire Japanese workers. He cautioned, however, that hiring the Japanese was actually an economic liability because they formed work cooperatives, thereby driving up wages over time. In his personal notes for "The Japanese Evil," Pomeroy mapped the different areas of town and the number of acres Japanese owned in each section.[42]

Pomeroy's speech articulated the growing concerns over Japanese in the agricultural industry. By 1920, of the 440,000 acres of land cultivated in Los Angeles County, an estimated 5 percent was operated by Japanese, mostly through leases. Between 1910 and 1920, the number of Japanese-owned farms tripled, and the total acreage farmed by Japanese increased more than seven-

NATALIA MOLINA

fold.[43] The Japanese produced crops that others had resisted farming because they were labor intensive, such as strawberries. Japanese success with certain crops, such as fresh berries and celery, led critics to portray them as monopolizing these crops. As we have seen, the belief that Japanese farmers presented unfair competition to white farmers ultimately led to the 1913 and 1920 Alien Land Acts.

Furthermore, Pomeroy linked what he characterized as rising Japanese birthrates with the Japanese position in the agricultural industry, implying that the Japanese economic stronghold would only increase as the population grew. He included in "The Japanese Evil" a chart comparing births in the county from 1915 to 1919 using the categories *white, Japanese, Mexicans,* and *others.* With 27 percent of births in the rural areas of the county, the Japanese were portrayed as a growing racial threat. In a separate chart, Pomeroy tracked births per district throughout the unincorporated areas of the county, specifically indicating where Japanese births outnumbered white births. As if these numbers were not already alarming enough, health department officials pointed out that it was difficult to obtain accurate birthrates for the Japanese in the rural communities and that actual Japanese birthrates could be even higher.[44] Such concerns of course call into question the accuracy of the numbers Pomeroy used in the first place.

Clearly, if birthrates were held up as evidence of the threat that the Japanese posed, then Japanese women were targeted as particular threats. Once in the United States, they could both give birth to Japanese Americans and work in the fields. Pomeroy characterized these births as "startling" since they represented the "growth of a large American citizenship, yellow in color."[45] As American citizens, Japanese Americans had the right to purchase land, thereby undermining the intent of the 1920 Alien Land Act.

In addition, Pomeroy and others considered Japanese women working in the fields alongside men to be transgressing the limits of prescribed gender roles; if they were working in the fields, then they could not be at home, raising their children properly.[46] (Ironically, American gender ideology was being used to judge a group considered inassimilable.) Underlying these critiques were concerns that Japanese farmers had an added advantage when they worked in family units in the fields. (Interestingly, similar critiques were not directed at Mexican women, who also toiled alongside their families as agricultural laborers.) Citing as evidence health department as well as independent university studies, Pomeroy suggested to the Los Angeles County Board of Supervisors that the federal Children's Bureau be called in to educate Japanese women about American notions of child care and to enforce regulations requiring the registering of births.[47] Such a request demonstrates how the head of one department could potentially set in motion a racially based agenda in another institution. In addition, the specific request for help in compelling the registration of births speaks to how the politics of race influenced how and why statistics were gathered. Thus, attention to public health issues, such as birthrates, could simultaneously medicalize and engender the Yellow Peril.

As seen from the ways that politicians and sociologists appropriated Pomeroy's concerns and statistics, Pomeroy helped construct the prevailing racial ideologies of his time. In addition, he was not alone in espousing such views within the medical community. Others explicitly made links between the increase in Japanese birthrates and increased Japanese economic power. Some doctors strongly vocalized their concerns over race suicide in legitimate scientific arenas. In a regional medical journal, Dr. W. O. Henry urged "well bred white women" to procreate and warned them that, if they did not "bear sufficient children, the Japanese and other foreign women [would] keep up the needful human production, just as the Japs and foreigners [would] meet the farming needs of the country when American men fail or refuse to do it," thereby tying economic and racial fears together. Henry went on to ask: "Will it be the cultured, civilized, educated American women or must we depend upon the foreign, ignorant, uncultured, and half civilized?" He compared the urgent need for white women to procreate to France's need to raise its birthrates after World War I. Interestingly, racial fears also drove France's population campaign, one that labeled some women, such as midwives and abortionists, as traitors to the state.[48]

Suggesting that high birthrates substantiated claims of an emerging Japanese stronghold was only one example of medicalized nativism directed against the Japanese. In addition, notions of Japanese farmers as spreading disease through the produce they cultivated also helped marginalize the Japanese community. Every aspect of Japanese farmers' lives came under scrutiny. Because many Japanese farmers lived on the same land that they cultivated, their housing became an issue for public forums. Japanese often lived in inexpensively constructed homes that housing and health officials portrayed as inferior to "typical" housing found in Los Angeles, such as the California bungalow and the craftsman-style home.[49] Not taken into account was the fact that the Alien Land Acts of 1913 and 1920 left most Japanese the option only of leasing land for three years at a time, thus reducing any incentive to build more permanent housing. Health and housing officials depicted all Japanese housing as unsanitary, and, by extension, they reasoned that those unsanitary conditions could spread to the produce that the Japanese cultivated. Despite the limited staffing in the health department, Pomeroy proposed that funds be made available to hire someone "who could devote his entire time" to monitoring Japanese-operated farms.[50]

Public health officials played a key role in promoting the image of Japanese farmers as disease carriers. The issue of sanitation on Japanese farms became particularly prominent in discussions of the spread of typhoid. Notably, typhoid cases remained distinctly low during the 1910s and 1920s. Nonetheless, public health officials began raising the specter of disease with regard to Japanese produce. They argued that the types of produce that the Japanese farmed, such as berries, were ideal carriers of typhoid since people generally consumed them raw. Furthermore, in correspondence with the Los Angeles County Board of Supervisors, as well as in open forums and published articles directed at both the public health community and a general audience, Pomeroy depicted Japanese farmers as harbingers of disease. A 1920 medical journal noted his opinion that an increase in typhoid-fever rates could be traced back to the food supplied by the "Japanese farmers who disregarded the health laws of the state."[51] Pomeroy's revised opinion was in keeping with stricter attitudes toward Japanese in 1920, most notably, the revised Alien Land Law Act of 1920.

The attitudes of public health officials also went beyond the scope of the public health forum. The Board of Supervisors relied on Dr. Pomeroy's opinions on matters pertaining to what it termed the "Japanese Question in Los Angeles."[52] Pomeroy's viewpoints, which were given credibility by their acceptance by scientific authority, had the potential to spark legislation targeting Japanese. This was not the first time that public health discourse shaped urban legislation during the Progressive era. In 1912, arguing that Chinese vendors undermined white vendors in the city's marketplace, and citing sanitation reasons as well, Los Angeles City officials had passed an ordinance forcing Chinese vendors to relocate their stalls from the city's general market area to a more isolated marketplace created specifically for them. Seven years later, addressing concerns over the potential of Japanese-cultivated produce to spread typhoid, Pomeroy cited the case of the Chinese vendors as a precedent for enacting an ordinance that would "[prohibit] the sale of infected or unwholesome fruit and vegetables," an ordinance specifically targeting Japanese farmers and vendors. Pomeroy's reference to the 1912 ordinance demonstrated how previous racialized legislation paved the way for future racialized legislation. The proposed ordinance would expand the authority of health officials by declaring all fruit and vegetable stands subject to inspection. Moreover, vendors themselves would be subject to physical examination.[53] In this way, the specter of disease was mobilized to increase the regulatory powers of the newly emerging health department.

Thus, the public perception of the Japanese had, through the lens of the Yellow Peril, come to be that of a community simultaneously inassimilable and economically threatening. Medical discourse helped expand how to measure the Japanese as a threat by focusing attention on birthrates and a perceived ability to spread disease through agricultural produce. Public health officials in Los Angeles, with the power of their emerging profession and department behind them, identified these issues and determined to resolve them, thereby bolstering their department's and their own professional authority. In the process, they expanded understandings of what the category *Japanese* meant in the early twentieth century and circulated this expanded racial category throughout the nation.

### Sanitizing the Mexican Workforce

While public health officials could use their authority to restrict a group's social and economic position in the United States, they could also do the opposite. This section provides an examination of how public health officials helped make the Mexican workforce more acceptable to the general public, largely by offering programs to Mexicans that emphasized so-called American models of health and hygiene, thereby assuring the general public that, because Mexicans could, unlike the Japanese, be brought to conform with American standards, they posed no threat to the white majority. Such assurances were necessary as many opposed Mexican immigration and fought for tighter border restrictions throughout the 1910s, during which period Mexicans were stepping in to replace the Japanese workforce, just as the Japanese had earlier stepped in to replace the Chinese workforce. Still, Mexicans posed less of a threat than the Japanese did because they worked primarily as laborers and did not purchase farmland. They were, thus, largely welcomed, especially by Southwestern capitalists, who saw them as both a necessary and a docile workforce more likely than not to return home to Mexico at the end of the harvesting season.

Mexican birthrates did not elicit the same level of concern from health officials in the 1910s as did Japanese birthrates. One reason was that the Mexican population in the United States was, as we have seen, growing most rapidly through immigration. Another reason was that Mexican birthrates were lower than Japanese birthrates. For example, while Japanese births in the unincorporated areas of Los Angeles County accounted, as we have seen, for approximately 30 percent of all births from 1915 to 1919, Mexican births in the same areas accounted for only about 13 percent of all births in 1916 and 1917, just over 17 percent in 1918, and just under 19 percent in 1919.[54] Despite the slight increase in the latter, because Mexican birthrates were charted in conjunction with Japanese birthrates, concerns over the former were eclipsed by concerns over the latter.

Faced with both a temporary and a permanent Mexican population, public health officials dealt first with the immediate health risks, especially infant mortality rates (IMRS) and disease outbreaks, both of which attracted particularly negative attention to the Mexican community. The shift in focus from birthrates to IMRS speaks to the different ways in which Mexicans and Japanese were racialized. The Japanese were perceived as an economic threat, so a focus on their health problems spurred punitive legislation. The Mexicans were perceived as an economic boon, as a much-needed source of cheap labor, so a focus on their health problems spurred attempts to improve their living conditions.

High IMRS among the Mexican community caused great concern for several reasons. First, because infants were considered more susceptible than adults to an unhealthy environment, IMRS had been used since the early 1870s as an important gauge of public health and, hence, a health department's efficacy. High IMRS among the Mexican community thus reflected badly on the nascent Los Angeles County Health Department. Second, the issue of IMRS itself appealed to the public at an emotional level, focusing as it did on infants and children. Third, the issue of IMRS had since the mid-nineteenth century been tied to immigration, rising national IMRS being seen as the result of increased immigration into East Coast cities and, thus, blamed on immigrants and "their filthy immigrant slums."[55] As a result, IMRS were elevated from a mere health problem to a bona fide social concern.

Indeed, Mexicans' IMRS were very high. Mexicans living in rural areas of the county suffered higher IMRs than any other ethnic group. IMRs were especially high among the Mexican agricultural workers who lived in the San Gabriel Valley: as many as three hundred deaths per thousand live births. The health department attributed the high Mexican IMRs to three factors: the fact that Mexicans were "absolutely ignorant of the fundamentals of hygiene";[56] their substandard housing; and their inadequate diet. As these factors were rooted in culture, not biology, public health officials advocated extending Americanization programs to the Mexican community to ameliorate their living conditions.[57]

Many of these Americanization programs targeted Mexican women. Some gave them health and hygiene instruction as a way of improving general living conditions.[58] Others covered topics ranging from the care of pregnant women and newborns to the proper way to clean homes and prepare meals. Dr. Charles Bennett, a member of the Los Angeles County Health Department's advisory board, argued that such efforts were necessary to "reduce the possibility of bodily disease" and, thus, "conserve the energy of [Mexican] laborers for efficient work."[59] In enlisting the help of Mexican women, health officials demonstrated that they did not view them in the same way as they did Japanese women, that is, as undermining white labor. Even though Mexican women too worked in the fields, they also provided the unpaid labor at home (cooking, cleaning) that enabled their husbands to be more productive workers in the fields or on the railroad lines.

These programs addressing health and housing problems were part of larger efforts intended to attract Mexican laborers to work sites. Some employers believed that, if they offered sound housing and a healthy environment, Mexican workers would be more willing to stay in their work camps, rather than seek better wages and conditions elsewhere. Dr. Charles Bennett, chairman of the joint building committee of a housing colony for workers of a lemon- and orange-packing house, gave it as his opinion that improved housing and health programs would be necessary "in [the] competition for serviceable labor." Women and children were integral to such goals. Bennett considered Mexican women to have a calming effect, helping Mexican men feel more settled in their work sites. He also advocated hiring men with families because "heads of families [make] the most reliable workers. The single man is universally restless and forever moving about."[60] Thus, health programs, especially those centered on Mexican women and children, not only improved health conditions for Mexicans but also made of them a more reliable and productive workforce.

Public health officials also promoted the idea that disease in Mexican work camps could be contained. That idea was put to the test when, in the summer of 1916, a case of typhus broke out in a Southern Pacific Railroad camp near Palmdale (twenty miles north of Los Angeles), where twenty Mexican men lived in a bunkhouse.[61] Typhus fever is an infectious disease caused by rickettsia, a bacteria-like microorganism. The symptoms can include fever, headaches, chills, and general pains followed by a rash. Both body lice and vermin can transmit typhus. The first case was a Mexican laborer who had been recruited by the Pacific Electric Railway. In total, twenty-six cases of typhus were reported in the four-month period from June to October 1916. Five Mexicans died in the outbreak.[62]

Contrasting how health officers handled the typhus outbreak among Mexicans to how they promoted the possibility of disease transmission by Japanese farmers demonstrates how they inverted their racial logic depending on the immigrant group with which they were dealing. During the typhus epidemic, health officials did promote ideas that constructed Mexicans, like the Japanese before them, as diseased and inferior to white Americans, but they also stressed that they could help Mexicans by advising them on how to adopt white American notions of health and hygiene. And, in order to gain a sense of living conditions with which they were dealing and assess the health of the Mexican laborers and their families, they began monitoring the work camps, in one three-month period inspecting seventy-three railroad camps and thirteen Mexican villages.[63] They also drafted regulations for all Mexicans living in the camps. Because they attributed the outbreak of typhus cases to Mexicans, all the regulations revolved around the proper way for Mexicans to conduct themselves.

To contain the outbreak, cleanup campaigns were initiated in the railroad camps and villages. County health officials conducted hygiene, sanitation, and education programs. They also used cyanide gas to destroy pests in thirty of the railroad camps.[64] (No consideration seems to have been given to how cyanide gas might have affected the Mexican residents of the camps.) Such efforts were classified as a "campaign against filth and lack of personal hygiene."[65] The Mexicans themselves were, thus, cast as solely responsible for the outbreaks. (No mention was ever made of the railroad companies' provision of inferior living conditions.) And public health officials were cast as solely responsible for the remedy.

Although public health officials spoke of Mexicans as disease carriers, ignorant, and unhygienic, they also candidly suggested that Mexicans could be rehabilitated. Just months after the typhus epidemics, Dr. Pomeroy reported to the Los Angeles County Board of Supervisors that, "once the Mexican realizes hygiene and better sanitary conditions will prevent sickness, and his cooperation is secured, if proper supervision is given, we find rapid results can be obtained." Pomeroy continued: "[S]uccess is readily possible with a small outlay of capital."[66] The message was clear. If their efforts were properly funded, health officials could properly supervise and sanitize the Mexican workforce, enough to make it acceptable to white America. As an emerging professional class, public health officials needed the municipal resources for their programs.

In conclusion, by examining how health officials interpreted and dealt with issues such as the spread of disease and birthrates, one can see how they inverted racial logic, making Mexicans redeemable immigrants and Japanese unredeemable aliens. The underlying message of the attention given Japanese birthrates and Japanese farms was that the Japanese were economically threatening and socially unassimilable, further fueling attempts to ban emigration from Asia completely and to restrict the position of Japanese already in the United States. The underlying message of the attention given Mexicans' health and hygiene problems was that Mexicans, although, like the Japanese, inferior, culturally backward, and unhygienic, were, not an economic threat, but a source of cheap labor, and, as such, a redeemable population.

The 1924 Immigration Act prohibited Japanese immigration altogether but continued to allow Mexican immigration—although border-crossing policies became more restrictive[67]—sending a clear message on who policymakers considered to be of value. But regional laws, ordinances, and policies had already established the place of Japanese and Mexicans within the U.S. racial hierarchy. In many ways, the 1924 act formalized what had already been long-standing practice in California. While immigration acts policed the nation's borders, the policies and practices of local institutions, such as health departments, demonstrated how the border shifted to the interior as those local institutions regulated immigrant bodies in the rural and urban landscape.

*Notes*

1. Kraut, *Silent Travelers.*
2. Amy Fairchild argues that medical examinations served a dual purpose. They excluded some immigrants, but they also helped define who would be a potential worker in the

NATALIA MOLINA

U.S. industrial workforce and, thus, also worked as a method of inclusion (Fairchild, *Science at the Borders*).

3. Omi and Winant, *Racial Formation*, 56.

4. In my *Fit to Be Citizens*, I examine how public health programs did not lead to full social membership in U.S. society and how public health policies justified social and juridical exclusion of immigrants from U.S. society increasingly after the 1924 Immigration Act.

5. Kim, *Bitter Fruit*.

6. Almaguer, *Racial Fault Lines*, 186. Although the Alien Land Acts of 1913 and 1920 do not mention Japanese specifically, they were consistently applied to Japanese and, thus, racialized on enforcement. While both acts were essentially the same, the 1920 act was more detailed, elaborating on the 1913 act, and also penalized anyone who conspired to help in the illegal transfer of land. This added penalty speaks to how Japanese had been able to circumscribe the laws with the help of non-Japanese assistants (*Statutes of California* [1913], 206–8; *Statutes of California* [1921], lxxxiii–lxxxviii). For more on the strategies that Japanese used to combat these land acts, see Ichioka, "Japanese Immigrant Response."

7. Modell, *Racial Accommodation*.

8. "Americanization Is Favored by Japanese," *Los Angeles Times*, 25 May 1919.

9. Phelan, however, refused to debate the Japanese professor ("Japanese Undaunted by Phelan's Rebuff," *Los Angeles Times*, 22 October 1920).

10. Kurashige, *Celebration and Conflict*. Nayan Shah also demonstrates how second-generation Chinese Americans fought to be included in American social membership both symbolically and actually, arguing in favor of the entitlement to American programs such as public housing (Shah, *Contagious Divides*).

11. González, *Labor and Community*, and *Labor Organizing*.

12. Balderrama, *In Defense of La Raza*.

13. Letters written to the Mexican consul in Los Angeles, 1915–35, Archives of the Secretary of Exterior Relations, Mexico City.

14. Escobar, *Making of a Political Identity*; Gutiérrez, *Walls and Mirrors*; Sánchez, *Becoming Mexican American*.

15. African Americans constituted 2.5 percent of the total population of Los Angeles in 1900. African Americans predominately settled in the city, not the county, in areas such as the West Adams district.

16. Deverell, *Whitewashed Adobe*.

17. For two insightful studies that focus on Mexican communities in Los Angeles, see Escobar, *Making of a Political Identity*; and Sánchez, *Becoming Mexican American*.

18. Carr, *Los Angeles*, 233.

19. Guglielmo, *White on Arrival*; Ignatiev, *How the Irish Became White*; Jacobson, *Barbarian Virtues*, *Special Sorrows*, and *Whiteness of a Different Color*; Roediger, *Wages of Whiteness*.

20. For studies of whiteness and Mexicans in the American West, see Avila, *Age of White Flight*; and Deverell, *Whitewashed Adobe*.

21. Almaguer, *Racial Fault Lines*.

22. Ibid., 181.

23. Matsumoto, *Farming the Home Place*, 292.

24. For a discussion of the unionization of Japanese and Mexican farm laborers in southern California in 1903, see Almaguer, *Racial Fault Lines*, chap. 7.

25. Pomeroy, "Japanese Evil," 2.

26. Modell, *Racial Accommodation*, 39.

27. Dr. John Pomeroy to Los Angeles County Board of Supervisors, 19 June 1919, Los Angeles County Board of Supervisors. Interestingly, Pomeroy's comments link all Japanese in the United States to Japanese in Japan, regardless of generation, citizenship, or time spent in the United States.

28. "Phelan Ends So. Cal. Tour with Anti-Japanese Plea: Warns of Subtle Invasion and Predicts Victory of Land Bill," *Los Angeles Evening Herald*, 25 October 1920.

29. Los Angeles County Health Department (LACHD) Quarterly Health Report (QHR), 31 March 1917, 4, Department of Health Services (DHS) library.

30. Romo, *East Los Angeles*, 61.

31. U.S. Congress, U.S. Immigration Commission, *Report of the United States Immigration Commission*, pt. 25 (Washington, DC: U.S. Government Printing Office, 1911), 448–50, quoted in Gutiérrez, *Walls and Mirrors*, 52.

32. Sánchez, " 'Go after the Women.' "

33. The rapid growth of the Mexican community in the early twentieth century contradicted social Darwinist beliefs that, as an inferior race, Mexicans, like Native Americans, would inevitably die off. Such beliefs gained currency in the mid-1850s when advocates of Manifest Destiny argued that Mexicans would eventually disappear once Anglos had conquered the Southwest. The public frequently revisited and debated Mexicans' place in the United States in the early twentieth century as the Mexican population in the United States grew rapidly (Horsman, *Race and Manifest Destiny*; Hietala, *Manifest Design*).

34. LACHD, Memorandum to the *Los Angeles Tribune* (1917).

35. For general attitudes toward immigrants, see Higham, *Strangers in the Land*. See also Jacobson, *Whiteness of a Different Color* and *Barbarian Virtues*. On the racial underpinning of naturalization policy, see Haney-López, *White by Law*.

36. Mason and McKinstry, *Japanese of Los Angeles*, 32.

37. Pernick, "Eugenics."

38. The LACHD report states that Japanese births constituted one-third of the births in Los Angeles County (LACHD Annual Health Report [AHR], 30 June 1917, 28, DHS library), while, as we have seen, the LACHD memorandum to the *Los Angeles Tribune* article reports one-fourth.

39. Ibid.

40. Modell, *Racial Accommodation*, 22.

41. *Los Angeles Evening Herald Examiner*, 25 October 1920.

42. Pomeroy, "Japanese Evil," 2. Pomeroy's personal notes are handwritten on the back of the article, which is held in the DHS library.

43. Modell, *Racial Accommodation*, 99.

44. LACHD AHR, 1920, 31.

45. Pomeroy, "Japanese Evil," 2.

46. Ibid.; Burnight, "Japanese in Rural California."

47. Dr. John Pomeroy to Los Angeles County Board of Supervisors, 16 May 1918, Los Angeles County Board of Supervisors. It is not known whether the Children's Bureau came to the aid of the health department. For a history of the development of the Children's Bureau, see Muncy, *Female Dominion in American Reform*.

48. Henry, "Diseases of Women," 77. For a fascinating analysis of France's population campaign, see Koos, "Engendering Reaction."

49. Deverell, "Plague in Los Angeles."

50. Dr. John Pomeroy to Los Angeles County Board of Supervisors, 4 August 1922, Los Angeles County Board of Supervisors.

51. Editorial notes, *Southern California Medical Practitioner* 35 (1920), 95.

52. Los Angeles County Board of Supervisors Minutes, 26 July 1920, Los Angeles County Board of Supervisors.

53. Ordinance No. 26146 (n.s.) cited in Dr. John Pomeroy to Los Angeles County Board of Supervisors, 19 June 1919, Los Angeles County Board of Supervisors. See also Los Angeles City Health Department, Annual Health Report, 1915, 58–59, 63.

54. Annual Report of County Health Officer to Board of Supervisors, calendar year 1919.

55. Meckel, *Save the Babies*, 26–32.

56. LACHD QHR, 30 September 1916, 4, DHS library.

57. Yu, *Thinking Orientals*. Yu examines how, among sociologists in the early twentieth century, ideas about race shift from being rooted in biology to being rooted in culture. Ultimately, cultural practices are written onto the body in such a way that the distinction is insignificant.

58. LACHD QHR, 2 July 1917, 3, DHS library.

59. Charles Bennett, "Housing for Field Employees" (c. 1920), p. 11, University of California, Berkeley, Bancroft Library, Department of Industrial Relations, carton 43, folder 2.

60. Ibid., p. 2.

61. LACHD AHR, 30 June 1917, 12, DHS library.

62. Of the twenty-six typhus cases reported, twenty-two were among Mexican railroad workers (some in Los Angeles County), one was contracted in Los Angeles City, two (beyond the county railroad-camp cases) were contracted in Los Angeles County, and the point of origin of the last was unknown. The non–Los Angeles County cases include seven from Banning (Riverside County), one from Livermore (Alameda County), one from Bakersfield (Kern County), and three from Tulare (Tulare County), (*California State Board of Health Monthly Bulletin*, June–December 1916).

63. LACHD QHR, 30 June 1916, 4, DHS library. Dr. Pomeroy estimated that there were more than one hundred railroad camps, some forty Mexican villages, and a large number of wandering labor camps (LACHD AHR, 30 June, 1917, 13).

64. LACHD QHR, 30 September 1916, DHS library.

65. LACHD, Memorandum to the *Los Angeles Tribune* (1917), DHS library.

66. LACHD AHR, 30 June 1917, 16–17, DHS library.

67. Ngai, *Impossible Subjects*.

# 3   GETTING THE MEASURE OF TOMORROW

*Chinese and Chicano Americas under the Racial Gaze,*
*1934–1935 and 1942–1944*

Victor Jew

In the fifth year of the Great Depression, an anthropologist thought he saw a wonderful opportunity. What if a population of persons, descendants of immigrants who had moved to the United States decades earlier, were studied in depth in ways that had been impossible to pursue prior to the Depression? Moreover, what if this population, living as a separate community within a large U.S. city, promised to be the ideal anthropological subject? Here was a group that seemed to shun intermarriage with outsiders and had apparently kept themselves apart for at least three generations. Hence, social scientists might have access to a relatively "pure," inbred ethnic community living in twentieth-century America. Such a situation presented the chance to measure both racial continuities and racial discontinuities. In particular, some social scientists thought measuring this group might reveal the effects of exogenous, environmental factors—to be specific, the ways the American environment was thought to change "foreign" racial body types. This could yield results useful for comparing other immigrant communities, hence providing the basis for some larger generalizations useful to physical anthropologists and anthropometrists. The scientific effect would be similar to coming upon a lost tribe of persons suddenly made available for anthropological scrutiny.

In 1934 and 1935, a number of anthropologists believed that such an opportunity was within reach, and, for those academics, located in Berkeley and Palo Alto, California, the golden chance was no farther away than a trip up the coast or a ride across the bay. The new field now opened for fieldwork was in San Francisco, and the objects for study were those Chinese San Franciscans living in the city's Chinatown.[1]

An ethnic neighborhood that stretched across a grid of five east-west avenues and nine north-south streets, Chinatown contained most of the city's Chinese-descended residents. The idea that a government-funded effort might measure thousands of those inhabitants excited prospects rich with "practical and scientific possibilities" in the minds of supporters such as Professor R. L.

Olson of the University of California's Department of Anthropology. For him, the benefits of collecting data on a supposedly homogeneous population could confirm links between the U.S. environment and the "gross measurements" of "stature and weight" as well as the "conformation of the head," something Olson assured readers was "definitely" racial in origin.[2]

This story, largely neglected by both Asian Americanist historians and social historians of the Great Depression, contributes a page to a number of historiographies, but it is most telling as an account of American race discourse in the years preceding the modern civil rights movements. As will be shown, the anthropometry of 1934–35 was unavoidably implicated in dominant ideas about race in the United States and how Chinese Americans fit into this hierarchy in the 1930s.[3]

Being an Asian American case, the Chinatown anthropological study can discuss race in ways that go beyond the traditional black-white dyad. Being neither black nor white, this instance of American race history can be further developed when paired with another race-making story, one affecting a community that also sat askew the black-white model of race relations. Mexican American Los Angeles during the 1940s experienced an explosion of racialized public scrutiny that, while different from the Chinatown anthropometric gaze, was, nevertheless, similar in many respects and showed an overlapping of racializing maneuvers.

At first blush, these two stories seem more dissimilar than similar. The Chinese case in Depression-era San Francisco involved an attempt to collect data about Chinese residents. In the Mexican American example, city officials and public opinion shapers tried to explain alleged criminal propensities of Mexican American youths in wartime southern California. One was a foray into collecting social measurements; the other was a forum for announcing social opinions, some notoriously prejudged. Despite the differences in these cases, the act of juxtaposing them reveals larger commonalities, the rich dimensions of which allow for a number of interpretative gains. Both accounts start as familiar instances of dominant discourses "making" the subjected group identities of racialized communities. No doubt, this occurred in 1934–35 and 1942–44; coercive and dominant top-down identity work happened in these two cases. Yet both also illustrate the inner tensions and contradictions within such efforts, and, more important, they show the incompletion that could happen and the contestation that could arise.

There are other parallels. Both the 1930s Chinatown anthropometry and the 1940s Mexican American "crisis" were examples of applied social science urgently applied to well-established nonwhite communities. Viewed together, they reveal the faith placed in social science to make sense of "colored" populations that either fell outside the white–Negro relation (Chinese America) or sat uneasily in the middle of it (Mexican America). In these two instances, race-making discourses operated to fix in place two hard-to-fit populations, and the appeal to science served in both cases to generalize tendencies and supply a prediction of how these groups would conform to the American nation.

## The Subject

We can squeeze new meaning from these two episodes if we draw on concepts that have dealt with such matters as identity, race, and citizenship. One powerful set of concepts concerns the social and ideological processes that make subjects of human persons. Whether gauging self-fashionings or measuring subjectivations, these theories have clarified ways to think historically and specifically about the often-mysterious ways in which persons are made. For recent students of subject-making, these processes are both more dominating and less crude than a simple "hailing" of named persons into authoritatively organized subjected positions. Over the past twenty years, interpreters of the subjectivation process have stressed the possible room for maneuver that exists within the very naming and classificatory schemes of being made a "subject." While duly recognizing the oppressive power of a dominant society "organizing" persons and populations into positions, they have also insisted that such processes are never entirely complete, that they are not always successful, and that they are not achieved without some measure of resistance.

One way to make these contingencies vivid is to think through the metaphor of "chaining" suggested by Stuart Hall. Hall characterizes social identities as the possible and probable results of historical, contingent conditions, which take shape through the "articulation or 'chaining' of the subject into the flow of discourse." Further illustrating this concept of fitting persons into given discursive and ideological "already(s)," Hall described such processes as the "effecting of the join of the subject in structures of meaning."[4] While the metaphor of chains signals the disciplinary hailing of larger orders that create categories of identity and positions (*men, women, Chinese, Oriental, Mexican colony*), the notion of "effecting a join" emphasizes a sense of process, one that is not guaranteed despite much planning and design. Within this interval of power we can place the historical particulars of the Chinese who were measured and weighed by social science–guided relief workers in 1930s San Francisco and the Mexican American youths who were subjected to wholesale scrutiny in the public forums of wartime Los Angeles. As "Chinese" in the United States, those measured San Franciscans were already subjects occupying various positions (Oriental, male, female, child, Chinese), but the anthropometry of Chinatown in 1934–35 attempted to fit them into another "structure of discourse": the joining of Chinese American subjects into the contested anthropological category *Americanizable Asian immigrants*. For young Mexican Americans in 1942–44, the subject-making process was more beleaguered, but many sought a similar goal: to diagnose "typical" Mexican American youth criminality and "fix" its etiology, whether social, psychological, or biological.

## A New Laboratory

The Depression was a watershed for Chinese San Franciscans because, as the Asian American historian Judy Yung notes, "for the first time in their history, Chinese Americans, who had always been marginalized, became beneficiaries of federal relief programs."[5] This unprecedented inclusion coincided with Depression-era opportunities of another kind. While federal relief now seemed to encompass a heretofore-neglected Chinese American community in San Francisco, the economic depression opened the door to a heightened social organizing of the "Chinese" as a population. Not only would Chinatown see more social work activity (much of it done by its own second-generation Chinese American social work professionals), but it would also be the site of intensive social science–inspired observations.

It must be noted that this gaze was initially cast elsewhere, or, to put it differently, that it started with a different purpose. What eventually became the Chinatown anthropometry began as a project to measure malnutrition among Chinatown's youths. Two Chinese Americans, Dr. Charles A. Wong and Samuel Dunn Lee, wanted to address what had alarmed public health officials for at least ten years: the prevalence of hunger and undernourishment in the Chinese quarter. Wong and Lee saw a chance to collect empirical data to "determine the underlying causes of this serious condition" as well as question the applicability of San Francisco public school age-weight standards to Chinatown youths.[6]

In retrospect, such an investigation could have led to valuable short-term gains (focusing relief efforts to address chronic malnutrition) as well as potential long-term benefits—namely, a social critique that could highlight the structural poverty that most likely made that malnutrition chronic. But the task at hand—measuring hundreds of children—was huge, and the funds were as meager as the times. In 1934, Wong and Lee began what would become an incessant plea for continued monetary support. Eventually submitting an application to the California State Emergency Relief Administration (SERA) in December of that year, they decided to enhance their grant request with endorsements from social scientists—professionals who had been measuring humans for years. However, not only would these contacts open the door to endorsements; they would also make possible a friendly takeover of the project. The anthropologists and child welfare specialists contacted by the malnutrition study lost no time incorporating the Wong and Lee effort into long-standing anthropological investigations. For their part, Wong and Lee were only too glad to have the approval of scientists such as the famous Alfred Louis Kroeber and C. H. Danforth, the editor of the *American Journal of Physical Anthropology*. Getting those names meant getting funding from SERA and, later, the Works Progress Administration (WPA). Changing the project's dimensions to accommodate science was a small price to pay if it meant starting the malnutrition measurements.[7]

While stature and weight were the original measurement indices, advice from "the Anthropology Department and the Child Welfare Clinic at the University of California" counseled the project's designers that "some valuable anthropological material could be obtained by including other body and head measurements." The data collection could do more than just determine local malnutrition; it could throw light on the question of race adaptation to new environments, a question that had long intrigued anthropologists: "About the beginning of the century, Wissler and Boas in a study of European immigrants and their offsprings [*sic*], found that there were consistent and significant changes in body structure which definitely indicated that change in environment not only affected such gross measurements as stature and height, but also such definitely racial characteristics as conformation of the head."[8] Invoking these forebears would not only march-step the San Francisco study in a long line of inquiry; it would bestow an impressive intellectual legitimacy on a relief project that started with much more modest goals.

Invoking Wissler and Boas meant placing the Wong and Lee effort in the shadows of Clark Wissler (1870–1947) and Franz Boas (1858–1942), both eminent figures in U.S. anthropology. Their joint work, *Statistics of Growth*, was probably the precursor that the social scientists believed most relevant for the Chinatown work. Done on behalf of the U.S. Bureau of Education in 1905, this undertaking measured children's growth. That study would not be the end of either anthropologist's efforts at human bodily measurement. Wissler would engage in continued ethno-guaging, going on to publish *The Hard Palate in Normal and Feeble-Minded Individuals* (with Walter Channing) in 1908 and *Measurements of Dakota Children* in 1910. As late as 1936, one year after the Chinatown anthropometry, the sixty-six-year-old Wissler published the studies *Changes in Population Profiles among the Northern Plains Indians* and *Population Changes among Northern Plains Indians*. It was Franz Boas, however, who redirected the anthropometric gaze onto immigrants. Six years after doing his stint with the U.S. Bureau of Education, he would produce an enormous work on behalf of the U.S. Immigration Commission. Commonly known as the Dillingham Commission, and named after the U.S. senator who chaired it, the eleven-member body oversaw the eventual production of the *Reports of the Immigration Commission*, forty-one volumes about immigrants and their place in industrializing America. Boas's work resulted in volume 38, *Changes in Bodily Form of Descendants of Immigrants*.

Were there "bodily changes" in the U.S.-born second-generation children of immigrants? If there were, what larger consequences did these imply for U.S. immigration policy in 1911? Boas sought answers in measurements. He studied the growth of males and females from the following groups— Bohemians, Hungarians, Slovaks, Poles, "Hebrews," Sicilians, Neapolitans, the Scotch, and "miscellaneous Italian[s]." The bulk of Boas's final report was a massive accumulation of numbers. Volume 38 weighed in at 573 pages with a staggering 73 tables, 36 tabulations, and 53 figures, the latter displaying such data as "Comparison of Head Form of American-Born and Foreign-Born Hebrew and Sicilian Males," "Weights of Boys," "Excess of Weight of American-Born Boys over Foreign-Born Boys," "Length of Head of Foreign-Born and American-Born Bohemians," and so forth for each group studied.[9]

The sum of these measurements was meant to be greater than its numerous parts. The overall aim was to contest contemporary "scientific racism." While he gave credence to the body-measuring techniques of physical anthropologists, Boas was not an anthropologist of the old school; indeed, he posed a challenge to the legacies of Louis Agassiz and the nineteenth-century school of race immutability. Boas's liberal aim was to show the physical adaptability of immigrants, a bodily change that gestured toward an Americanizing transformation that would prove the mutability of presumed racial characteristics. He wrote: "The adaptability of the immigrant seems to be very much greater than we had a right to suppose before our investigations were instituted."[10]

It is not hard to see how the 1934–35 Chinatown effort was tweaked to continue this Boasian legacy. Anthropology professors at Berkeley and Stanford envisioned the Chinatown study as adding a brick to the edifice first built by Boas in 1905. Including the Oriental, specifically the generations of Chinese, would bring to the existing storehouse of measurements the decidedly non-"white" Asian dimension that was missing from an already impressive compilation of data measuring the "racial" traits of Europeans. Hence, the optimistic assessment of Stanford's C. H. Danforth that the Wong-Lee measurements might prove to be a "classic" in physical anthropology.[11]

The academic anthropologists prevailed. The project, officially WPA Project 3330,[12] pursued the kinds of measurements recommended by the scientists, and the final report explicitly endorsed the Berkeley and Stanford vision. Seeking to credit the relief project with some larger significance, the report noted favorably the project's incorporation into the anthropometric agenda: "The study . . . became more important in that it [became] interested in the physical changes as affected by the transfer of a race from one environment to another."[13] Thus, the report cast the project as having undergone a value enhancement as a result of its imbrication into long-standing anthropological concerns.

The academic anthropologists saw the "Chinese colony proper" as a promising new field site. It must be noted, however, that Chinatown had long beckoned anthropologists; it was just that the informants had seemed too few and the territory mysteriously off-limits. Prior to the Great Depression, "[f]ormer students . . . [had] experienced a great deal of difficulty," namely, noncooperation on the part of potential subjects. Wong and Lee, having adopted the anthropologists' project, wrote that Chinatown denizens had been "hesitant . . . to depart [sic] with information or permit observation and study."

VICTOR JEW

Thus, pre-Depression social scientists had been unable to "capitalize upon the research possibilities of Chinatown."[14]

Gaining access to this potential gold mine of "Gold Mountain" human data was a fortuitous by-product of the Great Depression.[15] In the words of Wong and Lee, a high percentage of Chinese were "employed in the luxury-class of employment, the family cook, bazaar keeper, and store clerk." Those so employed proved vulnerable to the downward economic and social spiral of the 1930s, and Chinatown Chinese were "the first to feel the effects of the economic depression and become dependent upon the relief organization." Thus, a newfound relation to state institutions and public policy "broke down the barriers which heretofore had made it impossible to enter Chinatown for research purposes." The project's staff hinted at a quid pro quo that emerged from the Depression's effects on Chinese San Franciscans. "The obligation of the Chinese people and those agencies for the assistance rendered by the S.E.R.A. during these trying times has opened up this avenue of cooperation."[16] A more somber assessment, one arrived at with the benefit of hindsight, might conclude not only that hard times and state relief made possible a new relation between Chinese San Franciscans and the Depression-era state, but also that they incorporated them into circuits of both social service and social surveillance.[17] But, in the mid-1930s, Wong and Lee were sanguine about the effort. They thought that the potential gains meant an advance for both the community and science: "The new Works program would enable us to obtain this very interesting material combined into one publication; no similar publication has yet been issued. The study of morbidity of racial groups that have moved to new environments has always interested scientists because it will be possible to observe if the American environment in contrast to that of the old country is producing any appreciable effects."[18] Thus, Chinatown in 1934–35 would supplement the work of anthropologists such as Boas, Wissler, "Spier, Shapiro and others" who "demonstrated that comparable changes [were] observed between adult and offspring in other immigrant groups, both Caucasian and Mongoloid."[19]

If those outside Chinatown needed to have this study's significance translated in lay terms, they could have turned to a local English-language newspaper. The *San Francisco News* ran a story with a headline announcing: "SERA Wants to See If Our Climate Changes Them." The opening paragraph declared: "Residents of San Francisco's Chinatown are to be measured and photographed by SERA workers in an effort to learn if the California climate and other factors in living conditions here have changed their racial characteristics." Aside from demarcating what was the preferred "normal" or dominant reading and social position that the *San Francisco News* privileged ("our climate" affecting "them"), the paper related the logistic scope of the upcoming study, noting that "four generations of Orientals" (comprising three thousand individuals) would be examined.[20]

As already mentioned, the study had undergone its own morbidity, shifting from a policy concern with children's malnutrition to an attempt to gauge environmental effects on "definite racial characteristics" as embodied in body structures. The racializing ambitions of that switch can be gleaned from the project's anthropometric procedures, which stated: "This study includes in its scope thirteen body and eight head measurements; [and] four observations of hair, eye (iris) and skin." Photography would be an important tool as well, and, by the end of the study, "three hundred photographs, full-face and profile, were taken of the children attending the St. Mary's Primary School." Older Chinatown schoolchildren were harvested for hair samples, which were "taken to the left of vertex" and "collected from the grammar and junior high school groups (up to 16 years of age)."[21]

In all, the Chinatown anthropometry took many measurements. The project weighed and measured 1,722 males and 1,219 females for a total of 2,941 Chinatown residents. Subjects' ages ranged from three years to "between sixty and seventy." Yet whether these numbers would lead to the anthropometric payoff was uncertain. Contributing to this fogginess were "on the ground" decisions that seemed to undercut the larger ambitions envisioned by the academic anthropologists. One decision seemed to particularly betray the expectations of lay non-Chinese San Franciscans hoping to know whether the Bay Area climate really did change the physical characteristics of those people they may have seen climbing up Jackson Street, walking down Grant Avenue, or watching the next generation play in the Waverly Place "Chinese Children Play Ground." For non-Chinese, the one facial feature that seemed to broadcast "the definitely racial characteristic" of "Orientals" was the eyefold. Yet the study held off from examining the slant of Asian eyes. Wong and Lee's final report recognized this when it conceded: "There may be some criticism as to the limited number of measurements and the inadequacy of observations taken, especially such important factors as eyefold."[22]

Moreover, the study weakened its scientific claims by not employing trained anthropologists in the actual measurements of Chinese bodies. The final report had to admit this major omission: "Too much emphasis cannot be made on the fact that the work was completed without the assistance of a professional physical anthropologist." Thus, the original project was encouraged by anthropologists, indeed, by major figures in that field, but the professionals left the actual measurements to WPA workers. Nevertheless, Wong and Lee made no further ado about the absence of professional physical anthropologists, and this missing link did not hinder WPA Project 3330 from pressing on in its diligent efforts to "secur[e] simple measurements and observations." Data were gathered from persons "all in good health insofar as school medical authorities could determine and after cursory examination of each individual." Excluded from the study were possible outliers, or those deemed abnormal. Falling into the outlier category would be individuals whose health was questionable, individuals who were possibly the result of "racial intermarriage," and the abnormal—those defined by the study as the obese. The latter were excluded because "the study was primarily interested in the normal development of the physical body."[23]

When examined, the subjects "were undressed to the waist and measurements were made while the individuals were bare-footed." For those culled from the schools, "observations and measurements were taken during the regular school hours, between 9 AM and 3 PM, in a standard classroom." For adults, measurements were taken in the work world—for example, in the office of the clerical staff of a construction project or in the offices of the anthropometric study. Using anthropometric head and body instruments loaned by the Department of Anthropology at the University of California, and borrowing a Toledo weight scale made available by the Toledo Scale Company, WPA Project 3330 measured the following according to Martin measurements: stature (Martin no. 1); acromion (Martin no. 8); radiale (Martin no. 9); stylion (Martin no. 10); iliospinale (Martin no. 13); sitting height (Martin no. 23); total reach (Martin no. 17); chest expanded and diminished (Martin no. 61); interspinous diameter (Cristal width); biceps; wrist; and weight. Head measurements were measured by head length and width, face width, jaw width, total face height, upper face height, nose height, and nose width. Regarding hair, eye, and skin, the following classifications were used. For hair, color was classified as black, dark brown, and brown. The form of hair was classified as straight, specified as either hair having an intercrest diameter of five to ten centimeters or hair having an intercrest diameter of less than five centimeters. Eye color was classified as black, dark brown, and brown. Finally, skin color was classified as brown, dark yellow, lemon yellow (light yellow), and white.[24]

The final report insisted that the aims of such data gathering were, ultimately, scientific and the benefits altruistic: "The primary purpose of this study was to accumulate a sufficient number of measurements to permit further research on the subject of the physical growth of Chinese as well as a study of the influence of environment on physical structure." To that end, other studies were contemplated, interestingly, to test for the effects of what might be called the *intersection of class and race*: "It was hoped that a similar study would be completed in Oakland, California, where the housing condition of the Chinese is recognized to be better, to ascertain further differences that might appear."[25] But, as hinted at in "further differences that might appear," the goal was, not to understand the social effects of socially constructed and lived circumstances, but to trace changes made on presumed core racial and racially inherited physicalities that allegedly verified race even if an American environment was suspected of rubbing away some of the more foreign bodily characteristics, thus rendering second and third generations of immigrant communities more American.

Despite the considerable effort that went into the measuring of thousands of Chinatown Chinese, the final results fell short of the scientific aspirations fostered by the university social scientists. There were never enough measurements for either a study of malnutrition or an ambitious anthropometry that could measure the difference that the U.S. environment presumably made on race. Assessing this effort from our perspective, the safest conclusion is that, at the very least, work was provided for Depression-era participants. In the end, the study produced a final progress report and a final report; however, no scholarly article resulted from the work, even though Wong and Lee thought the imprimatur of the *American Journal of Physical Anthropology* might induce more SERA funding and, perhaps, the investment of that journal's editor in publishing what he had at one time esteemed to be a coming "classic" in anthropological research.

It must be said that neither was the work of the Chinatown anthropometry entirely forgotten nor its scientific aspirations completely frustrated. During the Second World War, as part of a summing up of what SERA did during the 1930s, a valedictory report included mention of the Chinatown study. That wartime recapitulation, the one source for the only other mention of the anthropometry by a historian, told of how the schoolchildren's photographs, "along with samples of their hair," were sent to "museums all across the country."[26]

If the project went out with a whimper, it nevertheless gave social scientists at Berkeley and Stanford a chance to ponder the problem of Chinese America and its place in the firmament of humankind and human science. For A. L. Kroeber, a force in the anthropological universe, the stakes raised by the Wong and Lee project went well beyond measuring indices of malnutrition. The project promised to help "fix the place of the Chinese type in racial classification."[27] Kroeber's sense of "fix[ing] in place" was shared by others who too hoped the study of Chinese bodies might yield data that could determine knowledge about Chinese, Chinese Americans, immigration, and race. R. L. Olson, Kroeber's junior colleague at Berkeley, conveyed the notion of ramifying positivities when he casually said that such studies were of "great utility not only from the standpoint of theoretical science but also along the more practical lines of economic and political policy."[28]

Mentioning Kroeber's ambition easily incorporates the Chinatown anthropometry into the intellectual history of American anthropology, but, as an episode of U.S. social history, the Chinatown study leaves a mixed impression. The measuring of 2,941 people can be understood as a type of racialized subject-making, especially since the results were deemed capable of fixing the "Chinese type" within the physical anthropological schema. Yet we must proceed cautiously if we are to appreciate the complexities of the 1934–35 anthropometry, something best done by locating that episode within the larger pattern of Asian American history. Over the past thirty years, that history has become clearer owing to the efforts of Asian Americanist historians who have unearthed an impressive record of historical agency, and resistance against various forms of oppression, on the part of Asian American individuals and communities.[29] Yet the anthropometry of 1934–35 appears to be an anomaly within this larger narrative. How do we reconcile the measuring of nearly three thousand Asian bodies with the previous eighty years of strategic and canny Chinese American opposition to such harsh features of Exclusion-era life as discriminatory state statutes, racist local ordinances, and the daily intimidations carried out in the name of enforcing immigration restriction? It may seem bewildering to imagine nearly three thousand persons participating in any human-measurement project, yet the local and immediate context of the Great Depression and its effects on San Francisco's Chinatown residents goes far to explain this participation.

It must be remembered that the othering that adhered to the San Francisco anthropometry was one step removed: none of the non-Chinese academic anthropologists directly participated in the measuring of bodies; they stayed in Berkeley and Palo Alto while others collected the data. Oppression as such was not visibly displayed or directly applied at the different measuring sites in Chinatown. Had any of the project been connected with the U.S. Immigration Service or the immigration processing center at Angel Island in San Francisco Bay, the mass measuring would most likely have encountered nonparticipation, if not protest. Daily acts of anger and striking back at intrusive Exclusion inspectors who arrogantly ventured into Chinese American communities in San Francisco, Los Angeles, and New York were in the living memory of Chinatown adults.

Likewise, it must also be remembered that, in the 1930s, San Francisco's Chinese community witnessed a number of new social work interventions, none of which were racially othering, and most, if not all, of which were conducted by members of the U.S.-born twentieth-century cohort that styled itself the "Second Generation" of Chinese American promise. Those of this group who entered professional social work seized the Depression-era opportunity to conduct social welfare surveys that measured, not human bodies, but the indices of community survival, such as numbers of schools, hospitals, playgrounds, and day nurseries. The Chinatown anthropometry operated, as it were, in the tow of this environment of social work ferment.[30]

Given that young Chinese Americans were already interviewing Chinatown residents about how many hours they worked, whether their children were attended to during the workday, and whether the National Recovery Administration had improved their wages, it might have been easy to assume that body measurements were just one more type of data to be collected for the sake of progress and public health. After all, Dr. Charles Wong and Samuel Dunn Lee had initiated the study to fight chronic malnutrition. And Wong and Lee themselves were members of the new Chinatown Second Generation. Given the resemblance, it would have been easy to blur the lines between different types of social intervention and the myriad kinds of interviewing, social inventory taking, and measuring. Considering the times, it all could have seemed like progress.

*The Figure of Crisis*

Chinese San Francisco would not be the only racially marginalized community subjected to scrutiny. Four hundred miles to the south, and seven years later, Mexican Americans in Los Angeles were placed under various social microscopes and inundated with public diagnoses. From 1942 to 1944, they became the focal point of efforts that tried to appraise the Chicano place in the U.S. national future.

Much like the Chinatown anthropometry of 1934–35, the Mexican American moment of 1942–44 witnessed desires to "fix" into place a distressing present and uncertain future of a racialized minority group, and, not unlike the Chinatown study, these moves were steered from without, by persons who were not of the community being gazed at, measured, and talked about within dominant discourses.

For Mexican Americans in the 1930s and 1940s, the official discourses that often hailed a "Mexican American psychology" were theories and practices of criminalization, social pathology, and delinquency. Edward Escobar, a historian of Chicano Los Angeles, shows in his *Race, Police, and the Making of a Political Identity* that official discourses had been moving toward the view that Mexican Americans were habitually criminal. This ideological barnacle had been crusting for at least twenty years, since 1923, when the Los Angeles Police Department started its institutional tendency of attempting to correlate race and crime rates. While various reports and commissions proved inconclusive and ambivalent toward the question of Mexican American criminality, the 1920s and 1930s witnessed Los Angeles law enforcement's growing investment in a "fully developed theory of Mexican criminality" that would, according to Escobar, "dominate relations between the police and Mexican Americans in . . . subsequent decades."[31]

By the 1940s, the local state in Los Angeles and the national government had already rehearsed ways to discipline the "Mexican" problem in the United States. The Depression era had witnessed mass "repatriation," the "sending back" to Mexico of persons of Mexican descent. That the hybrid Mexican American identity could be vexed, problematic, confusing, and easily subjected to abuse was clearly evidenced in the fact that some citizens of the United States born to Mexican immigrant or second-generation parents were also "repatriated" to Mexico alongside so many unwanted "foreigners."

These efforts at disciplining Chicano deviance took a heightened form with the wartime crisis of 1942–43. The home front moral panic that engulfed Los Angeles brought to a climax an array of anti–Mexican American ideas. But, while these were consistent with decades of previous practices, they did not go unchallenged in 1942. Curiously, elements within Los Angeles officialdom generated dissent within this moment of dominant-directed subject-making.

Catalyzing these developments was a crisis lasting two years in the history of World War II–era Los Angeles. From 1942 to 1944, a citywide turmoil about its Chicano youths roiled the southern California metropolis. This tumultuous episode reached its peak amid the unsettled contradictions and conflicts of the home front during the Second World War.

## A Crisis Sparked

It began with a mystery. On 2 August 1942, a wounded young man was discovered near a gravel pit known as Sleepy Lagoon. Identified as José Díaz, he would later die from his head injuries. While the circumstances surrounding his fate have remained inconclusive, the local press jumped to the conclusion that "Mexican Boy Gangs" had murdered Díaz.[32] Journalists circulated these stories as avidly as they had stirred hysteria about alleged Japanese American subversion just months earlier.

The death of José Díaz sparked a wave of anti-Mexican sentiment that escalated into a fury of violence, mobbing, and mutilating in the late spring of 1943. In June of that year, Los Angeles saw a citywide disturbance carried out by the forces of order: U.S. Navy and Army personnel on furlough and members of the Los Angeles Police Department went on a rampage against Mexican American youths that lasted eight days. The controversy over Mexican Americans did not abate with the end of the June 1943 rioting, however. Before two years had passed, the crisis was resituated in the judicial chambers, where a controversial trial convicted seventeen Chicanos for the death of José Díaz, a decision that would be eventually overturned by an appeals court. The Díaz incident did more than set off a riot of violence against young Mexican Americans. It also sparked a fiery debate about the nature of the Mexican American population in Los Angeles. Following the death of José Díaz, the Los Angeles County Grand Jury convened hearings to inquire into that very issue.

As if on cue, the voices that criminalized Mexican American youths spoke first and forcefully. If there was one opinion that set the terms for the 1942 debate, it was that offered by an official within the Los Angeles County Sheriff's Office. Captain Edward Duran Ayres of the Los Angeles County Sheriff's Department testified to what he believed was the key underlying factor for why a "certain element of the Mexican population . . . [committed] a great proportion of crime." That "certain element" was the Chicano youths of Los Angeles—the wartime Second Generation of the 1940s. Arguing that they committed the lion's share of the city's crime, Ayres pressed for a final solution based on a steely-eyed diagnosis of bedrock underlying causes. "To get a true perspective of this condition we must look for a basic cause." To Ayres this meant finding a source more determinative than even "social discrimination" against Mexican Americans. For the Captain, the key fundamental fact underlying all Mexican American delinquency was "the biological basis."[33]

Biology was destiny, and, for Captain Ayres, it was the peculiar biology of inherited race traits that made Mexican Americans born criminals. When it came to that population, Ayres saw persons in whose bloodlines lay a persistence of savagery: "When the Spaniards conquered Mexico they found an organized society composed of many tribes of Indians ruled by the Aztecs." By recounting that fact, Ayres was not merely reciting a history lesson; he wanted to forge a biological-historical connection that could draw on the 1510s to explain the 1940s. Recalling a schoolroom truism about Mexico at the time of the Spanish Conquest, he said that the Aztecs were "given over to human sacrifice," with as "many as 30,000 Indians . . . sacrificed on . . . heathen altars in one day, their bodies being opened by stone knives and their hearts torn out while still beating." Moving from Montezuma to his own embattled present, Ayres said that such savagery and its propensities persisted in the bloodlines of contemporary Chicano Los Angelenos. The reason was biological fate. "This total disregard for human life," as evidenced by the Aztecs' mass human sacrifices, "has always been universal throughout the Americas, among the Indian population." Ayres assured his audience that this was a truth "which of course is well known to everyone."[34] And it was this enduring Indian presence in the racialized figure of the hybridized Mexican that posed a problem, for both the modern Mexican government and Los Angeles County.

The "miscegenated" history of Mexican identity, what Ayres called the "Indian" element, had racial ramifications. Even in the hands of those less sensationally racist than Ayres, the *mestizaje* of Mexicans in the United States could be inflected with race meanings that inherently privileged white against colored. For one social scientist, T. J. Woofter Jr., writing in 1933, the Mexican population in the United States could be parsed according to its mixed heritage, but this would have explicit racializing meanings for "whitened" or darkened subjectivities. Of the million and a half persons of Mexican descent living in the United States as of 1930, Woofter wrote: "About 65,000 were enumerated in 1930 as 'white Mexicans' or those of Spanish descent." The remaining 1.4 million were "of Indian and Negro descent."[35] The attention to mestizo Mexican America was a way to mark off "white Mexicans" from those of "Indian and Negro" heritage. Implicitly hierarchical in the way these notions operated in a context that privileged whiteness, mestizaje in the hands of Edward Duran Ayres could serve as an open-ended warrant to find in the "Indian" element the roots of a Mexican American "disregard for human life."

According to Ayres, the ancient savage impulse was yet lurking about in southern California, and its incorrigibly different ways were clearly manifested when contrasted with "Caucasian" behavior. Said Ayres: "The Caucasion, especially the Anglo Saxon, when engaged in fighting, particularly among youths, resort to fistcuff [sic] and may at times kick each other, which is considered unsportive, but this Mexican element considers all that to be a sign of weakness and all he knows and feels is a desire to use a knife or some lethal weapon. In other words, his desire is to kill, or at least let blood."[36]

Ayres's racial theory of Indian heritage allowed him to color most Mexican Americans in Los Angeles as nonwhite and, hence, potentially savage. His racial worldview also released him to find commonalities between Chicanos and other human types that were possibly akin to Indians. For Ayres, these nearby relatives would be Asians. Thus, Ayres offered his fellow citizens of Los Angeles a racist multiculturalism that could link the city's second-generation Mexican Americans with various types of "Orientals."

Emphasizing the "Indian" element within the Mexican American, Ayres claimed that it was "evidently Oriental in background" and continued to manifest itself in the Mexican's display of "Oriental characteristics," the most telling being "his utter disregard for the value of life." Ayres's Orientalism did not stop with general claims about purported Asian "characteristics." His race theories began to proliferate, branching off into a range of Asian identities. Surveying Asian populations in southern California, he explicitly discussed Filipinos, Chinese, and Japanese. Among these, he seized on Filipinos as being the most violent. "[C]rime [sic] of violence . . . is quite prevalent [among them]," he asserted, reaffirming the relevance of the putative "biological aspect."[37]

The biological took on a life of its own in Ayres's comments. Ayres painted a picture of the ineradicable racial strains spreading like a contagion, and his account likewise traversed the globe to trace that contagion's growth. He cited ethnologists who lumped Filipinos into the category *Malayan*. For many in Los Angeles, this would have been a familiar classification. Throughout the 1920s, city officials grappled with the legal ramifications of assigning Filipinos to the classification *Malay*; however, in the racial imagination of Edward Duran Ayres, that classification could now mean so much more. In a feat of racial logic made possible by these ethnological schemes of classification, Ayres argued: "The Filipino is a Malay, and ethnologists trace the Malayan people to the American Indian." With that shoe dropped, the other soon fell as well. Malayans traced to Indians could, in turn, be traced specifically to those Indians living "from the southwestern part of the United States down through Mexico, Central America and into South America." The importance of this linkage lay in the added assertion that "[t]he Malay is even more vicious than the Mongolian—to which race the Japanese and Chinese, of course belong." For Filipinos, American Indians, and, thus, Mexicans, the final verdict was, indeed, quite dismal: "In fact, the Malay seems to have all the bad qualities of the Mongolian and none of the good."[38]

Ayres's racial theories had connected a great portion of the world to devise an answer to Mexican American criminality in Los Angeles. But, once started, the biological dynamo could not easily stop, and Ayres, perhaps wishing to explain all nonwhite deviance, then cast one last heave of the racializing dragnet to haul in every possible manifestation of colored misbehavior. He finished his analysis by roping African Americans into his racial assessment: "As for the Negro, we also have a biological aspect." The Negro's biological aspect, "to which the contributing factors are the same as in respect to the Mexican," pointed to a reinforcing racial crisis in Los Angeles: the Mexican American (Indian)—Filipino—Negro strains causing a crisis in public order. Furthermore, in Ayres's assessment, the similarity between blacks and Mexicans "only aggravate[d] the condition as to the two races."[39]

It is sobering to remember how consequential this doctrine of race immutability was in 1942. Examining another Asian American—Latino comparison reveals this. That these ideas could implement broad and far-reaching racial discrimination was tragically shown in Los Angeles nine months prior to the grand jury's Mexican American forum. In February 1942, the head of the U.S. Western Defense Command claimed that Japanese Americans were suspect as a "race" because the strains of disloyalty continued across generations, that, indeed, this taint extended past the immigrant generation to infect every Japanese American all the way down to posterity's vanishing point in the future. As is well-known, that opinion was used to justify the chain of executive order, congressional act, and military proclamation that resulted in the forced mass removal of Issei and Nisei from the West Coast.

It probably is the case that, however disturbing its tenets, Ayres's testimony from 1942 does not surprise us. The dominant discourse in Los Angeles had been entertaining these notions since the 1920s, and their concentrated form in 1942 merely distilled those alchemies. But, however predominant they were, it is significant to note that Ayres's words did not go unchallenged. His theories provoked a sharp rebuttal from Mexican American activists in Los Angeles, many of whom had been battling derogatory representations for some time. Expressing fierce protest at Ayres's words were voices that spanned the spectrum of Mexican American political positions in southern California, from Bert Corona, Luisa Moreno, and Josefina Fierro to the "centrists" such as Eduardo Quevedo and Manuel Ruíz.

From within official Los Angeles governance, two members of the Los Angeles County Grand Jury also acted to challenge Ayres's musings. Harry Henderson and Harry Braverman organized a Special Committee on Mexican American Issues, thus supplying a forum for a second round of public hearings in October 1942 that rang a second round in the debate about "Mexican relations" in Los Angeles.

Those who participated in that fall meeting took special care to dispute the notion that Aztec "propensities" continued into twentieth-century Los Angeles. Patently ridiculous, said Carey McWilliams, the chief of the Division of Immigration and Housing for the California Department of Industrial Relations. "I know of no scientific warrant for the doctrine that there is any biological predisposition on the part of any race toward certain types of behavior."[40] On the matter of Aztec immutability and Mexican biological determinism, an anthropologist from the University of California, Los Angeles, testified: "No where among these people . . . do we find any lust for blood, any human sacrifice, or any inborn desire to kill."[41]

While Ayres had seemed to offer a comprehensive social explanation that was breathtaking in its reach and internal consistency, his opponents countered with an argument that was equally forceful in its coherence. They fired back that, if there were differences to be explained, they were best understood as the result of "culture," not biology. Citing the anthropologist Ruth Benedict, McWilliams said: "Man is not committed in detail by his biological constitution," thus making possible his claim that the "problem of Mexican youth in Los Angeles County is, in the widest sense of the term, a problem of cultural conflict."[42]

From August to October 1942, official Los Angeles debated the meaning of the "special Mexican relations"[43] crisis in terms of biologism versus culturalism. Biologism was blunt and most likely appealed to many whites. Its opponent, culturalism, would eventually win educated public opinion during the postwar years; however, culturalism was not without its problems, and these could be seen in the 1942 debate with Ayres.

While an improvement over biological arguments, culturalism could, nevertheless, cage already othered minorities into racially typed generalizations. Culture-based arguments could be a step backward as well as forward. Despite their good intentions, some antibiologists merely exchanged culture for biology; the underlying determinism and essentialism remained intact. This could be seen in the thoughts of Emory Bogardus, a sociologist at the University of Southern California who established himself as a major student of Mexicans and Filipinos in the United States. On the matter of criminality, Bogardus would deny any inherited Mexican tendencies toward antisocial behavior, but his etiology of cultural causes was composed of essentializations merely translated into broad "cultural" terms. As Escobar notes: "[Bogardus] explained what he believed to be an 'abnormal' crime rate among Mexicans on cultural traits. Mexicans' proclivity for stealing . . . resulted from 'the peon[s'] . . . little training in the meaning of private property'; their involvement in violent crimes stemmed from Mexicans' 'uninhibited emotions'; and Mexican juvenile delinquency developed from a generational conflict between traditional parents and youth trying desperately to fit into modern American society."[44]

That culturalism could recapitulate biologism's all-encompassing and stereotypical judgments reveals the limits of liberal race reform discourses as they wrestled with the nakedly racist formulas of Captain Ayres. Even a civil rights leader and trenchant social critic such as Carey McWilliams suffered from such limitations. Addressing the grand jury, McWilliams dismissed the biological argument, but he also transmitted one of its strains when he said that "[t]endencies toward certain types of behavior are to be found . . . in [the] cultural heritage" of a people. While sounding different from Ayres—explicitly deny-ing the notion that such tendencies were carried "in the blood stream"—he nevertheless came close to saying something very similar.[45] The wording "ten-dencies toward certain types of behavior" and the alleged roots of those ten-dencies in "cultural heritage" could devolve into a notion of culture that was static, unchangeable, immutable. In less sympathetic hands, such progressive culturalism could transmute into regressive race typing.

Perhaps this point was too fine to make in 1942, especially in the heat of battling Ayres. Indeed, the pitfalls of an undertheorized and "essentializ-ing" culturalism were probably imperceptible to those grappling with a then-dominant racial biologism. We should not be surprised if the more high-minded saw themselves fighting a prejudice that many U.S. whites believed to be "naturally" true. Nevertheless, this limit needs to be appraised, especially since it operated as a limit, however permeable, on the discursive possibilities for publicly imagining a subject position for Mexican American Los Angelenos different from that proposed by Ayres.

An unfortunate instance of this boundary is evident in a public rebuttal to anti-Latino racism, one that may have circulated more widely than the com-ments mobilized by the grand jury's special committee on "Mexican relations." In his local newspaper feature "Column Left," the essayist Al S. Waxman wrote of the Chicano crisis in 1943 and tried to tell his fellow white southern Califor-nians of the structural and social disabilities that racism had put on Mexican Americans. Waxman argued: "Unfortunately, here in this nation, particularly in Southern California, they are not 'accepted.' They have had to face every sort of discrimination that can be heaped upon a minority group. They have been denied the right—which they have sought—to contribute to the war effort; they have been denied the right to work in defense plants (it took a presidential order to get them jobs as laborers); the armed forces have even been reluctant to accept them."[46]

Nevertheless, Waxman felt compelled to preface this social criticism by giving a nod to cultural understandings of racial difference as were probably certified by many racial culturalists at the time. "Mexicans as a race are easy going, peace-loving people," wrote Waxman. He probably understood himself to be disputing Ayres's contentions about Aztec violence; nevertheless, he reinforced a stereotypical approach to evaluating Mexicans as a race by saying: "Those who are familiar with their history will remember that the outstanding thought which comes to mind in thinking of Mexico and its people is: Fiesta,

VICTOR JEW

siesta, mannana [*sic*], religion." To his credit, Waxman would not leave "Mexicans" in the dustbin of unchangeability. Seeking to assimilate them into a forward-moving history of the United States, itself a problematic gesture that necessarily presupposed a notion of forever-backward Mexico, he argued that Mexican Americans had added to their cultural legacy the "progressive" elements of democracy, antifascism, and organized labor.[47]

In retrospect, defending Mexican Americans against the Aztec biologism of Ayres was easier than defining the modern Mexican American in Los Angeles, a job that both disputants in 1942 were attempting to do in their own ways. Hampering even race liberals in this effort were the very words that were available for publicly discussing Mexican American Los Angeles. What was handy worked ham-handedly in not conveying the complexities of being Chicano in 1940s America. Moreover, the public discourse showed its inability to discuss those complexities by its linguistic poverty: there were only so many conceptual coins that circulated when it came to talking about Mexican Americans, and there seemed to be no great desire to mint any that were new and insightful. Two aspects that seemed beyond anyone's reach in this debate touched on the question of assignments: how to assign Mexican Americans racially and where to assign them nationally.

From early on, race was recognized as a problematic nonfit for Chicanos, who did not fit easily within hegemonic black/white categorizations of race. Moreover, the war years seemed to put a premium on the possible Asianness of Mexican-descended residents of Los Angeles. This was deemed especially true at a time when the newspapers portrayed the city's Chicano youths as subversive threats, a fearful characterization similar to that put on Japanese Americans, who, by August 1942, had been emptied out of the city. Finally, the very location of the Los Angeles barrio was discursively cast as something both inside and outside the U.S. body politic. Not unlike the curious Los Angeles River, which periodically surprises that city's residents with its winter overflows, the figuration of the young Mexican American Angeleno spilled over into other identity conundrums.

Traditional categories of race created a borderland for Los Angeles–area Latinos, one whose borderline moved them backward and forward in social circumstance. Carey McWilliams shared this with the Los Angeles County Grand Jury in the fall of 1942. "Mexicans are listed in the census as 'white persons,'" wrote McWilliams, "and ethnically, there is no doubt but that the classification is correct." According to this sentence, McWilliams appeared to accept the U.S. central state's organization of "Mexicans" as a normative certainty. "No doubt," he wrote, they should be classified as "white," most likely because they could not be classified as "black" according to his implied commonsense categorization. McWilliams was able to identify and exploit the inescapable irony for "ethnically" white Mexicans who were nonetheless living in a de facto racially segregated southern California. "Nevertheless," McWilliams continued, "it must be recognized that many Mexicans have what might be called a degree of color visibility." The "degree of color visibility" would lead to the "natural and inevitable" state of being "objects of race prejudice."[48]

If there was a gap between ethnographic racial classification and actually lived race assignment, another fissure broke along the lines of national belonging. Officials in Los Angeles routinely described the Mexican American community with a word that located Mexican America as enigmatically both internal and external to it. Just as Mexican Americans occupied a twilight zone of racial classification and racialized experience, so did Mexican America in Los Angeles occupy an ambiguous site, both inside and outside the overlapping and blurred distinctions between the United States and Mexico.

The word of choice to name Mexican American southern California was *colony*.[49] It is important to note how often and how casually officials and prominent individuals in Los Angeles used that term to describe the Mexican Americans in their midst. A range of persons used it in the 1940s. Whether it was Captain Ayres or Ruben A. Calderon, president of the Mexican American War Savings Committee, it seemed commonsensical to name the city's Mexican Americans as an outpost of Mexico. Even as far away as Washington, DC, the coordinator for inter-American affairs used the term. Nelson Rockefeller wrote that he was happy that "a group of interested civic employees" in Los Angeles were trying to "contact the various groups of the Mexican colony with a view to promoting such activities as recreation programs and goodwill meetings."[50]

The term *colony* came to encompass all persons of Mexican descent whether twentieth-century immigrants or descendants of those who had inhabited what came to be known as the "American Southwest" for hundreds of years prior to the U.S. conquest and colonization in 1848. In the 1940s, the word effected a discursive obfuscation that left white Angelenos blind to the ways that demographic changes had rendered it unintelligible and useless as it was used by whites. The idea of a "colony," even with specific reference to Mexican Americans, systematically failed to recognize a sizable U.S.-born cohort that was in the throes of self-consciously grasping and grappling with the two-ness of being Mexican American. The persistent use of the label *colony* sustained the more general confusion over where to meaningfully locate the Chicano crisis of 1942 and how to assign it a national identity. Even the sympathetic October 1942 grand jury meeting revealed this confusion. The title of the committee that convened this forum to specifically refute Ayres was the "Special Mexican Relations Committee" of the Los Angeles County Grand Jury.[51] To many Mexican Americans, the name itself exposed a serious blind spot shared by Los Angeles County officials on both sides of the debate. Those officials seemed mired in a vocabulary that could not name the new realities that were stirring in Boyle Heights, the "Jimtown" districts of West Whittier, the "section surrounding the Pio Pico School" in the Ranchito School District, and the poverty-stricken Hicks Camp in El Monte.[52]

*Colony* signified confusion, but one can argue that, by 1942, its persistent use also disclosed an inability to deal with white anxieties provoked by the sudden emergence of a new Mexican American Los Angeles. This emergence—a showing up on the public radar screen—acquired urgency because it took the form of the high-profile crisis that stretched from the Sleepy Lagoon arrests, through the servicemen's riot of 1943, to the trial of the accused murderers of José Díaz. Mexican Americans suddenly became newly noticeable. Significantly, a sympathizer with the new Chicano Los Angeles captured that sense of officialdom caught unawares. The civil rights advocate Carey McWilliams testified before the October 1942 grand jury symposium and noted that "[o]ur local problem" was "in truth . . . merely one aspect of a much larger national problem." The predicament was that the "colony"—whether in Los Angeles or expanded to include all Mexican American communities throughout the nation—had grown to surpass the comforting limit that the word *colony* seemed to describe and vouchsafe. "Just how large is the Mexican population in the United States?" asked McWilliams. Asking that simple question, he suggested, would make the issue "immediately apparent," and he hoped that his audience might consider the consequences of disfranchising a population that the National Resources Planning Board had estimated "as high as 3,500,000."[53]

According to McWilliams, that figure would have surprised the compilers of a major social survey that had been conducted ten years earlier. In 1933, then-President Herbert Hoover commissioned a massive inquiry into the social trends of the United States. In McWilliams's reading of that document, the presence of Mexican America barely registered: "Since the Mexicans are the newest of the large immigrant groups, there has not been sufficient time to rear a large second generation born of parents of this nationality." In the short span of time between 1933 and 1942, the Mexican population had, indeed, crossed the threshold of producing a "large second generation" born in the United States: "[W]e are just beginning now, in 1942, to feel the impact of this second-generation problem in the Mexican group."[54] When McWilliams said that, he was sounding an alarm of sorts for progressive purposes as he hoped that wartime Americans could be moved to enfranchise the sizable "Mexican" population and its increasingly visible U.S.-born cohort. One could argue, however, that this tocsin sounded in the episode of the Chinese anthropometry as well. While not as loud or direct, one might contend that the San Francisco measurement study attempted to address a similar issue as that faced by Los Angeles during the Mexican American crisis of 1942. A new ethnic reality was emerging, however sequestered it was within the city's "Chinese colony." This was an uncertain future that had to be measured, both literally and figuratively, and, thus, be more efficiently governed as well as more scientifically understood.

## Conclusion

Both the Chinatown anthropometry and the Mexican American moral panic were instances of officially sanctioned activities that can be seen as dominant modes of subject-making facilitated by various arms of the central state and the local state. In the Los Angeles episode, the efforts to grapple with the Mexican American crisis happened, in this essay's focus, through the Los Angeles County Grand Jury. The San Francisco example from 1934 to 1935 could not have proceeded very far without the support of SERA and the WPA. More significantly, these moments of racialized subject-making flowed through channels banked by dominant privilege; for the most part, the talk recorded in this essay reflected the assumptions and public speaking positions of those "outside" the Chinese quarter and the Mexican colony. Even in the case of the Chinatown anthropometry, which witnessed the indispensable role of two Chinese Americans in starting the measuring project, the overriding hand belonged to the white academic social scientists. Dr. Charles Wong and Samuel Lee could not have gone far had they not adjusted their proposal from measuring malnutrition to measuring racial adaptation.

As sanctioned discursive moments, both instances of subject-making were attempts at gauging the present and the future of these two racialized communities. But it must be noted that official endorsement and dominant discourses were not the only sites from which to construe the identities and futurities of Chinese San Francisco and Chicano Los Angeles. At this very time, for both Chinese America in the 1930s and Mexican America in the Depression and war years, a growing U.S.-born "second-generation" was grappling with its new presence as a sizable critical mass of U.S.-born citizens who were still negatively racialized as Oriental and Mexican. These young Chinese Americans and Mexican Americans worried the hyphen of their dual positionalities through numerous public discussions and debates that jostled the key question, Where does my future lie? For debaters in the Chinese American context, the two roads diverged at the ocean's shore: one path stayed in San Francisco, while the other found promise across the ocean in China. Likewise, the "Mexican American generation" wrestled with what America could offer even as it withheld so much.

Thus, something was afoot during the 1930s and 1940s for these racialized communities that were neither black nor white. For the younger members of these "colonies," defining the future meant inventing new meanings for the doubledness of being raced Americans. For those on the outside of these groups, they now realized that peoples and communities that had been left unattended or partially noticed now required closer scrutiny. It would not be too far-fetched to say that, for everyone involved, the situation approached various thresholds of crisis the particulars of which seemed galvanized by the larger national crises of depression and world war. As such, the various participants in these two episodes would have appreciated how one social critic of the time understood the idea of "crisis." For Antonio Gramsci, it was a moment of critical caesura and unbearable tension—when the old had not yet died and the new had yet to be born.

## Notes

1. Dr. C. H. Danforth, a professor of anatomy at Stanford University and a formative intellectual influence on the San Francisco study, wrote: "If you succeed in carrying out your plan in such a manner that the data will be beyond question, the results should be a classic which will be consulted for many years to come" (quoted in "Final Progress Report to State Emergency Relief [sic] on Project Number 2-F2-230, A Study of Prevalent Diseases

amongst the Chinese. A Physical Anthropological Study of Chinese" [hereafter "Final Progress Report"] [1935], a copy of which can be found in the storage holdings of the library of the Institute of Governmental Studies, University of California, Berkeley).

2. R. L. Olson to Sam D. Lee, 2 November 1934, accompanying "Final Progress Report."

3. In terms of results, the project seemed to have two identities that may have reflected the pull of two purposes, a theme suggested by this essay. The two identities can be seen in the wording of the titles of the two reports that emerged from the measuring project. Contrast the full title of the "Final Progress Report" (see n. 1 above) with "Final Report. Anthropometric Study of the San Francisco Chinese. Official Project 65-3-4229. W.P.A. Project 3330. Submitted to Dr. James B. Sharp. State Coordinator of Statistical Projects" ([hereafter "Final Report"] [n.d.], a copy of which can be found in the storage holdings of the library of the Institute of Governmental Studies, University of California, Berkeley). Both reports were submitted by "Thomas A. Wong, MD," supervisor, and "Samuel D. Lee, AB, Author and editor of the project."

4. Hall, "Who Needs Identity?" 6.

5. Yung, *Unbound Feet*, 180.

6. "Final Report," 1.

7. The list of endorsers included: "Dr. C. H. Danforth, Professor Anatomy [*sic*], U. of Stanford [*sic*], Director of Amer. Journal of Phy. Anthro.; Dr. A. L. Kroeber, Professor of Anthropology, U of C; Dr. R. L. Olson, Associate Prof.; Dr. E. W. Gifford, Curator, Museum, U. of C.; Dr. K. Klimek, Polish Anthropologist on U.C. Campus [*sic*]; Dr. Agnes Fay Morgan, Prof. of Household Science, U of C; Dr. Nancy Bayley, Child Welfare Bureau, U of C" ("Final Progress Report," 1–2).

8. "Final Report," 2, 2–3.

9. U.S. Immigration Commission, *Reports of the Immigration Commission*, vol. 38, *Changes in Bodily Form of Descendants of Immigrants*, 61st Cong., 2d sess., 1911, S. Doc. 208, ix, xi.

10. Ibid., 2.

11. C. H. Danforth to Samuel Lee, 20 February 1935, accompanying "Final Progress Report."

12. It was also given the identifications Project No. 2-F2-230 and Official Project 65-3-4229.

13. "Final Report," 3.

14. Ibid., 1–2.

15. *Gold Mountain* is the English-language translation of *gam saan*, the term used by Guangdong residents to describe California.

16. "Final Progress Report," 2.

17. This opportunity for now reaching the Chinese was matched by the mobilizing of resources, also made possible by the Great Depression and the New Deal: "The S.E.R.A. made possible the contribution of this material to the field of Anthropology by not only furnishing the clerical aid and investigators but also lending the prestige of the organization. This project would be a herculean task for individual initiative or under private endowment because of the hesitancy of schools and other agencies to co-operate" (ibid.).

18. Ibid., 6.

19. R. L. Olson to Sam D. Lee, 2 November 1934 (n. 2 above).

20. "Article Written Up in S.F. News" included with "Final Progress Report," a typed copy of "Chinese to Get Pictures Taken: SERA Wants to See if Our Climate Changes Them," *San Francisco News*, n.d.

21. "Final Report," 8, 9.

22. "Final Report," charts following 8 (numbers of subjects), 8 (ages of subjects), 9–10 (quotation).

23. Ibid., 9–10: "When there was some question regarding the physical condition of the person, or the possibility of factors entering in because of racial intermarriage, the individual was excluded. The abnormal cases, such as obesity, were omitted since the study was primarily interested in the normal development of the physical body. The subjects were undressed to the waist and measurements were made while the individuals were bare-footed" (10).

24. Ibid., 13. The full set of indices for "Body Measurements" were as follows: "Stature, Martin No. 1; Acromion, Martin No. 8; Radiale, Martin No. 9; Stylion, Martin No. 10; Iliospinale (Iliocristale), Martin No. 13; Sitting Height, Martin No. 23, modified (The subject was seated on a flat top box forty five centimeters high. Some of the subjects were unable to touch the floor with their feet from this height, particularly those of the younger age groups); Total Reach, Martin No. 17 (This measurement was taken on a movable measuring rod on the wall with subject's arms held horizontally and with no extra stretching on the part of the subject); Chest, Expanded and Diminished, Martin No. 61, modified (These measurements were taken with a steel tape around the chest anteriorly at the level of the nipple line, and posteriorly directly below the angle of the scapula in both boys and girls. The arms were held normally at the side of the body); Interspinous Diameter (Cristal Width), Martin No. 41 (It should be noted here that the pressure was exerted in placing the measuring points exactly on the mid-point of the anterior superior spine); Biceps, Martin No. 65; Wrist, Martin No. 67, modified (The circumference of the wrist was obtained by placing the steel tape along the styloid prominences); Weight, Martin No. 71, modified" (ibid., 11–12).

25. "Final Report," 13.

26. Chun, *Of Orphans and Warriors*, 20. The summary report was produced by the California State Emergency Relief Institute as "A Report of the State Emergency Relief Institute of Governmental Studies Administration, 1935–1944," cited in Chun, 20.

27. A. L. Kroeber to Charles Wong, 26 March 1935, accompanying "Final Progress Report."

28. R. L. Olson to Sam D. Lee, 2 November 1934 (n. 2 above).

29. Samples of this scholarship, specifically on Chinese America, include Lee, *At America's Gates*; Salyer, *Laws Harsh as Tigers*; McClain, *In Search of Equality*; Chan, ed., *Entry Denied*; and Wong and Chan, ed., *Claiming America*.

30. "Survey of Social Work Needs of the Chinese Population of San Francisco, California," SERA Project no. 262-156 (1935). (The SERA project number is curiously illegible because it was rendered in what appears to be a stylized attempt to mimic Asian forms of calligraphy.) A copy can be found in the storage holdings of the library of the Institute of Governmental Studies, University of California, Berkeley.

31. Escobar, *Making of a Political Identity*, 131.

32. Ibid., 207.

33. Edward Duran Ayres, "Statistics," May 1943, Foreign Relations Bureau (typewritten document in John Anson Ford Papers, Huntington Library, San Marino, California), 1. Ayres actually discussed "a number of factors" when diagnosing the purported "great proportion of crime by a certain element of the Mexican population." He devoted the first five paragraphs of his notorious remarks to the discussion of social predicaments of Mexican American Los Angelenos. He mentioned such problems as poverty, lack of employment, low wages, segregation in the workplace and in housing, and Jim Crow–like discrimination

in theaters, restaurants, and parks. Nevertheless, he chose to discount these factors and emphasize what he called the "basic cause . . . more fundamental" than the social maladies he had already noted. Moreover, that basic cause, his "biological basis," consumed the lion's share of his comments (1).

Ayres translated Spanish-language documents for Los Angeles County. Apparently, he did this in his capacity as an officer with the Foreign Relations Bureau. This translation duty was noted in Ruben A. Calderon to John Anson Ford, 22 April 1943, John Anson Ford Papers.

34. Ayres, "Statistics," 1.

35. Woofter, "Status of Racial and Ethnic Groups," 561.

36. Ayres, "Statistics," 2.

37. Ibid.

38. Ibid., 3.

39. Ibid.

40. Testimony of Carey McWilliams, Chief, Division of Immigration and Housing, Department of Industrial Relations, State of California, in "Papers Read in Meeting Held October 8, 1942, called by the Special Mexican Relations Committee of the Los Angeles County Grand Jury," John Anson Ford Papers.

41. "The Problem of Crime among the Mexican Youth of Los Angeles," testimony of Harry Hoijer before the Los Angeles County Grand Jury, in "Papers Read in Meeting Held October 8, 1942."

42. Testimony of Carey McWilliams.

43. This was the name given to the special committee of the Los Angeles County Grand Jury convened to investigate the problem of Mexican American criminality. The title as given in the papers that issued from the 8 October 1942 meeting was the "Special Mexican Relations Committee."

44. Escobar, *Making of a Political Identity*, 114.

45. Testimony of Carey McWilliams, 2.

46. Al S. Waxman, "Justice?" *Column Left*, undated clipping, John Anson Ford Papers. Handwritten on this clipping is "Eastside Journal 1 / 20 / 43."

47. Ibid.

48. Testimony of Carey McWilliams, 4. McWilliams cited Robert Park for the latter observation.

49. It must be noted that *colonia*—a term referring to a community of residence—was often used by Spanish-speaking Los Angelenos to describe their neighborhoods, especially if they lived in rural areas near El Monte. In this essay, I am referring to how the English word *colony* was used by Anglo government officials to describe the Mexican American presence in the United States. Words, as we know, are always hard to pin down, especially when recovered by historians. In this way, it could be argued that *colony* acquired othering connotations when deployed by government officials gazing on 1940s Mexican Americans. It is likewise noteworthy that contemporaneous documents also described Chinese American Chinatowns, similarly, as *colonies*.

50. Nelson A. Rockefeller to John Anson Ford, 2 July 1943, John Anson Ford Papers.

51. "Index" to "Papers Read in Meeting Held October 8, 1942."

52. Stephen J. Keating, Secretary, Citizen's Committee for Latin American Youth, to John Anson Ford, 6 May 1943, John Anson Ford Papers.

53. Testimony of Carey McWilliams, 2.

54. Ibid., 3.

*Part Two* **CONTRADICTIONS OF COALITION**

Méndez v. Westminster *Reexamined*

Toni Robinson and Greg Robinson

The history of struggles for civil rights by Latinos and Asians offers a revealing window into the complexities of relations between racialized groups. Although the two communities have at various times joined together in movements for fair housing, equal employment opportunity, and integrated schools, their collaboration has been marked by tension and conflict as well as solidarity. A prime example of both the promise and the limitations of intergroup coalition is the 1946–47 federal court case *Méndez v. Westminster School District of Orange County.*[1] The *Méndez* case, which put an end to the exclusion of Mexican American children from "white" schools in Southern California, is a bellwether event in the history of equal rights in the United States. Not only did the court's decision represent a major advance for Mexican Americans in their quest for equality, but it also led directly to the repeal of all school segregation laws in California, which, until then, had been the largest state to maintain separate schools for minority populations. The *Méndez* case can, thus, be seen as the first victory in the postwar legal struggle against segregation in primary education that climaxed with the Supreme Court's epochal ruling in *Brown v. Board of Education* in 1954.[2]

*Méndez* has been enshrined both in historiography and in popular memory as a precursor to *Brown*, a challenge to racial discrimination by minority group representatives. In accordance with this view, the numerous historical exhibits, articles, lectures, and commemorations of the *Méndez* case have tended to highlight the participation as amici curiae of civil rights organizations such as the National Association for the Advancement of Colored People (NAACP), and, to a lesser extent, the Japanese American Citizens League (JACL), with the League of United Latin American Citizens (LULAC) as well as the involvement of NAACP Chief Counsel Thurgood Marshall. They thus portray the case as a golden moment of intergroup unity among Latinos, Asian Americans, and African Americans.

A notable illustration of the tendency to view *Méndez* as a landmark of (inter)racial struggle is the work of the historian Ronald Takaki, whose "multicultural history of America in World War II" provides the following commentary on the case:

> The Mexican-American struggle for justice expanded [after World War II] to the right to equal education. In the 1946 case of *Méndez v. Westminster School District of Orange County*, the U.S. Circuit Court of Southern California declared that the segregation of Mexican children violated their right to equal protection of the law guaranteed to them under the Fourteenth Amendment and therefore was unconstitutional. To support the *Méndez* case, amicus curiae briefs were filed by the American Jewish Congress, the National Association for the Advancement of Colored People, and the Japanese American Citizens League. Together, they won a victory over prejudice in education. The *Méndez* decision set a precedent for the historic 1954 *Brown v. Board of Education* decision.[3]

This is all inspiring, and for many people it is clearly empowering. However, it is important to guard against romanticizing the *Méndez* decision as the product of a united front of minority groups. In actual fact, what the events of *Méndez* reveal most strongly are the tensions and complexities present in partnerships against discrimination among groups such as Japanese Americans and Mexican Americans and the contingent nature of their self-identification as racial or ethnic minorities. The goals of the groups involved in *Méndez* were divergent and even contradictory, and the participants adopted differing legal strategies to support their respective goals. The racial factor, which ostensibly united them, was at the center of their dispute. The final court decision, and the nature of the "victory" won by the minority groups, was laced with ambiguity and irony.

## Roots of the Case for Mexican Americans and Japanese Americans

For both Mexican Americans and Japanese Americans, the roots of the *Méndez* case can be found in the Immigration Act of 1924, which severely restricted European immigration to the United States and completely barred immigration from Japan. In the years following passage of the act, Nikkei (ethnic Japanese) communities in California, home of some 70 percent of mainland Japanese Americans, remained stigmatized by nativist prejudice. Issei (first-generation) immigrants were forbidden to own agricultural land or become naturalized citizens, while their native-born Nisei (second-generation) chil-

TONI ROBINSON AND GREG ROBINSON

dren, although U.S. citizens, were subjected to widespread economic discrimination and anti-miscegenation laws. In a few areas, notably the districts of Florin and Walnut Grove near Sacramento, Nisei children were required by law to attend separate "Oriental" public schools.[4]

Japanese American communities divided over the response to such discrimination. Issei continued to favor close ties with Japan, and some sent their children back to their homeland to be educated. However, a handful of Nisei organizations, notably the JACL, founded in 1930, challenged their elders for dominance within Nikkei communities. The JACL restricted its membership to American citizens, and its leaders advocated a platform of Americanization, including exclusive loyalty to the United States and protest against anti-Japanese discrimination through the defense of citizenship rights. JACL leaders strenuously rejected any suggestion that their Japanese ancestry made them in any way different from other Americans.

Meanwhile, immigration from the Americas, especially Mexico, remained unrestricted throughout the 1920s. During the years that followed 1924, waves of Mexicans were drawn or recruited to work in the United States, notably in California, whose population of Mexican ancestry more than tripled. By 1930, ethnic Mexicans were the state's largest "minority group."[5] During the Depression years, the Mexican American population of Southern California continued to grow—although much more slowly—despite the imposition of immigration restrictions and the deportation of tens if not hundreds of thousands of Mexicans and Mexican American citizens as supposedly "illegal" aliens. The vast majority of the new immigrants settled in Southern California. Most took up jobs in agricultural areas, where local farmers (whites as well as some Japanese Americans) sought laborers to pick their crops.[6] Others settled in urban areas—the 1940 U.S. Census counted 219,000 people of Mexican ancestry in the Los Angeles area, of whom 65,000 were Mexican born.[7]

The expansion of the Mexican American population was matched by a heightening of barriers of inequality against Mexican Americans. Although Mexican Americans, unlike Asian Americans, were not targeted by statewide race-based legislation such as anti-miscegenation statutes, they were, nonetheless, forced to live in segregated districts and barrios and sometimes excluded by local ordinance or custom from public facilities such as swimming pools and stores.[8]

Mexican Americans were also frequently placed in separate and markedly inferior "Mexican" schools.[9] Significantly, although sections 8003 and 8004 of the California Education Code did not list children of Mexican ancestry as a group that could be segregated, white educators and school psychologists in Southern California believed Mexican American children to be inferior and, thus, more in need of "Americanization"—that is, the assimilation of U.S. values and customs—than of a traditional academic education. They also used linguistic difference as a pretext for segregation. Mexican American groups tried repeatedly to contest such discrimination. In 1931, parents of Mexican American children in Lemon Grove, with aid from the Mexican consulate in San Diego, brought legal action against the placement of their children in a segregated school and won a writ of mandate from the Superior Court of California admitting the children to the "white" school.[10] However, the ruling in the Lemon Grove case did not seem to have set a precedent for other school districts.

A decade later, LULAC picked up the struggle. Founded in Texas at the end of the 1920s, LULAC was an organization of young lawyers and middle-class professionals. Like the JACL, its membership was restricted to citizens of the United States. It was dedicated to promoting the assimilation of "Americans of Mexican ancestry" and to challenging discrimination against them. During the 1930s, LULAC instituted legal action challenging the placement of Mexican Americans in segregated schools in Texas but achieved only inconclusive results.[11] In 1941, LULAC moved its efforts to California and assisted in a lawsuit brought by two Mexican American families in Los Angeles County's Ranchito school district whose children had been barred from the district's new elementary school and forced to attend an older school in another district. The complainants' attorneys asserted that there were no county ordinances permitting such segregation and claimed that it would be in the best interests and "promote the Americanism" of the children to send them to the white school.[12] In order to illustrate the injustice of the segregation, they pointed to the fact that Nisei students in the district were not segregated and had enrolled freely in the new school.[13] The suit failed to end the segregation—Judge Emmet Wilson ruled that the school board had the power to assign children as it saw fit and found that the placement of Nisei children was irrelevant. Similarly, in nearby Orange County, where Mexican American children made up one-fourth of the total student population, some 70 percent of Mexican American children were, by 1934, attending predominantly segregated elementary schools.[14] In contrast, the entire ethnic Japanese population of Orange County was, by

TONI ROBINSON AND GREG ROBINSON

1940, only 1,855, and the small fraction of Japanese American children in the student population attended "white" schools.[15]

## Effects of World War II
### THE JAPANESE AMERICAN INTERNMENT

World War II fundamentally reshaped both groups. In the days following the Japanese attack on Pearl Harbor, over a thousand Issei were arrested and interned as potentially dangerous enemy aliens. In February 1942, following a pressure campaign by West Coast military officials and political and economic interest groups, President Franklin D. Roosevelt signed Executive Order 9066, under which all Japanese Americans, whether Issei or Nisei, were forcibly expelled from the West Coast without trial and shipped under armed guard to a network of barren camps in the interior. There they remained confined behind barbed wire, for the most part until the end of the war. Following the evacuation order, the Japanese Americans were forced to abandon most of their land and possessions or sell them off cheaply, and the once-prosperous community was impoverished. The traumas of imprisonment and the rigors of the camp experience triggered widespread psychological disturbance among the inmates and brought about the breakdown of existing community and family structures.[16]

Following their release from confinement in 1942 and 1943, the vast majority of the Japanese American camp inmates chose eventually to return to California and the other West Coast states, although the federal government endeavored to persuade them to resettle in other regions and the Pacific Coast remained closed to them until 1945. The readjustment after return was difficult. The returnees were subjected to widespread discrimination and terrorist attacks by resident white bigots. The federal government offered no police protection or financial aid to assist Japanese American resettlers in California, while the state legislature tried to discourage the former inmates from returning by barring Japanese aliens from various professions and by bringing escheat proceedings to strip the Nisei of title to the landholdings purchased for them by their Issei parents. Many returning Japanese Americans were forced to settle in urban areas, despite housing scarcities and high rents, and were squeezed into overcrowded apartments or mobile homes in ghettos and barrios alongside African American and Latino neighbors. One important change from the prewar years, however, was that the old Oriental schools were abandoned and Japanese American children throughout the state were enrolled in integrated schools.

Both the wartime confinement of the Nisei and their postwar resettlement experience contributed to reshaping their political orientation after 1945. The post–Pearl Harbor internment of influential Issei community leaders and the subsequent overall stigmatization of the Issei in the camps as "enemy aliens" left the Nisei with the chief responsibility for leading and representing the Japanese American community. The JACL, partly as a result of its (still-controversial) decision to cooperate with the federal government in executing the removal and confinement of Japanese Americans, emerged during the war years as the dominant Nikkei voice. Yet the JACL perceptibly shifted its platform at this time. It remained committed to its Americanization program—indeed, JACL members, like other Japanese Americans, seem to have absorbed from their mass incarceration the lesson that only through assimilation to (white) American norms could they hope to avoid a repeat of their exclusion. On the other hand, the JACL became markedly more assertive in demanding civil rights for Japanese Americans.[17] The injustice of the government's wartime actions against the Japanese Americans, coupled with the spectacular military record of Japanese American GIs, made the JACL especially impatient to secure full citizenship rights and eliminate further discrimination. Under the leadership of A. L. Wirin, a Los Angeles lawyer and director of the Southern California American Civil Liberties Union (ACLU) who had become JACL counsel during the war, and his law partner, JACL President Saburo Kido, the JACL instituted lawsuits challenging California's Alien Land Act and its discriminatory commercial fishing laws.[18]

Furthermore, in sharp contrast to the pre–World War II era, when advocacy of multigroup alliances by Japanese Americans was limited to a few newspaper columnists and progressive political organizations, community voices united in support of coalition-building. JACL leaders such as Larry Tajiri and Mike Masaoka and Japanese American newspapers such as the *Pacific Citizen*, the *Colorado Times*, and the *Utah Nippo* urged the Nisei to recognize that they were a minority group with the same problems as other racial and ethnic minorities and that it was in their own interest to support civil rights for all. JACL representatives joined interracial committees, and local chapters sponsored joint events with groups such as the NAACP. Most significant, the JACL counsel A. L. Wirin collaborated with the NAACP attorney Loren Miller in a series of legal cases challenging restrictive covenants against nonwhites in housing. In July 1946, the JACL established a special defense fund for civil rights cases to finance the organization's participation in litigation involving other racial minorities.[19]

## THE MEXICAN AMERICAN COMMUNITY

Although in a different way than for the Japanese Americans, the Second World War was a defining moment for Southern California's Mexican American community, one that energized community leaders to press for civil rights. By 1940, the majority of the ethnic Mexicans in the United States were American citizens, and they came of age during the war years. Nationwide, as many as 350,000 Mexican Americans, of whom Californians constituted a significant fraction, served in the armed forces. As was true for the Nisei, the distinguished military service record of Mexican American GIs bolstered the community's self-confidence and sharpened its awareness of unequal treatment for its members.[20] Meanwhile, as a result of wartime labor shortages, tens of thousands of Mexican American workers were hired for jobs in U.S. shipyards and other war industries—17,000 in the Los Angeles shipyards alone by 1944.[21] The ethnic Mexican population was also swelled by the arrival of a wave of migrant laborers recruited to the United States under the bracero program, 120,000 per year by 1946.[22]

The community was also drawn together by outbreaks of wartime bigotry. In August 1942, after José Díaz, a young Mexican American, was found unconscious and dying on a road in Sleepy Lagoon, on the outskirts of Los Angeles, detectives instituted mass arrests of Mexican Americans. Twenty of these arrestees were subsequently brought to trial, in an atmosphere marked by baseless newspaper stories of a "Mexican" crime wave and a presiding judge later found by a higher court to have been biased against the defendants. Although no proof was ever presented that Díaz had been murdered, let alone by any of those charged, twelve of the defendants were found guilty of murder and eight of lesser offenses by an all-Anglo jury.[23] In June 1943, following a long campaign of sensationalist stories in the popular Hearst press about the depredations of Mexican American gang members in "zoot suits," white Anglo soldiers and sailors went on a rampage, seizing young Mexican American (plus some African American and Filipino) pachucos, beating them, and stripping them of their clothing. Local police then arrested the victims.[24] In response to these events, Mexican American activists from groups such as the Spanish Speaking People's Congress and the Coordinating Council for Latin-American Youth sought to combat discrimination and lessen ethnic tensions through lobbying and public education campaigns and by forging coalitions with Anglo liberals, African Americans, and others, most notably in the Sleepy Lagoon Defense Committee.[25]

The various Mexican American groups also grew more assertive in fighting for integration and defending civil rights. As before World War II, a major vehicle of activism was LULAC. At the close of World War II, fueled by the presence of returning veterans, LULAC renewed its desegregation efforts. In 1945, it established its first permanent California chapter in Santa Ana in order to supplement the efforts of a local Latin American organization to organize parents and demand integrated schools. Along with the Coordinating Council for Latin-American Youth and the Federation of Hispanic American Voters, LULAC encouraged Mexican American parents in El Monte to demand educational equality for their children and joined a lobbying campaign to persuade the California State Assembly to repeal sections 8003 and 8004 of the state education code.[26]

## DIFFERENCES BETWEEN JAPANESE AMERICANS
## AND MEXICAN AMERICANS

Although both the Mexican American and the Japanese American communities underwent a significant transformation during World War II and intensified their campaign for equality in its aftermath, they pursued opposite strategies in pursuit of that goal. As noted, the JACL became heavily invested in intergroup alliances. Conversely, despite the support that they received from African Americans and Japanese Americans during the war, Mexican American leaders chose to distance themselves from such coalitions. For example, Mexican American organizations did not join in the multigroup legal struggle against whites-only restrictive housing covenants during the first postwar years. On the contrary, some Mexican Americans continued to reside in housing covered by such covenants. In February 1945, Superior Court Judge Alfred E. Paonessa dismissed a suit by property owners in El Monte who sought to bar Mrs. Nellie Garcia from occupying property covered by a covenant barring occupancy by those of the "African and Asian race" and by "those of

TONI ROBINSON AND GREG ROBINSON

the Mexican race." At the request of David Marcus, Garcia's attorney, Paonessa ruled that no cause of action applied in the case since there was no "Mexican race."[27] Furthermore, LULAC and the other organizations did not coordinate their lobbying efforts against educational segregation with the JACL or the NAACP even though Japanese Americans were still formally subject to separate schools under California law and many black children were required by local school districts to attend segregated schools. (The *New York Times* reported that, in late 1946, under the threat of a lawsuit, the Riverside school district abandoned its long-standing custom of segregated schools for African Americans and Mexican Americans.)[28]

Mexican American leaders fighting discrimination may have been fearful that associating with nonwhite minority groups might lead to their being categorized as nonwhite. The historian Mario García has noted, for example, that the leaders of the Coordinating Council for Latin-American Youth rejected any suggestion that Mexican Americans were a "minority" and explicitly distanced themselves from African Americans:

> Fearing that any attempt to classify Mexicans as people of color might subject them to "legal" forms of discrimination and segregation, the Council rejected any implication that Mexicans were not white. The Council's insistence that Mexicans were white also appears to have stemmed from the historic ambivalence and insecurity of Mexicans on both sides of the border concerning their racial status. These feelings often led to a denial of possessing Indian blood.

> Council members . . . drew distinctions between Mexican Americans and Afro Americans as a way of trying to avoid the stigma of racial inferiority imposed on blacks. . . . [They] focused on ethnic rather than racial discrimination . . . [and] insisted that Mexicans were white and hence no different from other ethnic groups such as the Irish, Italians or Germans."[29]

In brief, then, Japanese Americans, who rejected any question of cultural specificity attached to their group heritage, nonetheless predominantly saw themselves as a nonwhite minority and sought to ally with other nonwhite groups. In contrast, Mexican Americans, who expressed pride in their particular ethnic and cultural legacy, were inclined to conceive of themselves as white and refused interracial solidarity. The historian Neil Foley has commented that Mexican American leaders recognized that their citizenship rights depended on being able to claim that they were white:

As whites of a different culture and color than most Anglo whites, many middle-class Mexicans learned early on that hostility to the idea of "social equality" for African Americans went right to the core of what constituted whiteness in the U.S. Whether or not they brought with them from Mexico racial prejudice against blacks—and certainly many Mexicans did—middle-class Mexican leaders throughout the 1930s, 40s, and 50s went to great lengths to dissociate themselves socially, culturally, and politically from the early struggles of African Americans to achieve full citizenship rights in America.[30]

This basic contradiction between the position of Mexican Americans and that of Japanese Americans would suffuse the campaign against segregated schools that both groups undertook in the postwar era.

## *The* Méndez *Case*
### ORIGINS

In September 1944, Gonzalo Méndez, a Mexican-born tenant farmer who had moved during the war to the town of Westminster in Orange County and settled on the property of an incarcerated Japanese American family,[31] attempted to enroll his children at Westminster's white school. School authorities refused to admit the children and ordered them enrolled in Hoover elementary, a Mexican school. Méndez joined forces with members of the Latin American Organization, a group of Latino World War II veterans in nearby Santa Ana angered over the segregation of their children. In March 1945, Méndez, William Guzman, Frank Palomino, Thomas Estrada, and Lorenzo Ramirez brought a lawsuit on behalf of their children and the five thousand other children of "Mexican and Latin descent" in the four school districts of Orange County with segregated schools, seeking to challenge the discriminatory policy. Méndez and his co-complainants hired the Los Angeles attorney David Marcus, who had previously defended Nellie Garcia in the restrictive covenant case against her, to represent them. Marcus filed a petition alleging that the school districts' maintenance of separate schools deprived the petitioners of the educational benefits enjoyed by white or Anglo children solely because of their Mexican or Latin descent. It thus constituted arbitrary discrimination in violation of the due process and equal protection clauses of the Fourteenth Amendment to the U.S. Constitution and should be enjoined.[32] In their answer, the defendants (respondents) claimed that the separation of pupils

TONI ROBINSON AND GREG ROBINSON

was practiced for the sole purpose of instructing the children of Mexican descent in the English language and was in their best interest.

## ARGUMENT

The *Méndez* case was heard in late 1945 by Senior Justice Paul J. McCormick of the federal district court in Los Angeles. The defendants aggressively moved to dismiss the action for lack of subject matter jurisdiction. They argued that the lawsuit raised no federal issue, education being exclusively a state matter, and that the school districts were governed under state law. The judge denied the motion and set the case down for trial. At the trial, David Marcus called as witnesses a number of educational and social science experts who testified that the segregation of Mexican American children as practiced by the defendants was both contrary to modern educational understanding and injurious to its victims. The petitioners also introduced evidence that directly contradicted the school boards' claims that the segregation was necessitated by the alleged English-language deficiencies of the supposedly Spanish-speaking "Mexican" children. The defense attorney Joel Ogle countered that, in *Plessy v. Ferguson*, the Supreme Court had long since settled that "separate but equal" racially segregated facilities were constitutional.[33] Ogle introduced evidence showing that the physical facilities, teachers, and curricula afforded the Mexican American children were equal or even superior to those available to the Anglo children.[34]

## THE QUESTION OF RACE

During the trial, Marcus and Ogle entered into the crucial stipulation that race was not an issue in the case. The defendant school districts had initially argued that Mexican American children were not members of the white race, in connection with the argument that their segregation should be upheld under the precedent of *Plessy*. However, after one school official testified that the segregation was a necessary result of the inferiority of the Mexican American children to white children and another spoke of the segregation as being based on the "social problem" created by the presence of the Mexican Americans,[35] Ogle changed course. Presumably realizing that he had more to lose by presenting a policy based on open bigotry than from conceding that Mexican Americans were "white," he agreed to stipulate that there was no question as to racial difference or racial segregation in the case. He thereafter defended the segregation solely as a rational response to the Mexican American children's alleged lack of proficiency in English.[36] Marcus and his clients, meanwhile, were clearly aware of the "social value of whiteness" and the potential detriment to Mexican Americans of being classed as a nonwhite race.[37] Accordingly, they too agreed to the stipulation that the segregation of Mexican Americans was not a matter of racial discrimination.

## THE LOWER COURT RULING

On 18 February 1946, Judge McCormick ruled in favor of the petitioners, finding that the school districts' actions violated their rights under both the Fourteenth Amendment to the U.S. Constitution and California state law. His decision took a powerful swipe at the constitutionality of race- or ancestry-based public school segregation. Such segregation, the judge stated, hindered the Mexican American children from developing "a common cultural attitude . . . which is imperative for the perpetuation of American institutions and ideals" and harmed them by "foster[ing] antagonisms in the children and suggest[ing] inferiority among them where none exists."[38] McCormick thus directly anticipated the language of the future chief justice Earl Warren (then the governor of California) eight years later in *Brown v. Board of Education*.[39] Moreover, Judge McCormick declared: "[T]he equal protection of the laws . . . is not provided by furnishing in separate schools the same technical facilities, text books and courses of instruction to students of Mexican ancestry that are available to the other public school children regardless of their ancestry. A paramount requisite in the American system of public education is social equality."[40]

Although Judge McCormick recognized that English-language deficiency was the only tenable ground on which segregation could be defended, he nevertheless found that it was not the true basis for the defendants' practices. The evidence showed, in fact, that the children were actually segregated on the basis of their "Mexican" or "Latinized" names and, in some cases, their appearance. Damningly, Judge McCormick characterized the defendants' methods of determining language knowledge as "illusory." Such testing of children as was done to determine their English proficiency was, he found, "generally hasty, superficial and not reliable." Further, while any English-deficient Mexican American children who were starting school could reasonably be segre-

TONI ROBINSON AND GREG ROBINSON

gated by classroom for special instruction for a short time, the defendant school districts maintained entirely separate schools for all Mexican American students through the sixth grade—and, in two instances, the eighth—far longer than could possibly be justified by any alleged language deficiency. Indeed, "Spanish-speaking" children in "Mexican" schools were actually held back in learning English by their lack of exposure to its use. Rather, McCormick stated, it was clear that the defendants singled out Mexican American children as a class for segregation solely on the basis of their ancestry, a practice forbidden by the education law of California and a distinction "recently" declared by the U.S. Supreme Court to be "odious" and "utterly inconsistent with American tradition and ideals."[41]

## *The* Méndez *Appeal*
### APPELLATE BRIEFS AND ARGUMENTS

Almost immediately after McCormick issued his judgment, however, the defendants filed an appeal with the Ninth Circuit Court of Appeals. In an attempt to make the best of an unfavorable situation, Ogle argued that, given Judge McCormick's ruling that the defendants' segregation practices were irreconcilable with California law, those practices could not be considered "state action" under the Fourteenth Amendment and, therefore, that the federal courts had no jurisdiction over the case. Thus, he effectively conceded that the policy was illegal but claimed that this was a matter for the state courts to decide. David Marcus (joined by the appellate attorney William Strong) emphasized McCormick's finding that the defendants' discrimination was harmful to the petitioners as well as his conclusion that Mexican Americans were not a group for whom a school district could establish segregated schools under sections 8003 and 8004 of the California Education Code.[42] Although he noted McCormick's finding that segregated schools were unconstitutional, his argument rested primarily on the fact that Mexican Americans were not listed as a group that could be segregated. Similarly, during oral argument, Ogle insisted that, although segregation violated California law, it had been upheld by the U.S. Supreme Court when "equal facilities" were provided for minority groups. According to a newspaper account, Marcus countered that those other cases all dealt with racial segregation and were, thus, irrelevant to the matter at hand: "Marcus said there was no real racial question in this case, because Latins are Caucasians. But that, he went on, makes the discrimination even more dangerous; if condoned by the courts it could lead to discrimination on the ground of nationality, religion and social or economic position in all parts of the country."[43]

## PUBLIC COMMENT

Even before oral argument was held, the case had begun to attract nationwide attention. Judge McCormick's ruling, with its departure from the courts' habitual dependence on physical equality of facilities, was widely commented on in media reports and law journals.[44] The *New York Times* commented that *Méndez* was a "guinea pig case" on the issue of segregated schools and was being closely watched by representatives of other minority groups, and the *San Francisco Chronicle* called the case "[o]ne of the most important ever to come under Federal jurisdiction in this area."[45] The writer and activist Carey McWilliams, reporting on the case for the *Nation*, added that, if *Méndez* went to the U.S. Supreme Court, it could "sound the death knell of Jim Crow in education." McWilliams asserted that the exclusion of race as an issue in the case was actually advantageous because it meant that the courts could examine the effects of separate schools on children without their attention being diverted by arguments about racial difference: "With the 'racial issue' not directly involved, the court will be compelled to examine the social and educational consequences of segregated schools in a realistic manner." McWilliams also underlined the historic and multigroup nature of struggles against segregated schools in California by referring to the suit filed in federal court by President Theodore Roosevelt in 1907 to halt the San Francisco school board from segregating Japanese public school children.[46] The American Jewish Congress, hoping to arouse public interest in the case, financed the distribution of numerous reprints of McWilliams's article.

## THE AMICUS CURIAE BRIEFS

The widespread press coverage reflected the widespread belief that the *Méndez* case would set an important legal precedent. As a result, a number of different ethnic and political organizations moved to submit amici curiae briefs in support of the Mexican Americans. The briefs varied widely in their legal reasoning and in their strategies, but all differed significantly from those advanced by Marcus. The most powerful was that of the American Jewish Congress, which

TONI ROBINSON AND GREG ROBINSON

was drafted by the African American lawyer Pauli Murray. It asked the appellate court to overturn segregated schools as a violation not only of Fourteenth Amendment equal protection guarantees but also of federal government treaty obligations under the UN Charter. It urged the court to reject the *Plessy v. Ferguson* "separate but equal" standard. The brief asserted that segregation by official action of a group considered "inferior" according to prevailing community standards was "a humiliating and discriminatory denial of equality" to that group even if the physical facilities with which it was provided were equal to those of the "better" group.[47] Another striking appellate amicus brief was filed by the attorney general of the state of California, Robert Kenny, who wished to maintain his reputation as a strong defender of the rights of minorities. Kenny likewise insisted that sections 8003 and 8004 of the California Education Code violated the Fourteenth Amendment. Moreover, he cannily argued, even assuming that those school segregation laws were constitutional, the defendants' segregation practices were prohibited by the sections of the education code that mandated the free and universal admission of all children to the state's single standardized public school system. Nor did persons of Mexican descent fall into the single exception to that mandate by being expressly listed in the education code as a group for whom separate schools could be established.[48]

## THE JACL'S INTERVENTION

The JACL and the NAACP also intervened on the side of Méndez. The JACL, with A. L. Wirin and Saburo Kido "of counsel," was listed as a participating organization on the joint amicus brief that Wirin and Kido prepared on behalf of the Southern California ACLU and that was submitted in the name of the ACLU and the National Lawyers Guild's Los Angeles chapter.[49] Although the JACL had never before intervened in a civil rights lawsuit involving other minority groups, Wirin and Kido were well aware that the symbolic presence of the Japanese Americans—just months after the end of their wartime ordeal— would be a potent signal to the court of the importance of the *Méndez* case and of the potential consequences of upholding inequality. As a result, Wirin and Kido sought and received permission from JACL leaders to place the organization's name on the brief.

While Marcus's primary contention was that the segregation of Mexican American children was unlawful because Mexican Americans were not listed as one of the named groups for whom separate schools could be created under the very explicit California school segregation statutes, Wirin and Kido argued that the school segregation laws—which continued to stigmatize Japanese Americans—were themselves unlawful and should be voided.[50] Taking off from the NAACP brief (which Loren Miller had previously shared with Wirin), they began their argument by asserting that segregation on the basis of ancestry violated the Fourteenth Amendment. They contended that that amendment's equal protection clause protected citizens, aliens, and "all minorities, whether racial or religious, as well as Negro, for whom it was originally designed," and made void any law that discriminated against one of those groups unless there was a reasonable basis for singling that group out.[51] Wirin and Kido then referred to a second wartime case involving Japanese Americans, *Korematsu v. United States*,[52] in which the U.S. Supreme Court had declared that "racial antagonism" could never justify restriction of civil rights. Using somewhat convoluted logic, they argued that such a declaration was authority for the proposition that the Constitution also forbade discrimination solely by reason of ancestry or national origin and that it thereby protected Mexican Americans.[53]

Wirin and Kido were careful to exclude any further mention of racial discrimination in their brief; instead, they thereafter focused exclusively on the unlawfulness of "arbitrary" discrimination owing to ancestry or national origin, or to what the brief called in the case of Méndez and the others "the accident of birth, that of Mexican or Latin descent." Wirin and Kido maintained that the Constitution forbade any law that singled out such a class without any reasonable basis: "If appellants can justify discrimination on the basis of ancestry only, then who can tell what minority group will be next on the road to persecution. If we learned one lesson from the horrors of Nazism, it is that no minority group, and in fact, no person is safe, once the State, through its instrumentalities, can arbitrarily discriminate against any person or group."[54] In addition to drafting the brief, Wirin participated in oral argument on behalf of the JACL, the only group other than the parties to actually present its case before the appeals court.[55] During his presentation, Wirin affirmed that Orange County's school segregation policy unquestionably violated civil rights.[56]

## THE NAACP BRIEF

The Wirin/Kido brief did not directly attack the *Plessy* separate but equal doctrine. In contrast, the NAACP brief was a straightforward attack on the

TONI ROBINSON AND GREG ROBINSON

California segregation statutes. Drafted by Robert Carter, and submitted in the names of Carter, Thurgood Marshall, and Loren Miller (the latter added because he was the only one of the three admitted to practice before the Ninth Circuit), the NAACP brief amounted to what Richard Kluger later called a "dry run" for the association's subsequent briefs in its Supreme Court challenges to Jim Crow schools.[57] The NAACP brief addressed the issue in *Méndez* as if it were a case of segregation based on race. Indeed, it radically conflated race, color, and national origin as equally protected categories on the basis of which the Fourteenth Amendment forbade discrimination. It argued that all distinctions based solely on "race and color" violated the Fourteenth Amendment. (Somewhat inconsistently, the brief referred to individuals of Mexican and Latin descent as "persons of this particular racial lineage," yet it also spoke of the non–Mexican American children as being "purportedly of the white or Anglo-Saxon race.") The NAACP brief further pointed to three of the wartime Japanese American internment cases as authorities for the proposition that, even though the Fourteenth Amendment and the rigorous standards embodied in its equal protection clause applied only to state governments, the fundamental concepts of due process embodied in the Fifth Amendment barred even the national government from making distinctions based on race or color except in extraordinary circumstances such as a war emergency. Seeking to persuade the appellate court that it was not required by *Plessy* to uphold "separate but equal" racially segregated schools, the NAACP argued that *Plessy* was not controlling on the *Méndez* case since *Plessy* had dealt only with railroads and was inapplicable to public education. Indeed, the NAACP asked the court to reject *Plessy* altogether, calling it "a departure from the main current of constitutional law" and a product of its time that was no longer "good law." Instead, the NAACP stated, the court should uphold the trial court and strike down public school segregation since "such discrimination contravenes our constitutional requirements."[58]

## ANALYSIS OF DIFFERENCES BETWEEN THE BRIEFS

Because their interests and agendas were disparate, the approaches and legal arguments employed by the attorneys for Méndez, the JACL, and the NAACP all differed widely. The Mexican Americans, who were not listed in the state's school segregation laws but were de facto enrolled in separate schools, primarily argued that the establishment of segregated, Mexican public schools for their children was, not just unauthorized by state law, but forbidden by it. The constitutionality of school segregation laws in general, and racial segregation in particular, occupied a very secondary place in their arguments on the appeal. Although they accepted the participation of other minority organizations such as the JACL and the NAACP, they did not request it.[59] Rather, they sought in both their appellate brief and their appellate argument to avoid any suggestion of a racial difference between themselves and the defendants. Conversely, the California school segregation law explicitly targeted Japanese children, although, by 1946, all separate "Asian" schools had been eliminated.

The JACL's primary goal, by contrast, was to strike at any law that singled out a group for disparate treatment solely on account of race, ancestry, or national origin, which were, it maintained, all equally prohibited classifications under the Fourteenth Amendment. This position was presented in even more radical terms in the NAACP brief, which not only contended that the disparate treatment of any group on the basis of race, color, national origin, ancestry, or "racial lineage" was forbidden by the Constitution, except in highly specialized circumstances, but also invited the court to hold the long-established "separate but equal" *Plessy* doctrine inapplicable to public school segregation, if not completely outdated and void. Curiously, although both the JACL and the NAACP briefs cited the U.S. Supreme Court's opinion in *Korematsu*—a case that had reached the Supreme Court after the Ninth Circuit asked it for guidance on deciding the central issues—neither organization attempted to invoke the principle of "strict scrutiny" that the Supreme Court had just begun to formulate in *Korematsu* and that paved the way for the Court's epochal 1954 *Brown v. Board of Education* decision.

## THE APPELLATE COURT'S DECISION

The Ninth Circuit Court of Appeals issued its decision on 14 April 1947 (a corrected version followed that August). Although the Ninth Circuit unanimously upheld Judge McCormick's judgment and injunction, it clearly retreated from his ringing denunciation of segregation. Focusing on narrow legal issues, the court declared that California's omission of Mexicans from its statutory list of groups whose children could be placed in segregated schools required it to hold that the defendants' segregation practices were entirely without legal authorization and incompatible with California law.[60] Furthermore, in language that decisively rejected the expansive JACL and NAACP positions, the appellate court summarily declined to answer the question of whether the state could constitutionally establish segregated schools for children on the basis of either race or ancestry provided equal facilities were afforded the segregated group. Instead, the court declared: "There is argument in two of the amicus curiae briefs that we should strike out independently on the whole question of segregation. . . . [J]udges must ever be on their guard lest they rationalize outright legislation under the too free use of the power to interpret. We are not tempted by [that] siren [song]. . . . [W]e are of the opinion that the segregation cases do not rule the instant case and that is reason enough for not responding to the argument that we should consider them."[61] The court observed that all the cases cited by the defendants that had upheld the constitutionality of "separate but equal" facilities involved segregation of people of different races, or what it termed "children of parents belonging to one or another of the great races of mankind."[62]

The court then noted the lack of scientific support for making racial distinctions, stating: "Somewhat empirically, it used to be taught that mankind was made up of white, brown, yellow, black, and red men. Such divisional designation has little or no adherents among anthropologists or ethnic scientists. A more scholarly nomenclature is Caucasoid, Mongoloid, and Negroid, yet this is unsatisfactory, as an attempt to collectively sort all mankind into distinct groups."[63] Following this reasoning, and also noting that the parties had stipulated that there was no race segregation issue in the case, the court concluded that Mexicans were not a separate race from whites. Nowhere in California law, declared the court, was there any suggestion that segregation could be made "within one of the 'great races.' "[64] Without statutory or constitutional authority for the placement of children in segregated schools on the basis of ancestry, it could not lawfully be done. The question of whether laws permitting or mandating the public school segregation of children of African or Asian ancestry—that is, members of the other "great races"—were or were not constitutional thereby remained unanswered until the 1954 decision in *Brown v. Board of Education* (which notably did not cite *Méndez* as a precedent).

## The Aftermath of Méndez

Despite the overly dry and legalistic language that the appellate court employed in its *Méndez* decision and the narrow and restrictive reading that it gave to the issue of segregation, the case set off an important legal chain reaction. Its first result was to provide ammunition for the liberals in the California legislature who had already sought to overturn the school segregation laws as outdated and prejudicial. Less than two months after the initial appellate court ruling, the legislature, encouraged by State Attorney General Kenny, voted decisively to repeal secs. 8003 and 8004 of the State Education Code. Governor Earl Warren, who as chief justice of the United States would later write the companion Supreme Court opinions in the cases of *Brown v. Board of Education* and *Bolling v. Sharpe*,[65] signed the repeal into law.

The case also provided a precedent for the striking down of exclusion of Mexican Americans from public facilities in other states. Several weeks after the *Méndez* victory, LULAC activists brought a lawsuit in federal court in Texas, where state laws mandated segregation of Mexican Americans, to end such segregation. In the 1948 case of *Delgado vs. Bastrop Independent School District*,[66] school segregation in Texas was overturned. The *Méndez* and *Delgado* decisions, in turn, gave rise to a trend of court cases challenging the exclusion of Mexican Americans as "other whites" in different areas of public life. This legal campaign climaxed in the case of *Hernández v. State of Texas*,[67] decided by the U.S. Supreme Court just weeks before the justices announced their *Brown v. Board of Education* decision. In *Hernández*, the Court ruled that, under the Fourteenth Amendment, Mexican Americans could not constitutionally be segregated on the basis of their ancestry. Thus, almost eight years after *Méndez*, the Supreme Court finally endorsed the doctrine initially enunciated by Judge McCormick and passed over by the Ninth Circuit Court of Appeals.

In the months that followed, some of the major figures in *Méndez* reunited for a new struggle against school segregation in Southern California. The NAACP, represented by Loren Miller, and the Alianza Hispano-Americano, represented by Ralph Estrada and A. L. Wirin, sponsored a joint lawsuit against officials in the El Centro school district, who had long maintained a policy of segregating both African American and Mexican American students, and who had instituted a discriminatory school transfer policy in the wake of *Brown* to evade desegregation. Following a defeat in the lower court, in the summer of 1955 the case of *Romero v. Weakley* was heard before the Ninth Circuit Court of Appeals.[68] In support of the appellants, the JACL (represented by Frank Chuman), the ACLU, the American Jewish Congress, and the Congress of Industrial Organizations (represented by the JACL attorney Fred Okrand) collaborated on an amicus brief that referred prominently to both the *Brown* and the *Méndez*

TONI ROBINSON AND GREG ROBINSON

cases. In October 1955, the court struck down the policy, applying the logic of *Hernández* to school segregation.[69]

## Conclusion

In the years following *Hernández*, under leaders such as César Chávez and Dolores Huerta, Mexican American movements embraced more confrontational protest tactics such as boycotts. In the process, Mexican American and Chicano groups moved toward alliance with African Americans on different issues, including voting rights legislation and affirmative action. However, disagreements among Mexican Americans and legal scholars over the nature of their group identity and interests remain explosive. While some Mexican American or Chicano writers have argued that Mexicans in the United States are akin to a racial minority in status and should benefit from similar legal protections, many Mexican Americans are still identified, or identify themselves, as "white."[70]

Yet, if the *Méndez* case did not lead Mexican Americans to identify themselves as a racial minority in common cause with Japanese Americans or African Americans, it did help cement the alliance between the JACL and the NAACP. In the months that followed the appellate decision, Wirin and Kido deepened their collaboration with Loren Miller in fighting restrictive covenants against nonwhites. In late fall 1947, the JACL submitted an amicus curiae brief to the Supreme Court in support of the NAACP's suit in the case of *Hurd v. Hodge*.[71] This case, with its companion case, *Shelley v. Kraemer*,[72] struck a major blow against residential restrictive covenants by ruling them judicially unenforceable. The NAACP reciprocated in early 1948 with an amicus brief in support of the JACL's Supreme Court appeal in *Takahashi v. Fish and Game Commission*,[73] which struck down state laws that discriminated against nonwhite aliens "ineligible to citizenship."[74] Meanwhile, the two groups pursued their joint commitment to end educational segregation. Indeed, when A. L. Wirin became involved as an adviser in the *Delgado* case, NAACP lawyers lent him the transcript of their 1946 Texas law school desegregation case, *Sweatt v. Painter*,[75] so that he could peruse it for "ideas on the Mexican Children segregation case in San Antonio."[76] The two groups' alliance remained in effect through the *Brown v. Board of Education* case, in which the JACL was the sole non–African American racial minority organization to participate as an amicus curiae.

Both the postwar collaboration between African Americans and Japanese

Americans and the continuing debate over the identity of Mexican Americans underscore a central lesson of the *Méndez* case, namely, that solidarity among victims of discrimination is possible but that it is neither automatic nor easy to maintain. Advocates of civil rights too often envision alliances between people of color as natural and unproblematic. In fact, while representatives of racialized minority groups can and do come together at various times, their interests, attitudes, and priorities are often quite different. Furthermore, in the face of a dominant culture of white supremacy, which generates and reproduces inequality through laws based on racial distinctions, it is tempting and sometimes profitable for members of a racialized group to identify themselves with the white population and to seek equality by distancing themselves from more identifiably nonwhite minorities. As a result, multigroup coalitions against racial discrimination are fragile and can be difficult to hold together for long periods of time. If the *Méndez* case presents an example of a genuine victory won through the joint action of an interracial coalition, it also reveals why such victories are difficult to achieve and relatively rare.

## Notes

Portions of this essay appeared, in somewhat different form, in Toni Robinson and Greg Robinson, "*Méndez v. Westminster*: Asian-Latino Coalition Triumphant?" *Asian Law Journal* 10, no. 2 (May 2003): 161–83.

1. *Méndez v. Westminster School District of Orange County*, 64 F.Supp. 544 (1946), decided by U.S. District Court for the Southern District of California, central Division.

2. *Brown v. Board of Education*, 347 U.S. 483 (1954).

3. Takaki, *Double Victory*, 223. For other sources that highlight the interracial aspect of the case, see Arriola, "Knocking on the Schoolhouse Door," 203–4; Robbie, *For the Sake of the Children*; and Ruiz, "We Always Tell Our Children That They Are Americans." For the equation of *Brown* and *Méndez*, see, e.g., Jim Newton, "Ahead of the Curve on Integration," *Los Angeles Times*, 16 May 2004, M3. See also the Web sites http://www.Equal Terms.org and http://www.mendezvwestminster.com.

4. Sections 8003 and 8004 of the California Education Code permitted individual school districts the option of providing separate schools for "Indian children or children of Chinese, Japanese, or Mongolian parentage" and forbade the children of these groups from attending other schools once such separate schools were established. The law originally provided for the educational segregation of African Americans as well, but, following civil rights protests by black Californians, the law was amended in 1880 to remove black children from the list of groups that could be segregated. Although the law included "Mongolian" children starting in 1885, "Japanese" children were not explicitly listed until 1921 (Wollenberg, *All Deliberate Speed*, 24ff.). In 1940, under pressure from the Florin JACL, the local school board ended segregation ("Sansei Voted as President of Students," *Rafu Shimpo*,

6 December 1940, p. 1, col. 2). The Walnut Grove Oriental school remained open until mass removal in 1942.

5. "A History of Mexican Americans in California" (http://ohp.parks.ca.gov). After 1930, mass deportations and forced repatriations, as well as heightened work-visa requirements, sharply reduced the flow of migrants from Mexico.

6. See, e.g., García, *World of Their Own*; and Camarillo, *Changing Society*.

7. González, *Labor and Community*, 7.

8. García, *World of Their Own*; González, *Labor and Community*. See also Sánchez, *Becoming Mexican American*.

9. Wollenberg, "*Mendez v. Westminster*," 317–20.

10. Superior Court of the State of California, San Diego County, Writ of Mandate, 13 February 1931. See Alvarez, "National Politics and Local Responses." (We are indebted to Anne Knupfer for this reference.) Alvarez refers to the case only as "the Lemon Grove case."

11. San Miguel, "Separate and Unequal Schools."

12. Petition for a Writ of Mandate, *Joseph Chacon et al. v. Ranchito School District of Los Angeles County*, Superior Court for the County of Los Angeles, Civil Care, ser. I, no. 469887; "Pupil's Segregation Called Un-American," *Kashu Mainichi*, 12 November 1941, p. 1, col. 1; "Audiencia judicial sobre un caso de prejuicios raciales," *La Opinion*, 17 November 1941, p. 1, col. 1.

13. Petition for a Writ of Mandate (n. 12 above), 6. The local Japanese American press prominently featured the case. The Nisei columnist Ted Uyeno was outspoken in his support for the Mexican Americans: "We cannot view with apathy any unjust and discriminatory regulations imposed upon the minority racial elements in this country. . . . Children of Latin descent must not be segregated in separate schools. Let's be sure we stand united to defend equality for all people" ("Lancer's Column," *Rafu Shimpo*, 16 November 1941, p. 4, col. 4).

14. Alvarez, "National Politics and Local Responses." See also Greenfield and Kates, "The Civil Rights Act of 1866," 682.

15. U.S. Bureau of the Census, "Japanese Population of the State of California, by County, 1890–1940," in U.S. Congress, House of Representatives, *National Defense Migration* (Washington, DC: U.S. Government Printing Office, 1942), 97; Wollenberg, *All Deliberate Speed*, 73; Arriola, "Knocking on the Schoolhouse Door," 176–77.

16. See, e.g., Robinson, *By Order of the President*.

17. See, e.g., Kitano, *Japanese Americans*; and Hosokawa, JACL in Search of Justice.

18. Chuman, *Bamboo People*.

19. "Form Antidiscrimination Body to Seek Fair Play," *Rafu Shimpo*, 23 July 1946; "JACL Establishes Defense Fund for Civil Rights Cases," *Pacific Citizen*, 7 December 1946.

20. García, "Americans All."

21. Leonard, "Brothers under the Skin?" 192, 195–96.

22. McWilliams, *Brothers under the Skin*, 129. It remains an open question to what extent the recruitment of the braceros was designed to fill shortages in farm labor supply caused by the removal of Japanese Americans.

23. Perrett, *Days of Sadness*, 314–16; McWilliams, *North from Mexico*, 228–51. The verdict was subsequently overturned on appeal.

24. McWilliams, ibid. See also Mazón, *Zoot Suit Riots*.

25. García, "Americans All." The Sleepy Lagoon verdict prompted both African Americans

and Japanese Americans to defend publicly the rights of Mexican Americans. For African American reactions to the Sleepy Lagoon case, see Kurashige, "Transforming Los Angeles," 280–82; and Leonard, "'In the Interest of All Races,'" 333–34. Among the Japanese American commentaries was an editorial in the 30 January 1943 *Manzanar Free Press* denouncing the verdict and prejudice against Mexican Americans: "The maladjusted, socially ostracized, misunderstood group of 219,000 Mexican Americans in Los Angeles had lived in what social investigators had repeatedly described as disadvantaged areas. The authorities ignored this until the war broke out and the murder in August 1942 forced attention on this group." A group of Japanese American schoolchildren at Manzanar, learning of the case in their social studies class, collected ten dollars, which they contributed to the Sleepy Lagoon Defense Fund (*Japanese American Committee for Democracy Newsletter*, March 1944, 5).

26. García, "Americans All." In 1945, the assembly voted to repeal secs. 8003 and 8004, but the legislation subsequently died in the state senate.

27. Judgement of Dismissal, *A. T. Collison and R. L. Wood v. Nellie García et al.*, Superior Court of the County of Los Angeles, Civil Case ser. I, no. 498206, 9 February 1945. See also "Judge Rules in Covenant Suit," *Los Angeles Times*, 17 February 1945.

28. Lawrence E. Davies, "Segregation of Mexican American Students Stirs Court Fight," *New York Times*, 22 December 1946, sec. 4, p. 6, col. 4.

29. García, "Americans All," 285, 287.

30. Foley, "Partly Colored or Other White," n.p. See generally Foley, "Becoming Hispanic"; and Almaguer, *Racial Fault Lines*.

31. Robbie, *For the Sake of the Children*; César Arredondo, "Court Case Changed O.C. Schools," *Orange County Register*, 24 September 2002, p. s3, cols. 1–5.

32. Petition, *Westminster School District et al. v. Gonzalo Méndez*; Arriola, "Knocking on the Schoolhouse Door." Arriola describes Marcus as "an African American civil rights lawyer" (193), but this is inaccurate; Marcus was Jewish. At the time of trial, A. L. Wirin and Loren Miller each submitted an amicus curiae brief, Wirin on behalf of the ACLU, Miller in the name of the National Lawyers Guild.

33. *Plessy v. Ferguson*, 163 U.S. 537 (1896).

34. Wollenberg, "*Mendez v. Westminster*," 325–26; González, *Chicano Education*.

35. *Méndez v. Westminster*, record of trial, pp. 116, 121, and passim, cited in *Westminster School District of Orange County, et al. v. Gonzalo Méndez, et al. Motion and Brief of the United Jewish Congress as Amicus Curiae*, 17; *Westminster School District of Orange County, et al. v. Gonzalo Méndez, et al. Brief for the American Civil Liberties Union, and the National Lawyers Guild, Los Angeles Chapter as Amicus Curiae*, 16.

36. Ogle's decision not to assert that Mexicans were Indians and, thus, subject to the California school segregation law may have constituted lawyer's error. The question of the Mexicans' racial classification had never been judicially determined in California. A Fifth Circuit judge had ruled in the Texas immigration case *In re Rodríguez* (81 F. 337, W.D. Texas, 1897) that Mexicans were probably not classifiable as white but were, nevertheless, admissible as immigrants (see Steven H. Wilson, "*Brown* over 'Other White,'" par. 12). That decision later underwent various challenges and seems not to have been universally applied. For instance, when city and county officials in El Paso and elsewhere attempted in 1936 to classify people of Japanese and Mexican ancestry as "colored" for statistical purposes, the attorney George Rodriguez sought an injunction, arguing that the anti-

miscegenation provisions of Texas penal code defined those with pure or mixed Negro ancestry as "Negroes" and all others as "white" within the meaning of the law ("New Ruling in El Paso Imperils Nipponese Status," *Kashu Mainichi*, 14 October 1936, p. 1, col. 4). In any case, the decision was not binding on California, which was in the Ninth Circuit. In 1929, California Attorney General Ulysses S. Webb had issued an advisory opinion that segregation of schoolchildren of Mexican ancestry was not supported by law because they were members of the white race, but the opinion was nonbinding and does not seem to have influenced the Lemon Grove case. In 1931, Assemblyman George Bliss, who had established a segregated Mexican school in his hometown of Carpinteria on the grounds that it was an "Indian school," introduced an amendment to secs. 8003 and 8004 to provide for segregation of "Indian" children "whether born in the United States or not," presumably as a means to provide legal support for the segregation of Mexican Americans. The assembly, anxious to avoid alienating Mexico through such a provision, killed the bill (Alvarez, "National Politics and Local Responses," 44).

37. For more on "whiteness," see, e.g., Haney-López, *White by Law*; and Lipsitz, *Investment in Whiteness*.

38. *Méndez v. Westminster School District* (n. 1 above), at 549.

39. See, e.g., Warren's comment: "To separate [children in grade and high schools] from others of similar age and qualifications solely because of their race generates a feeling of inferiority as to their status in the community that may affect their hearts and minds in a way unlikely ever to be undone" (*Brown v. Board of Education* [n. 2 above], at 494).

40. *Méndez v. Westminster School District* (n. 1 above), at 549.

41. Ibid., at 550, 549, 548. Ironically, the language quoted by McCormick came from *Hirabayashi v. United States*, 320 U.S. 81 (1943), one of the "internment" cases that upheld the constitutionality of wartime restrictions imposed on Japanese Americans on the basis of their ancestry.

42. *Westminster School District of Orange County, et al. v. Gonzalo Méndez, et al.; Brief of Appellants; Westminster School District of Orange County, et al. v. Gonzalo Méndez, et al. Appellees' Reply Brief.*

43. "School Segregation Case Is before U.S. Court Here," *San Francisco Chronicle*, 10 December 1946. When one of the judges, Clifton Matthews, suggested that segregation was a long-standing practice, Marcus countered that it was, in fact, "recent."

44. Ferg-Cadima, "Black, White, and Brown," 20.

45. Davies, "Segregation of Mexican American Students Stirs Court Fight" (n. 28 above); "School Segregation Case Is before U.S. Court Here" (n. 43 above).

46. McWilliams, "Is Your Name Gonzales?" 302–3.

47. *Westminster School District of Orange County, et al. v. Gonzalo Méndez, et al. Motion and Brief of the United Jewish Congress as Amicus Curiae.*

48. *Westminster School District of Orange County, et al. v. Gonzalo Méndez, et al. Motion and Brief of the Attorney General of the State of California as Amicus Curiae.*

49. *Westminster School District of Orange County, et al. v. Gonzalo Méndez, et al. Brief for the American Civil Liberties Union, and the National Lawyers Guild, Los Angeles Chapter, as Amici Curiae, A. L. Wirin, Saburo Kido, of Counsel for Japanese-American Citizens League*, 6. During the lower-court case, Wirin had been listed as "of counsel" on the amicus brief submitted in the name of the national ACLU, while the African American attorney Loren Miller had submitted a separate brief on behalf of the National Lawyers Guild.

50. Wirin clearly felt that a straightforward attack on secs. 8003 and 8004 of the state education code was necessary. Ten days after *Méndez* was argued, the *Utah Nippo* reported that Wirin's firm had commenced a separate action, sponsored by the ACLU and the JACL, directly challenging the constitutionality of the two statutes. The named plaintiff in that suit was Takao Aratani, a third-generation Japanese American and the son of a recently discharged Nisei GI. The complaint alleged that, since Aratani and all other Japanese American schoolchildren in California (none of whom were, in fact, attending separate schools) could be removed at any time to segregated schools, they were being unconstitutionally discriminated against solely because of their race. Just days later, however, the Wirin firm withdrew the complaint, stating that the immediate purpose of the suit had already been achieved inasmuch as Attorney General Kenny's amicus brief in the *Méndez* case had declared that the statutes in question were unconstitutional ("Legality of Segregating Grade School Children Challenged," *Utah Nippo*, 23 December 1946, p. 1, col. 3; "Class Segregation Suit Dismissed," *Utah Nippo*, 10 January 1947, p. 1, col. 3; see also "Charge Segregation in Suit," *Rafu Shimpo*, 13 December 1946, p. 1, col. 3; and "Kenny Raps Organizations on School Segregation Suit," *Rafu Shimpo*, 10 January 1947, p. 1, cols. 4–5).

51. *Westminster School District of Orange County, et al. v. Gonzalo Méndez, et al. Brief for the American Civil Liberties Union, and the National Lawyers Guild, Los Angeles Chapter, as Amici Curiae, A. L. Wirin, Saburo Kido, of Counsel for Japanese-American Citizens League*, 6.

52. *Korematsu v. United States*, 323 U.S. 214 (1944).

53. *Brief for the American Civil Liberties Union, and the National Lawyers Guild* (n. 51 above), 9. In view of the fact that the Supreme Court had actually ruled in *Korematsu* that the mass removal of Japanese Americans from the West Coast was constitutional, Wirin and Kido's argument is especially strained.

54. Ibid., 21, 17.

55. Lawrence E. Davies, "Pupil Segregation on Coast Is Fought," *New York Times*, 10 December 1946, p. 28, col. 1. Another sign of the JACL's interest in the *Méndez* case was the significant coverage that it received during 1946 and 1947 in the organization's newspaper, the *Pacific Citizen*, and in other Japanese American media (see, e.g., "Legality of California School Segregation Argued in Court," *Pacific Citizen*, 14 December 1946; "Segregated Schools," *Pacific Citizen*, 14 December 1946; and "School Segregation," *Pacific Citizen*, 19 April 1947).

56. "School Segregation Case Is before U.S. Court Here" (n. 43 above).

57. Kluger, *Simple Justice*, 399. Interestingly, the NAACP chief counsel Thurgood Marshall was not at all sanguine about the actual possibilities of an attack on the constitutionality of Jim Crow and preferred to build up a record of cases interpreting equality within separation. In a discussion of *Méndez* and other school segregation cases, Marshall wrote a colleague: "Frankly, and confidentially, and just between the two of us, there is serious doubt in the minds of most of us as to the timing for an all-out attack on segregation per se in the present United States Supreme Court" (Thurgood Marshall to Carl Murphy, 20 December 1946, Library of Congress, Washington, DC, NAACP Papers, Mendez case, legal files, ser. B, 1940–1960).

58. *Westminster School District of Orange County, et al. v. Gonzalo Méndez, et al. Motion and Brief for the National Association for the Advancement of Colored People as Amicus Curiae*, 4, 25, 31.

59. See Robert L. Carter to David C. Marcus, 13 September 1946 (Library of Congress, NAACP papers, Mendez case, legal files, ser. B, 1940–1960), informing Marcus of the NAACP's intervention.

60. *Westminster School District of Orange County et al. v. Méndez et al.*, 161 F.2d 774, 780 (9th Cir. 1947). The court stated that it arrived at this decision by applying the principle of legal interpretation "*Expressio Unius Est Exclusio Alterius*" (to state one is to exclude all others).

61. Ibid. The court's reasoning was extended in a concurring opinion by Judge William Denman, who had previously issued vituperative dissents in the *Hirabayashi* and *Korematsu* cases. Although Denman also avoided discussion of the constitutionality of separate but equal facilities for racial minorities, he warned that, if "the vicious principle sought to be established in Orange [County]" were permitted, it could easily extend to Italians, Greeks, Jews, or other "white" ethnics (ibid., at 783). In addition, Denman proclaimed that the school district officials who had brazenly admitted in their appellate brief that their actions violated California law should be arrested forthwith.

62. Ibid.

63. Ibid., at 780 n. 7. On the shifting and ambiguous bases of racial distinctions in U.S. law, see Haney-López, *White by Law*.

64. *Westminster School District v. Méndez* (n. 60 above), at 780.

65. *Bolling v. Sharpe*, 347 U.S. 497 (1954).

66. *Delgado vs. Bastrop Independent School District*, 388 W.D. Texas (1948).

67. *Hernández v. State of Texas*, 347 U.S. 475 (1954).

68. *Romero v. Weakley*, 226 F.2d 399 (9th Cir. 1955).

69. News release, *Alianza Hispano-Americano*, 10 October 1955; *Joe R. Romero, et al. v. Guy Weakley et al., Motion and Brief for the Japanese American Citizens League et al. as Amicus Curiae*, 2; University of California, Los Angeles, Library, Southern California Branch, Papers of the ACLU, School Segregation file, box 32.

70. See, e.g., Delgado and Palacios, "Mexican Americans as a Legally Cognizable Class," 323; and Greenfield and Kates, "The Civil Rights Act of 1866." See also generally Gutiérrez, *Walls and Mirrors*.

71. *Hurd v. Hodge*, 334 U.S. 24 (1948).

72. *Shelley v. Kraemer*, 334 U.S. 1 (1948).

73. *Takahashi v. Fish and Game Commission*, 334 U.S. 410 (1948).

74. See Greg Robinson and Toni Robinson, "*Korematsu* and Beyond: Japanese Americans and the Origins of Strict Scrutiny," *Law and Contemporary Problems*, vol. 68, no. 2 (spring 2005), 31–58.

75. *Sweatt v. Painter*, 339 U.S. 629 (1950).

76. A. L. Wirin to Thurgood Marshall, 31 October 1947, Library of Congress, NAACP Papers, Nisei folder 1, ser. B, 1940–1960.

## 5    THE POLITICAL SIGNIFICANCE OF RACE

*Asian American and Latino Redistricting Debates in California and New York*

Leland T. Saito

Redistricting, or the redrawing of political district lines following each decennial census to reflect changes in population, provides a unique opportunity to examine the relation between race and politics because the 1965 Voting Rights Act requires the recognition and protection of the political rights of ethnic and racial minorities. As part of this process, however, a group must establish that it is a "community of interest," that is, a population with shared social, economic, and/or political concerns. This compels groups that advocate for the use of race as a factor in redistricting to publicly and explicitly affirm the political significance of race.

In this essay, I examine contrasting views of society and race involving Asian Americans and Latinos through redistricting case studies of the New York City Council district that included Manhattan's Chinatown in 1990–91 and California's state political districts in 2000–2002. I document the debates and divisions within and across racial lines, analyzing the ways in which different positions in the redistricting process are rooted in the real, material interests of the participants emerging from their particular locations within the process and the constituencies that they serve. The configuration of districts directly affects the political power of racial groups, for example, by consolidating a group within a district and concentrating voting strength or, by fragmenting a group into two or more districts and possibly diluting its political impact. Because Latinos and Asian Americans generally live in multiracial regions and districts reflect that demographic reality, redistricting concerns involve the proportion of each group in a district and, therefore, imply the potential for conflict or alliances among groups.

Redistricting exemplifies the way in which government policies have defined and reflected racial categories and the tremendous social, political, and economic implications of such policies.[1] The struggle for political inclusion, mediated and constrained by political and judicial systems that historically have served to disenfranchise racial minorities, shows the complexities, contradictions, and structural impediments encountered by efforts to enfranchise minorities. The redistricting dialogue shows politics as a critical site through which subordinate groups understand, negotiate, and contest the meaning of their position as racialized minorities. Through their efforts, minorities force change in the political system, such as lawsuits based on the Voting Rights Act by African Americans and Latinos to challenge redistricting plans and to shift from at-large to district elections.

## New York City

In 1989, prompted by lawsuits charging racial discrimination and violation of the U.S. Constitution, the New York City Charter was amended to increase the number of city council districts from thirty-five to fifty-one, a change intended to increase the political representation of minorities. Working from 1990 to 1991, a districting commission created new council districts. As the redistricting process began, no Asian American had ever been elected to the city council or any citywide office. Because Chinatown contained the city's largest concentration of Asian Americans, the area offered the greatest opportunity for Asian American representation.[2]

Community activists agreed that uniting Chinatown within one district was the principal goal, ending the spatial fragmentation and dilution of political power that occurred in past redistricting plans. As Margaret Fung, the executive director of the Asian American Legal Defense and Education Fund (AALDEF, a New York City legal advocacy organization) explained: "[T]he voting strength of Chinese Americans has been diluted because Chinatown was divided into two state assembly districts. Moreover, Chinatown has also been split between two community board districts and two school board districts. This . . . has merely reinforced our community's inability to organize and develop a political cohesiveness."[3]

According to the 1990 Census, the city's population was 7,322,564, with 25.2 percent African American, 6.7 percent Asian American, 24.4 percent Latino, and 43.2 percent white.[4] Each of the fifty-one districts would require a population of approximately 143,579. With 62,895 in Chinatown, an additional 80,700 would be required to create a district.

The decision over which areas should be added to meet the population requirement was the fundamental issue that divided Chinatown activists, and two competing plans emerged in the debate, offering contrasting alternatives for Chinatown and its relation to the surrounding communities. One emphasized "descriptive representation"[5] and the historic opportunity to elect an Asian American, while the other supported a multiracial district based on similar political interests generated by the intersection of race, class, and neighborhood conditions. The areas to the north and east contained the Lower East Side, which historically has housed the city's immigrants and working classes. The Lower East Side remains a predominately low-income and working-class neighborhood with large numbers of Latinos, some African Americans, and Asian immigrants. With the effects of gentrification, however, a growing number of more affluent whites have moved into the area. The entertainment and residential districts of SoHo and Tribeca lie to the west, areas increasingly inhabited by middle-class and professional whites. With City Hall and the financial district's Wall Street a few blocks to the south, Chinatown occupied prime real estate, and conflict between the interests of developers and low-income residents fueled the political debate.[6]

Members of Asian Americans for Equality (AAFE, a Chinatown social service provider) proposed a district in which an Asian American could, they believed, be elected. Since Asian Americans did not have the numbers to elect a candidate on their own, AAFE understood that a successful campaign would need to create a multiracial coalition of voters, and, using data from a number of elections involving Asian Americans, it considered areas where such efforts have had a history of success. AAFE's plan followed the strengths of Margaret Chin, who was a member of Community Board 1 and had been elected twice in the 1980s as the Democratic Party state committeewoman from that area. As Doris Koo, the executive director of AAFE, stated at public hearings held in December 1990: "For an Asian American to win, he or she must build on the strength of a coalition of voters supportive of, and proven to have elected, minority candidates in the past. . . . Our objective is not to look for districts where Asians did well. Our objective is to look for districts where Asians have *won*."[7]

With this in mind, Koo/AAFE proposed that the core of Chinatown should be joined with areas to the west and south, that is, SoHo, City Hall, Tribeca, and Battery Park City, stating: "Asian candidates have done better than white candidates in the area West of Core, where one would assume white candidates with a liberal agenda would traditionally be at their best." The areas to the east of Chinatown were ruled out because data analysis showed that Asian American candidates did poorly in local elections there.[8] Antonio Pagan—the direc-

LELAND T. SAITO

tor of Coalition Housing, which built low- and moderate-income housing and a Puerto Rican candidate for city council in the Lower East Side—supported separate "Asian American" and "Latino" districts, stating at those same public hearings that he was "emphatically in favor and supportive of the creation of a Chinese seat or Asian seat at this moment . . . but we want to be able to elect our own."[9]

An alternative to AAFE's plan was developed by a variety of community activists and organizations—including AALDEF, the Community Service Society, and the Puerto Rican Legal Defense and Education Fund. Recognizing that no single ethnic or racial group in the area was large enough to constitute 50 percent or more of a district, residents formed the organization Lower East Siders for a Multi-Racial District, which, through its representative Elaine Chan, proposed at public hearings held in March 1991 a plan that would create a majority Latino, Asian American, and African American district based on the needs and interests of low-income and working-class residents.[10]

Chan—a city council candidate who withdrew from the race and the coordinator for the Lower East Side Joint Planning Council, a housing advocacy group—explained: "Asians, Latinos, and African Americans have had a historic working relationship on issues of common concern: housing, health care, immigration, day care, bilingual education, affordable commercial space, job training, and general quality [of life] issues."[11] At the November 1990 public hearings Chan had stressed the long history of multiracial activism in the area and how that defined and reinforced a tightly knit political community: "We represent more than thirty organizations on the Lower East Side that advocate for decent and affordable housing."[12] At the March 1991 hearings she stated: "Our plan, the United District, calls for a council district that closely resembles traditional Lower East Side boundaries as delineated by the parameters of Community Board 3."[13] Additionally, she refuted the assumption that Latinos would not vote for Asian Americans, noting that Latinos supported two Asian American candidates in the 1987 judicial race.[14]

Offering her interpretation of descriptive representation versus community empowerment, Mini Liu—another member of Lower East Siders for a Multi-Racial District—stated: "Yes, we want minority representatives. But we want minority representatives who are accountable to the Asians and Latinos on the Lower East Side, not just Asian and Latino faces in City Council, representing white middle and upper class interests."[15]

According to the New York City Districting Commission executive director Alan Gartner, the commission based the boundaries of the new district on AAFE's testimony, which represented, the commission believed, the majority opinion within the Asian American community. According to Gartner: "[AAFE] became the dominant player in the Asian American community. . . . The careful and comprehensive presentations of AAFE's Executive Director, Doris Koo, impressed the Commission and staff." AAFE proposed that the Asian American and Latino populations should be separated, and the commission agreed, stating that there was little statistical evidence that Asian Americans and Latinos would jointly support a candidate. Explaining why Asian American and white communities would be joined in the new district, Gartner stated: "The Commission hoped that a strong Asian-American candidate, with the support of the white, liberal areas surrounding Chinatown, could be elected."[16] In contrast, Margarita Lopez—a housing activist since moving to the Lower East Side in 1978 from her native Puerto Rico and a member of Lower East Siders for a Multi-Racial District—asserted that the commission ignored the evidence presented by Lower East Siders for a Multi-Racial District, evidence that clearly demonstrated, she believed, Latino support for Asian Americans, such as the successful efforts of Latinos to increase the number of Asian Americans on Community Board 3.[17]

Approved by the U.S. Justice Department on 26 July 1991, the districting plans joined Chinatown with areas to the west and created District 1, in which Asian Americans, at 39.2 percent of the population, constituted the largest group but accounted for only 14.2 percent of the registered voters. In contrast, whites constituted 37.2 percent of the population but accounted for 61.5 percent of the registered voters, Latinos constituted 17.4 of the populations and accounted for 15.5 percent of the registered voters, and African Americans constituted 5.8 percent of the population and accounted for 8.8 percent of the registered voters.[18]

Divisions in Chinatown did not divide neatly along racial and/or class lines but originated from a complex and often contradictory mixture of group and personal interests and histories that carried over into the redistricting dialogue and elections that followed. From the perspective of many Asian Americans, District 1 was inextricably linked with AAFE and its council candidate, Margaret Chin—overshadowing the actual political implications of their proposed district—since the organization had created and supported the general guidelines for the formation of the district.

AAFE—which originated in efforts in 1974 to force contractors to comply with city policies on minority employment and hire Asian Americans in the construction of Confucius Plaza in Chinatown—has provided a range of community services, such as building and renovating affordable housing, filing the lawsuit AAFE v. Koch to counter gentrification, providing information and training to small business owners, and enforcing tenants' rights.[19] From its indisputable progressive and community roots, however, by the 1990s AAFE had become, critics charged, a developer intent on following its own agenda,[20] and unilaterally promoting its own redistricting plan reinforced that image.

Kathryn Freed, Chin's major opponent, was the former chair of Community Board 1 and an attorney with a history of working for tenants' rights and affordable housing. Because of her stand on housing and employment issues and her support of multiracial coalition-building, Freed received the backing of the Asian American Union for Political Action,[21] whose members included supporters of the multiracial district. As Wayne Barrett of the *Village Voice* contended, however, Freed attended a dinner sponsored by a group that, because of its labor problems, Chin was criticized for supporting, and she also received contributions from real estate interests and garment manufacturers.[22]

In the Democratic primary, Freed emerged the victor with 42 percent of the vote, while Chin received 31 percent. Freed was elected with 53 percent of the vote in the 1991 general election, while Chin received 24 percent running on the Liberal Party ticket, and Fred Teng received 23 percent. Teng, a former board president of the Chinatown Planning Council and a Republican, received support from segments of the Chinatown business community. Although Asian Americans in Chinatown voted overwhelmingly for Asian American representation, the results of an exit poll conducted by AALDEF, a poll that surveyed 507 Asian Americans (predominantly Chinese) in Chinatown, demonstrate the heterogeneity of the community: 43.8 percent voted for Chin; 38.3 percent voted for Teng; 5.6 percent voted for Freed; and 12.2 percent declined to state or voted for another candidate.[23]

Although the districting commission crafted District 1 to support Asian American descriptive representation, the electoral reality was a district dominated by white voters. While white voters had supported Asian American candidates in previous local elections and Chin had attempted to build a campaign that went beyond Asian Americans, her campaign had apparently not laid the groundwork necessary to gain the endorsement of key West Side community leaders, and it also failed to generate compelling issues that would win the support of a majority of voters. In hindsight, the districting commission's reading of possible white support for Margaret Chin did not adequately consider interests within Chinatown, such as affordable housing and employment, that West Side residents did not share. Also, major concerns actively divided interests in the two areas, such as conflict over the expansion of Chinatown into the West Side. Clearly, many white voters crossed over, considering that Chinatown had a very low voter turnout and that only about 14 percent of the district's electorate was Asian American, but, whereas Chin had been elected to the Democratic Party State Committee in 1986 and 1988, apparently whites were reluctant to elect her to the much more significant position of council member. In the city council elections that followed, white candidates have continued to easily defeat Asian American candidates in District 1.

## California

In the 2000–2002 California redistricting process, the organizations advocating for the interests of African Americans, Asian Americans, and Latinos formed a cooperative working relationship. In contrast, after the process was complete, Latinos were sharply divided over a lawsuit filed by the Mexican American Legal Defense and Education Fund (MALDEF) against the state's final redistricting plan. As with the split among New York City Chinatown activists, the debate among Latinos over the MALDEF lawsuit revealed fundamental differences over the interpretation of the political relationship between whites and minorities.

Redistricting of the California State Senate, the California State Assembly, and the state's federal congressional districts was carried out by the state legislature.[24] Thus, politicians controlled the process that directly shaped their political opportunities. Understanding that these officials have not historically given adequate consideration to the concerns of minorities and, in fact, have actively worked against their interests, Asian Americans, African Americans, and Latinos all formed groups to participate in the process through research and advocacy.

The 2000 Census showed that, in terms of the single race count, African Americans constituted 6.7 percent of the state's population, Asian Americans 10.9 percent, Latinos 32.4 percent, and whites 46.7 percent. A comparison of the 1990 and 2000 Censuses showed that the Asian American population grew by 38.5 percent, the Latino population by 35 percent, but the African American population by only 4.3 percent, the latter actually losing ground in statewide percentage terms. The major change affecting the redistricting prospects of African Americans was the shift in population from areas of historically high African American concentration, such as the South Central area of Los Angeles County, to outlying multiracial regions, such as Riverside and San Bernardino Counties. For example, from 1980 to 2000, the city of Compton went from 73.9 to 40.3 percent African American and from 21.1 to 56.8 percent Latino.[25]

In terms of redistricting, with the second largest population in the state, rapid growth, and large population concentrations, Latinos were trying to build on their recent electoral gains. Asian Americans, although the fastest-growing population in the state, were residentially dispersed and, thus, worked to maximize the few areas of concentration that existed. African Americans worked to delay the probable decline in the number of elected African Americans owing to migration and new residential patterns.

Given that the forces of migration and resegregation have continued the historical pattern of multiracial minority communities, complicating redistricting (since what optimizes the representational interests of one group will not necessarily optimize the representational interests of other groups), what explained the high level of cooperation that developed among the African American, Asian American, and Latino redistricting groups? Recent U.S. Supreme Court decisions weakening the Voting Rights Act, a shared ideology of minority empowerment, and the experience of discrimination both in everyday life and in the political realm contributed to an understanding of the need for an alliance among people of color. In practical terms, since people of color constitute the majority of California's population, an alliance would represent an influential constituency.

An important legal decision that framed the New York City Chinatown redistricting was *Garza v. Los Angeles County Board of Supervisors* (1990),[26] in which a federal court ruled in favor of the Latino plaintiffs, a victory that emphasized the political rights of racial minorities and the prevention of vote dilution. U.S. Supreme Court decisions since then, however, have dramatically altered the legal framework, particularly with *Shaw v. Reno* (1993) and *Miller v. Johnson* (1995) deciding that race could not be the "sole" (*Shaw*) or "predominant" (*Miller*) factor in redistricting.[27]

The court decisions reducing the relative importance of race reaffirmed "traditional districting principles," such as "compactness, contiguity, and respect for political subdivisions or communities defined by actual shared interests."[28] Given the new legal framework and the shift away from race to "traditional" criteria, the complexity of redistricting criteria and the multiple ways that urban space can be divided up into divergent communities of interest, the state legislature's control over redistricting, and the history of gerrymandering that has led to the fragmentation of minority communities, African Americans, Asian Americans, and Latinos clearly recognized the importance of working together to combine their legal expertise, exercise the political leverage represented by their population numbers, and not allow the state legislature to pit one group against another.

Faced with these adverse conditions, the three groups established a dialogue from the beginning of the process, exchanging ideas, concerns, and information with the goal of developing maps that would support each others' interests. Stewart Kwoh, the executive director of the Asian Pacific American Legal Center (APALC), speaking during the September 2001 public hearings on the redistricting, explained: "It was . . . critical for us to have dialogue and collaboration with our counterpart civil rights organizations such as the Mexican American Legal Defense and Educational Fund, NAACP Legal Defense Fund, NAACP, the Southwest Voter Registration Education Project, the American Jewish Committee and many other community organizations."[29]

As stated in the handouts distributed by MALDEF in its community redistricting workshops: "The more leaders, organizations and members of the public the committee represents, the greater the clout of the committee and the community resources available to the committee. Furthermore, a unified minority community is more difficult for others to splinter or deny."[30] Kathay Feng, the project director of APALC's Voting Rights and Antidiscrimination Unit, also speaking at the September 2001 public hearings, explained: "We have come together on the principle that each of our communities has the right to full political representation in accord with the Voting Rights Act. At the same time we are united in saying that no community should gain at the expense of another."[31]

The level of cooperation and recognition of shared goals among the Asian American, African American, and Latino groups reached an unprecedented level in the history of redistricting in California. In addition to maintaining constant communication among their leaders, the groups coproduced a ninety-four-page handbook, *The Impact of Redistricting in Your Community*. The handbook included detailed sections on legal issues, practical guidelines on how to organize on a community level, and redistricting exercises to illustrate how legal and practical issues affect the process.[32] The groups also sponsored a one-day conference in Los Angeles that brought together the groups' leadership and community members from regions throughout the state and featured redistricting workshops and speakers from around the country.[33]

The state assembly and the state senate redistricting committees held public hearings, and Asian Americans, Latinos, and African Americans attended. Each group summarized its proposals for new districts and submitted maps that would optimize the political influence of their populations by keeping them intact, rather than split among different districts. After the state legislature revealed its preliminary plans in the first week of September, a *Los Angeles Times* editorial concluded that the map was aimed at protecting incumbents: "Consider the havoc that the Legislature is causing . . . through the congressional redistricting plan. . . . The same sort of gerrymandering occurs in the state Senate and Assembly plans as well—all in the name of party politics, to keep as many incumbent Republicans and Democrats as happy as possible. . . . As a result, the plans shatter the concepts of community of interest and compactness of districts, with a few exceptions, and largely thwart the desires of Latinos and Asian Americans to win additional seats in Congress and the Legislature."[34] In the joint senate and assembly public hearing following the release of the preliminary plans, Asian Americans, Latinos, and African Americans offered their critiques, focusing on areas of the state where concentrations of racial minorities had been fragmented among two or more districts.

Later that month, after minor adjustments, the state legislature passed the redistricting plan, and it was signed by Governor Gray Davis. "The maps produced this year are fair and balanced," Davis declared.[35] In contrast to the governor's assessment was the statement, "Redrawing California: An Incumbent Protection Plan," splashed in boldface type across the cover of the January 2002 issue of the *California Journal*, a monthly nonpartisan magazine that offers in-depth coverage of politics.

At the time of redistricting, there were four Asian Americans in the state legislature, all in the assembly. To use their limited resources most effectively, the members of the Coalition of Asian Pacific Americans for Fair Redistricting focused their efforts on the assembly plan, these districts being smaller than state senate and federal congressional districts in terms of population requirements and, thus, giving Asian Americans the best opportunity for forming an influential voting bloc. The Forty-ninth Assembly District in the San Gabriel Valley of Los Angeles County was of particular interest since it contained one of the state's largest and fastest-growing concentrations of Asian Americans in the contiguous cities of Monterey Park, Alhambra, San Gabriel, and Rosemead. Additionally, the Chinese American Judy Chu had just been elected to the assembly from this district. With a plurality of Latino voters, the district has had a history of electing Latinos. Chu's victory was due to her long record as a local council member who acted effectively on issues important to Latinos and whites as well as Asian Americans, such as improving local schools and health care services.

Asian Americans supported the new Forty-ninth Assembly District in the west San Gabriel Valley because the district shifted east, shedding some of its Latino population in East Los Angeles while increasing its Asian American numbers. The new district was 46.63 percent Latino (a 6.37 percent drop from 1991), 39.11 percent Asian American (a 2.95 percent increase), 12.10 percent white (a 3.39 percent increase), and less than 1 percent each African American and Native American (figures that remained unchanged since 1991). In comparison, the other assembly districts with Asian American representatives contained a much smaller percentage of Asian Americans, with 18.9 percent in District 16, 20.1 percent in District 44, and 16.6 percent in District 53.[36]

Demonstrating its understanding that this was a key area in the state for Asian Americans, MALDEF also supported the new District 49 even though other Latino individuals and groups speaking at the last set of public hearings criticized it because of the decreased Latino population in it. MALDEF's representatives explained their position by noting that the Latino population had been "diminishing" or experiencing "little growth" and recognized the continuing expansion of the Asian American population in the district, and they suggested that attention should focus on southeastern Los Angeles County, where the Latino population was growing at a rapid rate.[37]

The boundaries of the new state senate and federal congressional districts, however, fragmented the Asian American population in the San Gabriel Valley. The final plan divided Monterey Park, Alhambra, San Gabriel, and Rosemead into three state senate districts (21, 22, and 24) and two congressional districts (29 and 32). Monterey Park was split between the two congressional districts, disregarding traditional political boundaries, and adding to the problem of vote dilution. Since it had focused its redistricting efforts and analysis on the assem-

LELAND T. SAITO

bly districts, APALC did not consider filing a lawsuit based on the fragmentation of the San Gabriel Valley in the state senate and congressional districts. However, at the last public hearing held by the state legislature before the plans were approved, Kathay Feng stated: "We do ask that you revisit the Senate and congressional configurations which have carved this west San Gabriel Valley area up into so many pieces as to create a virtual glass ceiling for our community's representation at these higher levels of government."[38]

On 1 October 2001, MALDEF filed a lawsuit, *Cano v. Davis*, against the redistricting plan.[39] The lawsuit alleged that the boundaries of two congressional districts—one in the San Fernando Valley, the other in San Diego—were drawn to reduce the number of Latinos in each district, thereby protecting white incumbents. It also stated that an additional state senate district with a Latino majority should have been created in Los Angeles County. Antonia Hernandez, MALDEF president and general counsel, declared: "It is unacceptable and illegal to jeopardize the voting rights of historically disenfranchised minority voters. The district lines compromised the basic principles of community and the electoral process and are illegal."[40]

In a *Los Angeles Times* editorial, the Latina state senators from Los Angeles County, Martha Escutia and Gloria Romero, voiced strong opposition to the lawsuit, describing it as "frivolous and racially divisive." Escutia and Romero noted that the new plan maintains or strengthens thirteen state senate and federal congressional seats held by Latinos, that it creates a "new heavily Latino congressional district . . . in Los Angeles County," and that twenty-three of the twenty-six Latino state legislators voted for the plan. Commenting on Latino electoral success and what this means in terms of race, politics, and democracy, Escutia and Romero note that Latinos have been elected in districts "in non-Latino areas," demonstrating that:

> More and more, California is reaping the benefits of multiracial coalitions. The voice of Latinos in California is stronger because electoral politics and issues are no longer just about race. . . . Latinos need not limit themselves to only seeking office in "safe" Latino districts. We should not relegate ourselves to only a few court-imposed barrios. Our success lies in proclaiming that the Latino agenda is (and should be) the American agenda. . . . But, ultimately, we trust the voters. Most citizens cast their votes the American way—they vote for the most qualified candidate, regardless of race or gender. All we have to do is compete for votes the old-fashioned way: by earning them.[41]

Demonstrating not only the divided views among Latino progressives but also the reality of how politics works and the importance of backing longtime allies, Dolores Huerta, cofounder of the United Farm Workers, submitted a statement on behalf of the defendants in the MALDEF lawsuit. Huerta specifically praised Congressman Howard Berman of the San Fernando Valley district named in the lawsuit, stating that he "has always been one of our most effective political supporters."[42] Also at stake for Huerta was the fate of legislation that was, at that time, working its way through the state senate and assembly. The legislation would give "farm laborers the right of mandatory mediation in deadlocked contract negotiations" and was strongly opposed by large growers. The bill, characterized by the *Los Angeles Times* as "a triumph [for farm workers] unprecedented since the passage [in California] of the 1975 agricultural labor relations law," was signed by Governor Gray Davis on 30 September 2002.[43]

On 12 June 2002, the three-judge federal district court panel upheld the redistricting plan and dismissed the MALDEF lawsuit. The court opinion stated: "The essence of any successful vote dilution claim must be that the ability of a minority community to elect representatives of choice is adversely affected. . . . However, if a district is drawn in which Latinos constitute a plurality, non-Latino voters have shown that they are willing to vote for Latino candidates, and Latino candidates receive a majority of the overall vote with some regularity, then the most basic and necessary dilutive effect is lacking. . . . Latino candidates win elections in the territory that constitutes CD 28, and they do so with the support of non-Latino voters." The emphasis on incumbent protection is not seen as a problem for the district court judges because "the protection of an incumbent [is] a well-established legitimate districting criterion."[44]

## The Debate on Race and Redistricting

In New York City and California, the members of the community redistricting groups voiced their awareness of historical and contemporary discrimination. In contrast, in California, the Latino state legislators and the judges who ruled on *Cano v. Davis* noted that whites have voted for Latino candidates, and, in New York City, AAFE and the districting commission suggested that whites would support Asian American candidates. While none of the groups believed that discrimination had disappeared, their recommendations revealed contrasting interpretations of the contemporary significance of race in the redistricting process, voting patterns, and their perceptions of white voters.

During public hearings on redistricting, Asian Americans in California and New York City enumerated the government policies and practices that historically have disenfranchised and discriminated against Asian Americans, such as exclusionary immigration laws, the denial of naturalization to early immigrants, the incarceration of Japanese Americans during World War II, and gerrymandered districts. In fact, the option of creating districts with race as a factor was the direct result of the history of economic, political, and social discrimination faced by racial minorities in the form of residential segregation. Gail Kong, vice president of the Chinatown Voter Education Alliance, testified before the New York City Charter Commission:

> [W]e [Asian Americans] are a racial minority, which means that the inevitable burden of racism and discrimination persists with us. . . . I grew up in a California farm town, population 7,000, where one would expect that the residents, largely refugees from the Dust Bowl disaster, had precious little time to worry about discrimination. But they did find time to sign a petition barring my young, struggling parents from building their first home on the better side of town. That was even before World War II and internment. And all my Asian friends have a similar story. I am also frankly ashamed as a New Yorker, in liberal . . . New York City, that we're still under the jurisdiction of the Justice Department for our treatment of minorities.[45]

Thus, the U.S. government policies and institutions that created and enforced discrimination generated well-founded suspicion and distrust among racial minorities toward government agencies. For example, in the 1980s, scholars reported that the Census Bureau had provided confidential information from the 1940 Census to the War Department to help locate Japanese Americans for incarceration during World War II, an egregious violation of trust between the government and the public.[46] Furthermore, those who are lower income, immigrants, minorities, urban, and Democrats tend to be undercounted by the Census, a form of discrimination embedded in the census-taking process with consequences for redistricting.[47] For example, in the case of New York City's Chinatown, an undercount of Asian Americans in the 1990 Census resulted in an increase in the number of whites added to reach the required district population.

Feelings of betrayal about the 1990 Census undercount were expressed at a

1993 public forum on the completed redistricting process, underscoring the belief that the government discriminates against minorities. Responding to criticism that ethnic communities should have taken greater responsibility to ensure
an accurate census, Esmeralda Simmons—a former member of the districting
commission and the director of the Center of Law and Social Justice at Medgar
Evers College—cited U.S. government actions that stifled community efforts:

> E. SIMMONS: The idea that our communities did not get involved is very skewed
> because our communities were geared up to get involved until the INS [Immigration
> and Naturalization Service] decided to undo their commitment and do those raids
> immediately as the Census started. They said they wouldn't do raids. When they
> started doing raids, that was the end of the Census, and it was, in my opinion,
> deliberately timed. No one's going to sign up and say that they're here illegally and
> risk being deported. . . .

> ALAN GARTNER [executive director of the 1990 New York City Districting Commis-
> sion]: The Secretary of Commerce who made this decision was [President George]
> Bush's campaign manager two elections ago.

> E. SIMMONS: Exactly.[48]

As Simmons later stated: "They knew the Census was going on, and they
understood that it would have a discouraging effect, but they went ahead and
did it anyway."[49]

A history of racial discrimination also framed the redistricting testimony of
California residents, as exemplified by the remarks of the Japanese American
Thomas Ono, the cochair of the San Gabriel Valley group (affiliated with the
Coalition of Asian Pacific Americans for Fair Redistricting) and a resident
since 1977 of Monterey Park. At a public hearing, Ono explained how his
family's incarceration in a concentration camp and discrimination in housing,
employment, and health services shaped his understanding of the importance
of race in everyday life:

> I begin by sharing my background, for I believe it will help you understand the roots
> of my concerns. After the Second World War, my parents were released from the in-
> ternment camps and returned with nothing to Los Angeles, which remained largely
> segregated in its housing and employment. In 1948 I was born at the Japanese
> Hospital, Los Angeles, which was started in the 1920s because patients of Japanese
> ancestry were not accepted at other hospitals. My first residence was in a segregated

neighborhood near Little Tokyo in the present skid row area of Los Angeles. . . . In the early 1960s there was a community controversy over the continued use of a racially restrictive covenant to preclude a black family from moving into Monterey Park. As a result, the Monterey Park City Council was the first to pass a resolution denouncing the enforcement of illegal race covenants. This encouraged Asian and Pacific Americans to move into Monterey Park."[50]

Members of the African American Advisory Committee on Redistricting immediately followed the Asian American group at the public hearing. Coincidentally, but reinforcing the sense of shared purpose and history, Adrian Dove noted that his was the first African American family in Monterey Park that Thomas Ono had mentioned: "That was my family. . . . The day that I moved in, some members of the Nazi party picketed my house in Monterey Park. . . . And a car pulled up and George Brown came . . . to my house and said, 'I'm the mayor. I'm going to stay at your house.' . . . That's how I met George Brown, and Al Song [Korean American], and the particularly strong leadership that represented that area."[51]

Using redistricting to counter this history of discrimination and disenfranchisement resulted in two different strategies. Focused on election outcomes and descriptive representation, AAFE in New York City lobbied for a district favorable to its candidate, Margaret Chin, and Romero, Escutia, and the California district court noted the number of elected Latino officials. In contrast, the Lower East Siders for a Multi-Racial District and MALDEF supported substantive representation,[52] that is, districts that would enhance the political influence of communities of interest and their particular issues: low- and moderate-income people of color in New York and Latinos in California.

MALDEF's primary goal was analyzing demographic and political data with an eye toward developing districts that would keep Latino communities whole within a district and, if possible form the majority of the population, thereby providing an effective and influential voice for Latino voters. As a high percentage of a district's voters, Latinos could express their preferences at the ballot box and have an impact on the election process. Whether Latinos voted for a Latino candidate was not MALDEF's concern. Critics of its lawsuit who argued that the white incumbents in the disputed districts have long supported Latino issues were arguing a completely different point. The fact of Latinos voting for such white incumbents in no way invalidated MALDEF's strategy of developing districts that enhance the voice of Latinos.

Given the complexity of districts and the multiple interests within them, the Lower East Siders for a Multi-Racial District and MALDEF recognized that elected officials respond to varied and often conflicting voter concerns. The more the proportion and, thus, the voting power of a community of interest increases in a district, the more elected officials and candidates must pay attention to that community. It was this insight that drove MALDEF's and the Lower East Siders' primary concern with substantive representation. If whites represent the majority voting power in a district, the officials may have to respond to white, rather than Latino or Asian American, interests—even if the officials themselves are Latino or Asian American.

Critics of MALDEF's lawsuit and the Lower East Siders' proposal noted that whites have "gone beyond race" and will vote for persons of color. These critics, however, have not acknowledged that Latino and Asian American voters have also gone beyond narrow racialist thinking and will engage in crossover voting, that is, voting for candidates of a different ethnic or racial group. This was demonstrated by the 2001 election of the Chinese American Judy Chu in California's Forty-ninth Assembly District.

Because race still plays a critical role in voters' decisions, I would characterize crossover voting by Latinos and Asian Americans, not as *going beyond race*, but as a careful consideration of a candidate's political agenda and overall record, both of which include racial issues as a critical concern. Chu's electoral success reflects her ability to appeal to a wide range of groups—not just Chinese Americans in particular and Asian Americans in general, but whites and Latinos as well—because of her long record of supporting issues important to all residents (e.g., education and health services) and the distinct ways in which such issues affect particular groups (e.g., bilingual education and English-only policies). Chu was endorsed by prominent Southern California Latino officials, including Congresswomen Loretta Sanchez and Hilda Solis and Sheriff Lee Baca. As Solis explained: "The voters are growing more sophisticated in their choices. . . . Judy . . . is a bridge-builder with different groups. She is more than Asian American. She's dynamic, and she has helped the Latino community numerous times over the years."[53] Latinos voting for Chu was a clear example of substantive representation.

Simply citing the election of Latinos or Asian Americans in multiracial districts as evidence that voters have purportedly gone beyond race essentializes and trivializes racial categories by suggesting that the election of a Latino or an Asian American, regardless of his or her political ideology, record, and abilities, is an adequate indicator of political empowerment and the decreasing electoral importance of race.[54] In terms of such factors as class, nativity, political ideology, and religion, Latinos and Asian Americans are heterogeneous groups, and these differences are reflected in their voting patterns, making the *Latino vote* or the *Asian American vote* and *Latino politician* or *Asian American politician* complex and problematic categories. In a district dominated by Latino voters, for example, Latinos can work out their differences at the ballot box as part of the democratic process. But, as the number of Latino voters drops, other voters and issues increasingly enter the election process, and what was once a debate within the Latino community—however diverse—becomes a debate within and among a number of communities.

In the New York City case, the districting commission viewed Latinos and Asian Americans as rival racial groups and, to serve descriptive representation, separated them into different council districts. Yet, by linking whites with Asian Americans, the members of the commission did not adequately consider the ways in which whites act as a racial group. That is, through the past and present employment of such exclusion strategies as the use of literacy tests to block minority voting and the use of gerrymandered districts to dilute the po-litical power of minorities, not to mention their reluctance to vote for minority candidates, whites in New York City have acted to support their own racial privilege rather than political equality.[55] Implied in the commission's analysis was that whites would defer their own interests, recognize the merits of Asian American political representation, and support a qualified Asian American candidate. While strong Asian American candidates have run in every council election in the district in the decade following redistricting, only whites have been elected. Certainly, whites have joined with racial minorities to elect minorities, but this scenario primarily occurs when progressive whites need allies to supplant an entrenched group,[56] not when whites generally constitute a voting majority, such as in New York City's District 1.

While whites have voted for Latinos and Asian Americans—such as Califor-nia Congressman Robert Matsui, Washington Governor Gary Locke, and New York City Councilperson Margarita Lopez—these politicians generally have run "deracialized" campaigns to attract all voters in multiracial areas.[57] I suggest, however, that the racial identity of candidates gains added importance when a minority population becomes significant and that, at this "tipping point,"[58] the political importance of race is amplified when neighborhood interests and race create distinct communities, such as in District 1 and the clear differences in issues expressed by the white Westside residents. As a result, whites perceive a minority candidate as inextricably linked to that community, whether or not such a connection actually exists, as opposed to a candidate who will represent the entire district. In the case of Margaret Chin, even if she had developed a better strategy to attract whites, she may have failed to win those voters because of the way in which the council election was racialized. The lawsuits by racial minorities that initiated charter reform and resulted in the increase in the number of city council districts, public discussion by the members of the districting commission and Chinatown residents on the need for city council Asian American representation, and the existence of a large and rapidly expanding Chinatown within District 1 most likely converged to convince whites that Chin would represent the interests of Chinatown rather than the district as a whole.

Simply noting a group's racial identity does not predict the economic interests and ideological concerns that influence its position on redistricting. Asian American, African American, and Latino civil rights and community redistricting organizations in the Chinatown/Lower East Side area and California were able to work together because of their common interest in developing districts that considered minority political interests as such. Community groups understood the history of racial gerrymandering that fragmented their communities and diluted their political power. Community groups in California also understood that politicians, including Latino politicians, were focused on reelection and preserving their relations with other members of the state legislature and that, historically, the Democratic and Republican Parties have both focused their efforts on maintaining or increasing their political advantage, to the detriment of racial minorities. The California district court judges' adherence to traditional redistricting criteria continued to disenfranchise minority communities. As Morgan Kousser pointed out in his analysis of U.S. Supreme Court redistricting decisions: "Partisan, personal, and ethnic advantage were the real 'traditional districting principles' in North Carolina [i.e., *Shaw v. Reno*]."[59] By *ethnic advantage*, Kousser meant whites working to disenfranchise African Americans in the South.

In conclusion, redistricting is an arena in which contrasting definitions of *race* and *class* are put forward by various groups and acted on and given material form in the shape of the districts produced. Not only are districts a product of the debate on race, but they also shape future race relations by creating conditions that promote or discourage coalitions among groups. Residents within the same district have a reason to work together to lobby their shared representative. Fragmenting groups and placing them in separate districts erodes this basis for an alliance. Putting the Lower East Side and Chinatown in separate council districts disregarded the testimony of those who supported a multiracial district and spoke of the history of political alliances among Asian Americans and Latinos. Working-class Asian Americans and Latinos recognized their common subordinate position in the country's racial hierarchy. They understood that sharing residential communities, low-wage service jobs, and inadequate public services was the result of the discrimination that they experienced as racialized minorities. From this understanding, the label *people of color* goes beyond mere description and, instead, is transformed into a political identity based on a recognition of shared circumstances. Similarly, in California, dividing up concentrations of Latinos into separate congressional districts removes a political basis for collective action at the local level. By fragmenting communities of color in New York City and Latinos in California, redistricting continues the history of minority disenfranchisement through the political process.

## Notes

1. See Davidson and Grofman, eds., *Quiet Revolution*; and Kousser, *Colorblind Injustice*.
2. For a history of the redistricting process, see Gartner, "Redrawing the Lines." For a discussion of the charter revision process in New York City, see Mauro, ed., *Restructuring the New York City Government*.
3. Margaret Fung, written testimony delivered to the New York City Districting Commission (NYCDC), Public Hearings (PH), 1 November 1990, app. 3, vol. 2, n.p. The appointed members of New York City's fifty-nine community boards make recommendations to the city council regarding such issues as land use, budget priorities, and municipal services within their neighborhoods. New York City has thirty-two school districts covering elementary and middle schools, and each district has an elected board.
4. 1990 Census reported in *New York City Districting Commission Newsletter*, no. 10 (April 1991): 2.
5. Pitkin, *Concept of Representation*.
6. For an analysis of the debate among Chinatown activists over the proposed new boundaries of the Chinatown council district, see Saito, "Multiracial Political Coalitions." For a discussion of the structural impediments to minority empowerment through charter reform and redistricting, see Saito, "Sedimentation of Political Inequality."
7. Doris Koo, written testimony delivered to NYCDC, PH, 10 December 1990, app. 3, vol. 4, pp. 1–2.
8. Ibid., 4.

9. Antonio Pagan, oral testimony delivered to NYCDC, PH, 1 November 1990, app. 3, vol. 2, p. 226.

10. Elaine Chan, oral testimony delivered to NYCDC, PH, 21 March 1991, app. 3, vol. 7, p. 183.

11. Ibid., 184.

12. Elaine Chan, oral testimony delivered to NYCDC, PH, November 1, 1990, app. 3, vol. 2, p. 253.

13. Chan, oral testimony (n. 10 above), 182.

14. Keiko Ohnuma, "Asian Camps Split on District Lines for Lower Manhattan," *Asian-Week*, 26 April 1991, 1.

15. Mini Liu, oral testimony delivered to NYCDC, PH, 21 March 1991, app. 3, vol. 7, p. 290.

16. Gartner, "Redrawing the Lines," 68, 130.

17. Santiago, ed., *Redistricting, Race and Ethnicity*, 24.

18. Victor A. Kovner, Joel Berger, and Judith Reed, "Submission under Section 5 of the Voting Rights Act for Preclearance of 1991 Redistricting Plan for New York City Council" (plans submitted by the NYCDC to the U.S. Justice Department, 17 June 1991). The much lower percentage of registered voters among Asian American than among whites is explained primarily by the large number of immigrants among Chinatown residents. Naturalization and voter registration rates are also negatively affected by the lower levels of income, fewer number of years in the United States, and lesser English-language ability found among Chinatown residents. However, structural impediments have also depressed political participation among Asian American immigrants. These include a political system that appears nonresponsive and the inadequacy of registration and voter information in Chinese. For a discussion of these issues, see Ong and Nakanishi, "Becoming Citizens, Becoming Voters."

19. AAFE v. Koch 72 N.Y.2d 121; 527 N.E.2d 265; 531 N.Y.S.2d 782 (N.Y. 1988). See *Asian Americans for Equality: 1974–1994* (New York: AAFE, n.d.).

20. Andrew Jacobs, "What a Difference Two Decades Make: Asian Americans for Equality Is Attacked as the Establishment It Once Fought," *New York Times*, 12 January 1997, section 13, p.4.

21. Asian American Union for Political Action, letter stating position of the organization on the 1991 city council elections, 31 August 1991, held in Leland Saito's files.

22. Wayne Barrett, "Anatomy of a Smear: How a Former Reformer Set New Lows in New York City Politics," *Village Voice*, 5 November 1991, 11.

23. *Outlook* (the AALDEF newsletter), spring 1992, 1, 5.

24. The California state legislature is bicameral, with forty senators and eighty assembly members. All senators and assembly members represent single member districts, for a total of 120 senate and assembly districts. California has fifty-three federal congressional districts. There are no rules governing the redistricting process in terms of how state senate, state assembly, and federal congressional districts are drawn in relation to one another.

25. State population figures are taken from U.S. Census Bureau, "State and County Quick Facts, California," http://quickfacts.census.gov. The 1990 and 2000 population comparisons are taken from Maria L. LaGanga and Shawn Hubler, "California Grows to 33.9 Million, Reflecting Increased Diversity," *Los Angeles Times*, 30 March 2001, A1. For a discussion of African American migration patterns in the Los Angeles area, see Grant, Oliver, and James, "African Americans"; and Erin Texeira, "Migrants from L.A. Flow to Affordable Suburbs Such as Inland Empire," *Los Angeles Times*, 30 March 2001, U2. For

figures on the 1980 and 1990 Compton population, see 1980 Census of Population, vol. 1, "Characteristics of the Population," chap. C, "General Social and Economic Characteristics," pt. 1, "United States Summary," pc80-1-c1 (Washington: U.S. Government Printing Office, 1983), "Table 249: Persons by Spanish Origin and Race for Areas and Places: 1980," 1–411, and "Table dp-1: Profile of General Demographic Characteristics: 2000. Geographic Area: Compton City, California," 256 (available at http://www.census.gov).

26. *Garza v. Los Angeles County Board of Supervisors*, 918 F.2d 763 (9th Cir. 1990).

27. *Shaw v. Reno*, 509 U.S. 630 (1993); *Miller v. Johnson*, 515 U.S. 900 (1995). See Kousser, *Colorblind Injustice*, 5.

28. U.S. District Court, Central District of California, Cano v. Davis, cv 01-08477 mmm (rcx), Opinion and Order Granting Defendants' Motions for Summary Judgment, 12 June 2002, pp. 22–23 (available at http://www.cacd.uscourts.gov).

29. Stewart Kwoh, "Joint Hearing Assembly Elections, Reapportionment and Constitutional Amendments Committee and Senate Elections and Reapportionment Committee: Transcript of Public Hearing on Redistricting: Public Comment on Proposed Redistricting Plans Hearing at the State Capitol with Interactive Testimony from Los Angeles, San Bernardino, San Diego and Santa Ana," vol. 2, 5 September 2001, p. 563 (available at http://www.assembly.ca.gov).

30. William C. Velasquez Institute, "Fair Redistricting in the 2000's: A Manual for Minority Groups" (unpublished paper handed out at the "Community Redistricting Workshop" sponsored by the William C. Velasquez Institute, maldef, and the National Association of Latino Elected Officials, 6 February 2001, National City, California), 6.

31. Kathay Feng, "Joint Hearing Assembly Elections, Reapportionment and Constitutional Amendments Committee and Senate Elections and Reapportionment Committee: Transcript of Public Hearing on Redistricting: Public Comment on Proposed Redistricting Plans Hearing at the State Capitol with Interactive Testimony from San Francisco, San Jose, Monterey and Fresno," vol. 2, 4 September 2001, 47 (available at http://www.assembly .ca.gov).

32. Mexican American Legal Defense and Educational Fund, naacp Legal Defense and Educational Fund, and National Asian Pacific American Legal Consortium, *The Impact of Redistricting in Your Community: A Guide to Redistricting* (n.p., n.d.).

33. naacp Legal Defense and Educational Fund, Asian Pacific American Legal Center, and the Mexican American Legal Defense and Educational Fund, "Making Our Communities Count: United for a Fair Redistricting Process" (University of California, Los Angeles, 12 May 2001).

34. "The Politics of Map-Making" (editorial), *Los Angeles Times*, 7 September 2001, b14.

35. Carl Ingram, "Davis oks Redistricting That Keeps Status Quo," *Los Angeles Times*, 28 September 2001, b12.

36. Statistics available by district at http://www.assembly.ca.gov.

37. Amadis Velez, "Joint Hearing Assembly Elections" (n. 31 above), 80–82. For dissenting opinions, see, e.g., State Senator Richard Polanco, "Joint Hearing Assembly Elections" (n. 31 above), 80; and Alan Clayton, "Joint Hearing Assembly Elections" (n. 31 above), 145.

38. Feng, "Joint Hearing Assembly Elections" (n. 31 above), 5 September 2001, 349.

39. *Cano v. Davis*, 191 F.Supp.2d 1135 (C.D. Cal. 2001).

40. "maldef Sues State of California for Violating Voting Rights Act and Constitution with Redistricting Plans" (maldef press release, 1 October 2001).

41. Martha Escutia and Gloria Romero, "MALDEF's Lawsuit Is Racially Divisive," *Los Angeles Times*, 1 November 2001, B13.

42. Declaration of Dolores C. Huerta in support of Senate defendants' motions for summary judgment, 13 May 2002, 1. United States District Court, Central District of California, Cano et al. v. Davis et al., Case No. 01-084777 MMM (RCX).

43. Gregg Jones, "A Big Win for Farm Workers," *Los Angeles Times*, 1 October 2002, A1.

44. U.S. District Court, Central District of California, Cano v. Davis, CV 01-08477 MMM (RCX), Opinion and Order Granting Defendants' Motions for Summary Judgment, 12 June 2002, 27, 85–86 (available at http://www.cacd.uscourts.gov).

45. Testimony of Gail M. Kong before the New York City Charter Revision Commission, 8 June 1989, app. 10, no. 9, n.p. New York City had violated the 1965 Voting Rights Act, triggering its section 5 preclearance requirement, by using literacy tests into the 1960s. The literacy tests circumscribed the political participation of racial minorities as indicated by low voter turnout in presidential elections. For a discussion of this, see NYCDC, "A Short History of the Reapportionment of the City Council," in Kovner, Berger, and Reed, "Submission for Preclearance" (n. 18 above), app. 1, vol. 8 no. 19.

46. See Daniels, "Relocation of the Japanese Americans"; and Okamura, "Myth of Census Confidentiality." In March 2000, Kenneth Prewitt, head of Census 2000, issued two statements remarkable for their candor and forthrightness. In the first, he states: "In the spring of 1942, the Census Bureau cooperated with the war effort by providing special tabulations of the Japanese American population for counties and county subdivisions, and for some cities at the block level" ("Statement of Census Bureau Director Kenneth Prewitt on Internment of Japanese Americans in World War II" [Washington: U.S. Department of Commerce, U.S. Census Bureau, Census 2000, 17 March 2000]). Prewitt also noted: "The record is less clear whether the then in effect legal prohibitions against revealing individual data records were violated. . . . However, even were it to be conclusively documented that no such violation did occur, this would not and could not excuse the abuse of human rights that resulted from the rapid provision of tabulations designed to identify where Japanese Americans lived and therefore to facilitate and accelerate the forced relocation and denial of civil rights" ("Additional Comments by Census Bureau Director Kenneth Prewitt and the Role of the Census Bureau and the Use of Census Tabulations in the Internment of Japanese Americans in World War II" [Washington: U.S. Department of Commerce, U.S. Census Bureau, Census 2000, 24 March 2000]).

47. Sam Fulwood, "Census Method Hurt State, Study Finds," *Los Angeles Times*, 3 March 1999, A3; Soraya Sarhaddi Nelson, "Counting on an Accurate 2000 Census," *Los Angeles Times*, 5 November 1999, B2; Robert Rosenblatt, "Administration Says 2000 Census a 'Quality Count,' Won't Be Adjusted," *Los Angeles Times*, 3 July 2001, A6.

48. Santiago, ed., *Redistricting, Race and Ethnicity*, 32.

49. Esmeralda Simmons, telephone conversation with Leland Saito, 28 September 2000.

50. Thomas Ono, Assembly, California Legislature, Elections, Reapportionment and Constitutional Amendments Committee, "Transcript of Public Hearing on Redistricting, Identification of Communities of Interest," Los Angeles, 8 June 2001, 138, 144 (available at http://www.assembly.ca.gov).

51. Adrian Dove, Assembly, California Legislature, Elections, Reapportionment and Constitutional Amendments Committee, "Transcript of Public Hearing on Redistricting" (n. 49 above), 162–63.

52. Hero and Tolbert, "Substantive Representation."

53. Richard Winton, "Campaigning across Ethnic Lines," *Los Angeles Times*, 12 May 2001, section 2, p. 4.

54. For a discussion of racial representation, see Guinier, *Tyranny of the Majority*; and Saito, "Beyond Numbers."

55. Lipsitz, *Investment in Whiteness*; Mollenkopf, *Phoenix in the Ashes*.

56. See Browning, Marshall, and Tabb, *Protest Is Not Enough*; and Sonenshein, *Politics in Black and White*.

57. See McCormick and Jones, "Conceptualization of Deracialization"; and Underwood, "Process and Politics." The first Asian American member of the New York City Council was the Taiwanese immigrant John Liu, who was elected in 2001 from District 20 in Flushing, Queens, one of the most racially diverse areas of the city. Before the election, he worked as a manager at PriceWaterhouseCoopers, an accounting and financial services company. Among the top fund-raisers of the city council candidates, Liu ran a deracialized campaign that stressed delivering basic city services. His victory occurred in the same election as the businessman Michael Bloomberg's successful bid for mayor, illustrating, in part, the benefit that both candidates garnered by promoting the belief that successful businesspersons in private enterprise offer better management skills than do career public officials (see Karen Matthews, "Candidates Vying to Be the First Asian-American on New York City Council," Associated Press State and Local Wire, 17 February 2001; and Bryan Virasami, "Groundbreaking Win for Asian," *Newsday*, 8 November 2001, A56).

58. Lieberson, *Piece of the Pie*.

59. Kousser, *Colorblind Injustice*, 4.

*Part Three* **PERILS OF INCLUSION**

*Sexuality and Citizenship in Junot Díaz and Chang-rae Lee*

Andrea Levine

In the first story of Junot Díaz's collection *Drown*, two young Dominican boys—Yunior and his revered older brother, Rafa—spend their summer in the country with relatives, away from their Santo Domingo home. Their mother remains at her job in the capital; their father has been living in the United States for several years. On a bus ride one day to a neighboring village, the man next to Yunior purports to help him remove a grease stain from his pants: "He spit in his fingers and started to rub at the stain, but then he was pinching at the tip of my pinga through the fabric of my shorts."[1] Yunior "shove[s] the man against his seat," and hisses insults at him, but says nothing to Rafa. When, after a confrontation with the driver, Rafa succeeds in getting both boys off the bus without having paid the fare that they do not have and Yunior begins to cry, Rafa responds to his tears: "Are you always going to be a pussy? . . . You have to get tougher. Crying all the time. Do you think our papi's crying? Do you think that's what he's been doing the last six years?" (14). "The last six years" refer to the time that their father has been in the United States; Rafa implies that, unlike his younger brother, their father has been displaying the masculine self-sufficiency necessary to survive the travails of migration and seek success in North America. It is not clear whether Yunior's tears come in response to the bus driver's anger, his own poverty, or the actions of the man on the bus, but what is clear is that a suitably masculine relationship to the United States is invoked here in stark contrast to being a "pussy" in the campo, to the queer possibilities suggested by the stranger on the bus.

In this essay, I read both Díaz's *Drown* and Chang-rae Lee's Korean American novel *Native Speaker*, arguing that the dominant models of U.S. citizenship open to immigrants in these texts work to preclude potential alliances with other people of color—and, therefore, the development of anti-imperial subjectivities. This process, I suggest, is importantly facilitated by the promises of heteronormative masculine sexual fulfillment encoded within dominant constructions of U.S. national subjects.[2] Of course, the control of male sexuality has long functioned in the United States as a way to police racial discourse and to buttress white supremacy—certainly the most visible example of this has concerned the violent regulation of black male sexuality, especially in the American South. But even the important work that has illuminated the emasculating effects that immigration restrictions had on Chinese male laborers, for instance, has perhaps not fully accounted for the central role of sexuality in the ideological transformation of immigrants into U.S. national subjects. In his recent *Racial Castration*, David L. Eng takes on some of these questions, using psychoanalytic theory to investigate both the racially specific construction of Asian American male subjectivity and the "produc[tion] against these particularized images [of] the abstract national subject of a unified and coherent national body."[3] Sharing Eng's interest in the mutual constitution of sexual, racial, and U.S. national subjectivity, my essay considers not only the status of Asian American masculinity but also the broader appeal of the straight masculine paradigm for the interpellation of new U.S. national subjects across racial and ethnic borders. In reading two texts that pose distinct, uneven, but, at times, acutely pointed critiques of the processes and constraints entailed in the production of U.S. national subjects, it suggests the ways in which constructions of normative masculinity—and their frequent concomitant, feminine invisibility—can, at times, confound even those texts that would seem unabashedly to function as what Lisa Lowe has importantly called "critical acts."[4]

For the characters in Díaz's *Drown*, attaining the status of male sexual agent depends critically on economic reach, which is always imbricated with the United States. Yunior's brother, Rafa, always wears the same clothes when he visits his many girlfriends—"a shirt and pants that," Yunior says, "my father had sent him from the States last Christmas" (6). The outfit that Rafa chooses for his sexual adventures recalls Yunior's sexual encounter on the bus and Rafa's harsh reaction to his tears in its linkage of successful masculine sexuality with access to the products of labor in the United States. Rafa's access both to the material wealth of the United States and to his own idealized father are, of course, in reality pathetically circumscribed, as we see when he meets Ysrael, a young boy whose encounter with a wild pig has left his face grotesquely mangled. When Rafa and Yunior find him, Ysrael is playing with a kite that his own father sent to him from North America; in response, Rafa "frowns" enviously—and then breaks a bottle over Ysrael's head. Rafa's sexual conquests, too, are only partial ones; the girls he dates will sometimes let him, "if he's lucky, put it in their mouths or in their asses" (5). His sexual adventures, themselves figured as momentary avenues of escape from the hopeless boredom and poverty of life in the campo, are clearly depicted as offering only an approximation of the conventional heterosexual penetration he seeks. And, like the girl "who was pregnant and didn't give a damn about anything" (6), the girls who are willing to have intercourse with Rafa appear to do so more out of desperation than desire. Even Yunior and Rafa's father's experience suggests that, without economic agency, masculine sexuality can wind up as a kind of inadequate "perversion" for the would-be American. The collection's final story, "Negocios," chronicles the struggles of Ramon as a new, undocumented immigrant to the United States, alone in a roach-infested New York apartment, working "nineteen-, twenty-hour days, seven days a week." Ramon was "angry at the stupidity that had brought him to this freezing hell of a country, angry that a man his age had to masturbate when he had a wife" (179). In the Dominican Republic, Ramon had, not just a wife, but mistresses, while, confined to almost ceaseless labor in his newly adopted country, he is relegated to what he sees as the humiliating sexual postures of a teenager.

In the collection's title story, Yunior has become a New Jersey teenager and sometime drug dealer; he spends the summer before his last year of high school selling drugs and hanging out at the local swimming pool with his best friend, Beto, who is about to escape their neighborhood for college. "Twice. That's it," says Yunior, alluding to—and simultaneously disavowing—his two sexual encounters with Beto that summer. Yunior stays silent when Beto offers, " 'I'll stop if you want,' " but he remains "terrified [he] would end up 'abnormal,' a fucking pato" (104–5). Again, a kind of reluctant queerness lies in wait for Yunior, who believes that he has failed to negotiate the United States correctly, to construct an upwardly mobile, potentially powerful future. David Eng similarly reads "The Shoyu Kid," a text set in a Japanese American internment camp, arguing that, for a group of Japanese American boys who witness the homosexual molestation of another internee, the "scene ultimately encloses these young boys . . . within a profoundly negative identification with homosexuality, racialization, and alienation from the US nation-state."[5]

Right after their own homosexual encounter, Beto lies with his head in Yunior's lap while Yunior ruminates on his own lack of future possibilities: "I thought of how in high school our teachers loved to crowd us into their lounge every time a space shuttle took off from Florida. One teacher, whose family had two grammar schools named after it, compared us to the shuttles. A few of you are going to make it. Those are the orbiters. But the majority of you are just going to burn out. Going nowhere . . . I could already see myself losing altitude, fading, the earth spread out beneath me, hard and bright" (106). Yunior's teacher compels his students to witness the U.S. mastery of outer space while using this imperial imagery to dictate their exclusion from the state-sponsored mobility that the shuttles connote. He attempts to describe a kind of natural selection here, the successes—the "orbiters"—inexorably separating themselves from the rest, ascending away from their earthbound classmates. Yet the technological image itself returns to illuminate the fundamental complicity of the state in this ostensibly "meritocratic" process, just as the teacher's own socioeconomic advantage skews the evolutionary course he charts. As a result of his family connections, the teacher has the very power to name educational institutions, those ideological state apparatuses so central to the formation of U.S. national subjects. In another story, "Edison, New Jersey," the narrator, who works delivering pool tables to affluent suburban customers, explains: "Most of our customers have names like this, court case names: Wooley, Maynard, Gass, Binder, but the people from my town, our names, you see on convicts or coupled together on boxing cards" (130). Again, the narrator recognizes that the power to define—and, therefore, benefit from—such ostensibly "neutral" institutions as the legal system rests in the hands of the privileged Anglo few.

Yunior explicitly figures his own inevitable "burnout" as a phallic failure as well; he imagines "losing altitude," before colliding with the "hard" earth. Similarly, he assumes his queer, defeated posture with Beto only after he has rejected an opportunity to renegotiate his relationship to U.S. power—that is, after he has been approached by a military recruiter. The recruiter makes clear that he is selling a masculine version of the American dream. When Yunior protests that he "ain't Army material," the recruiter counters: "That's exactly what I used to think. . . . But now I have a house, a car, a gun and a wife. Discipline. Loyalty. Can you say that you have those things? Even one?" (100). The recruiter depicts, for one thing, a world of sexual autonomy and privacy that is clearly denied to Yunior. When Yunior and Beto lie in front of the television, after sex: "I had my eyes closed and the television was on and when the hallway door crashed open . . . I nearly cut my dick off struggling with my shorts. It's just the neighbor, he said laughing . . . but I was saying, Fuck this, and getting my clothes on" (106). Of course, Díaz works at the same time to expose the *price* of the sanctuary that the recruiter has purchased—to suggest the homophobic, gendered violence at the heart of the dream itself, which not only equates the possession of a wife with that of a house and a car but also makes the possession of a gun necessary to secure the rest of what the dream promises. The domestic sexual "security" that the state guarantees, then, has violence at its core; as Díaz goes on to suggest, it rests on the U.S. imperial project. And, as we shall see, that project itself both constructs and enables racialized forms of masculine sexual agency.

After their first conversation, Yunior takes care to hide from the recruiter, afraid he'll succumb to his blandishments: "He won't have to show me his Desert Eagle or flash the photos of the skinny Filipino girls sucking dick. He'll only have to smile and name the places and I'll listen" (100–101). The quotation explicitly links U.S. military power to transnational mobility and racialized sexual access. That is, by using "the skinny Filipino girls sucking dick" as an advertisement for what the U.S. Army has to offer, Díaz condenses imperial and sexual domination, turning the Asian women into agents of U.S. power, made to "service" those same soldiers whose nation occupied theirs. The U.S. Army, then, promises Yunior a chance to redefine his sexual status in relation to the state. No longer the "pussy" who cries or the passive partner in homosexual encounters, Yunior can readily become the dominant partner in a straight sexual scenario that turns on the subordination of the Asian woman while it promises to obscure his own racial and economic subjugation as a Latino within the United States.

It is here that Yunior's potential investment in this imperial narrative becomes clear. For, in another story, a set of "instructions" for dating girls of different racial backgrounds, the narrator explains how to share New Jersey neighborhood lore: "[S]upply the story about the loco who'd been storing canisters of tear gas in his basement for years, how one day the canisters cracked and the whole neighborhood got a dose of the military-strength stuff. Don't tell her that your moms knew right away what it was, that she recognized the smell from the year the U.S. invaded your island" (146). In strategically eliding the second part of the story—the 1965 U.S. invasion of the Dominican Republic—Yunior has chosen, partly in the interest of sexual viability, to suppress the humiliation of being *subject to* U.S. military power rather than the subject in whose name that power operates and, in effect, to align himself with U.S. interests. Yunior, then, chooses the version of the story that elides any correlation between himself and the Filipino girls in the photographs he never sees, any connection between himself and the feminized objects of U.S. force. To identify with U.S. power means in this text to refuse, on gendered grounds, the potential linkages *between* people of color, who share a history of relations to the U.S. "national interest" and imperial power. In spite of Yunior's denial, those operating on behalf of that national interest themselves posited an intimate relation between U.S. interests in Latin America and in Southeast Asia. Lyndon Johnson, for instance, "was convinced that the Dominican revolt had been planned in Moscow as a rejoinder to U.S. military operations in Vietnam"[6]—that, like Southeast Asia, Latin America was a theater for the playing out of cold war tensions between the superpowers.

In order to secure his chances with his dates, the narrator elides not only his family's part in his native country's history of military subjection to the U.S. nation-state but also its present *economic* dependence on the government. When preparing the apartment for a girl's visit, his first directive is to "clear the government cheese from the refrigerator" (143). Further, he removes all photographic evidence of his poverty-stricken relatives back in the Dominican Republic, hiding the trajectory that brought his family to North America in the first place. In the end, however, he confesses that these dates are unlikely to bring him any sexual rewards. In an echo of its opening lines, the story concludes: "[P]ut the government cheese back in its place before your moms kills you" (149). None of the forms of dissemblance that the narrator practices, then, can fundamentally alter his relation to the state—his family needs the food the U.S. government provides, and, as well as she knows the history of her native country's military domination by the United States, Yunior's mother cannot afford to deny this.

The narrator's strategies of self-presentation, all designed to enhance his sexual prospects, ultimately return him to a place where he is subordinate both to maternal authority and to the paternalistic power of a state that provides his family with handouts but fails to offer him anything approaching equal opportunity. His mother's unyielding dictates, meanwhile, make his "emasculation" coterminous with the maintenance of state power over him, as if these two positions are somehow one. As José Piedra argues in an essay with a different emphasis: "[C]olonialism could be described as a colonizing agent's 'systematic' bullying and sissification of a colonized target."[7] In *Drown*, the mother's implicit demand that the narrator return the "government cheese" to its proper

ANDREA LEVINE

place makes her, in effect, an agent of the colonizer's "bullying and sissifica-tion." At the same time, the state itself underwrites her ability to support her family as a single mother, facilitating her usurpation of the autonomy and authority that would more "appropriately" belong to the family patriarch.[8]

What the narrator's simultaneous elisions of his military and economic rela-tions to the U.S. government actually fail to register are precisely the linkages between these relations. That is, Díaz strongly implies that one legacy of U.S. imperialism in the Dominican Republic has been to render economic self-determination there untenable. In another story, "Aguantando," one set in the Dominican Republic, Yunior's grandfather "talked to [him] about the good old days, when a man could still make a living from his finca, when the United States wasn't something folks planned on" (72–73). The historian Eric Thomas Chester maintains that the years following the U.S. intervention have seen the "complete futility of every effort at social reform" in the Dominican Republic. The U.S.-trained and -supplied Dominican military has managed to stifle those dissenting voices protesting the nation's increasingly stark income inequality and lack of economic opportunity, as low-wage jobs accompanied the incur-sion of global (and, often, U.S.) capital into the country in the years following the U.S. invasion. Economic "stagnation and austerity" have persisted since the global oil crisis of 1973—a crisis that took place in the face of decreasing U.S. economic aid to the Dominicans "as memories of the uprising receded in Washington's collective memory." As Chester maintains: "[T]he country's bleak prospects have led many young people to search for a better future in a new country. Between 1966 and 1990, 10 percent of the entire Dominican population emigrated to the United States."[9] If the United States has, indeed, become something "folks plan on," Díaz suggests, this is (clearly) due in part to the long-term effects of U.S. military and economic policies in Latin America.

Further, in detailing the effects of the U.S. invasion on his own family, Yunior demonstrates a continuity between the U.S. military presence in the Dominican Republic and the economic domination that succeeded it. Their *abuelo*'s lament for the self-sustaining past comes in a story in which Yunior describes a photograph of his parents taken days before the invasion: "Mami had been pregnant with my first never-born brother" (69); when Yunior later describes "across [my mother's] stomach and back the scars from the rocket attack she'd survived in 1965" (71), it is obvious why Yunior's brother was never born. His family has experienced and suffered from the violence of U.S.

imperialism in the most immediate and intimate ways. But, as "Aguantando" makes clear, the subsequent neocolonial relation between the United States and the Dominican Republic, structured more by economic power than by military might, itself shapes and distorts family relationships. As Yunior explains in the story's opening lines: "I lived without a father the first nine years of my life. He was in the States, working, and the only way I knew him was through the photographs my moms kept in a plastic sandwich bag under her bed" (69). The story ends with Yunior's poignant, never-to-be-realized fantasy of a reunion with his father, Ramon, in which his father would display a sensitivity and compassion, a recognition of Yunior's individual subjectivity, of which the reader already knows him to be incapable. Rafa has his own telling fantasy about their father: "[He] used to think that he'd come in the night, like Jesus" (87). The rest of the text unravels these imaginings, all the way through the last line of the final story of the collection, which both voices filial desire and admits its inevitable unfulfillment. When Ramon finally decides to return to the Dominican Republic to bring his family back with him to the United States, Yunior explains: "The first subway station on Bond would have taken him to the airport and I like to think that he grabbed that first train instead of what was more likely true, that he had gone out to [his friend] Chuito's first before flying south to get us" (20).

Yunior wants to imagine his father rushing to reclaim the family he has left behind in pursuit of North American–style success. But Ramon is preoccupied with the friends he has made in the United States; he seeks to bring his family over primarily because he hopes that their arrival in the North will improve his fortunes. He feels no desperate desire for a reunion, and, at the end of the collection, Yunior is forced to confront the permanence of his father's emotional estrangement. The gap left by his father's absence, then, will never be closed, the structuring loss of the text never compensated for.

Just as Rafa's messianic hopes go unrealized, the whole text of *Drown* works to illuminate the failed promise of North America. From the first story, "Ysrael" (of course, the Promised Land), we arrive at a violently demystified version of the United States. Even once the characters in *Drown* have become U.S. citizens, they find that, in many cases, the spoils of capitalism are parceled out according to race. In the story "Boyfriend," for instance, the narrator chronicles the breakup of his upstairs neighbor's romance; he has witnessed her boyfriend in action around the neighborhood, trying to "get over on the whitegirls." He remembers what he takes as his own ex-girlfriend's similar betrayal: "Loretta's new boy was Italian, worked on Wall Street. When she told me about him we were still going out. . . . [S]he said to me, I like him. He's a hard worker. No amount of heart leather could keep something like that from hurting" (114). Díaz suggests, of course, that what Loretta treats as an individual trait—her new boyfriend's "work ethic," which she implies distinguishes him from the narrator—has everything to do with the socioeconomic opportunities open to whites, even white "ethnics," and systematically denied to the Latino narrator.

In "Edison, New Jersey," set predominantly in the white suburbs, the narrator works, as we have seen, delivering pool tables to customers who care only about "memoriz[ing] everything they own" (123) and keeping it safe from those who labor in their homes. On his delivery route, he meets a young Dominican woman who works as a maid in one of the houses, appears to be sexually involved with her white employer, and asks the narrator to drive her back to Washington Heights, the predominantly Dominican neighborhood in upper Manhattan. She takes all her belongings with her, not planning to return. A few weeks later, the narrator calls the suburban home that the woman has left, and she answers the phone. When the narrator reports this to Wayne, his co-worker, he responds: "Pretty predictable. She's probably in love with the guy. You know how it is." "I sure do," the narrator answers. "Don't get angry," Wayne tells him. The narrator replies: "I'm just tired, that's all" (139). The conversation testifies to the numbing repeatability of this narrative—there are no surprises left in the kind of racialized and gendered power that this affluent white man wields, both over his Latina female employee and over the narrator.

By contrast, the main characters in Chang-rae Lee's *Native Speaker* appear at first to have forged more secure trajectories, to have found some of what the United States promised to offer them. Henry Park, the Korean American narrator of *Native Speaker*, is a professional spy for a shadowy agency tied to government and big business and specializing in investigating ethnic minorities. Assigned to infiltrate the campaign offices of John Kwang, a Korean American councilman and successful businessman with aspirations of running for mayor of New York City, Henry is astonished by Kwang's "effortless" sense of entitlement to an "American" identity, his refusal to restrict himself to the Korean American community that, to Henry's parents, was the widest available world: "Before I knew of him, I had never even conceived of someone like him. A Korean man, of his age, as part of the vernacular. Not just a respectable grocer or dry cleaner or doctor, but a larger public figure who was willing to speak and act outside the tight sphere of his family, . . . [H]e didn't seem afraid like my mother and father, who were always wary of those who would try to shame us or mistreat us."[10] Henry imagines writing for his employers a history of John Kwang's life, one stretching from his boyhood in Korea—where his family and his village were "obliterated" by the Korean War—to his struggles as a young man in New York, "[w]here he first went to a real school and learned to read and write and speak his new home language. And where he began to think of America as a part of him, maybe even his" (211). Henry appears here to incorporate Kwang into the conservative plot that Lisa Lowe calls a "narrative . . . of immigrant inclusion—[a] stor[y] of the Asian immigrant's journey from foreign strangeness to assimilation and citizenship."[11]

It is telling that Kwang's "inclusion" demands that he offer a revisionist narrative of Asian American immigrant experience. In response to a black-led boycott of Korean-owned markets, Kwang speaks one day to an audience consisting of "an even mix of Koreans, blacks, Hispanics." Seeking to demonstrate what his Korean American constituents have "in common" with the Hispanics and African Americans in the crowd, to register their own experiences of subjection, he tells his listeners: "We Koreans know something of this tragedy. Recall the days over 50 years ago when Koreans were made servants and slaves in their own country by the Imperial Japanese Army. How our mothers and sisters were made the concubines of the very soldiers who enslaved us" (153). Kwang chooses to focus here on the Japanese imperialism that "cast [Koreans] as the dogs of Asia," never even mentioning the American war in Korea that killed his own family or any of the racial discrimination that Korean Americans, like other Asian Americans, encounter in the United States. In articulating his own claim on the United States, then, Kwang displaces the imperialist project so that it is external to America, confined as an intra-Asian phenomenon. As Lowe argues pertinently: "Most of the post-1965 Asian immigrants come from societies already disrupted by colonialism and distorted by the upheavals of neocolonialist capitalism and war. . . . In this sense, these Asian Americans are determined by the history of U.S. involvement in Asia *and* the historical racialization of Asians in the United States."[12]

The same is, of course, entirely true of Kwang, but there is an ellipsis in his narrative where U.S. intervention would be. Lowe maintains: [O]nce here, the demand that Asian immigrants identify as US national subjects simultaneously produces alienations and disidentifications out of which critical subjectivities emerge. These Asian immigrants retain precisely the memories of imperialism that the U.S. nation seeks to forget."[13] Like Díaz's Yunior, who rigorously works to suppress all material evidence of his own family's subjection to U.S. imperialism—even as the scars on Yunior's mother's body testify to the indelibility of that legacy—John Kwang, in his capacity as a political aspirant and the kind of "American" who really might become "part of the vernacular," has, in fact, *silenced* the "memor[y] of imperialism." While, as we shall see, his can be called a "critical" subjectivity to the extent that it refuses the easy certainties of U.S. racial discourse, it is less clear that his memories of imperialism enable the kind of critical subjectivity that Lowe describes.

Lee, however, does mark Kwang's potential disruption of the aspirational paradigm so often ascribed to the immigrant subject. *Native Speaker* shows us an effort to forge precisely the kinds of interracial and interethnic alliances that the state works, Díaz suggests, to undermine—in part, as we have seen, through its promise that male sexual agency hinges on an identification with U.S. military aims and a successful navigation of the U.S. economic order. Counting a wide range of ethnic groups among his followers—which, in the language of the media, means that he is "building an 'empire' from his 'ethnic base' " (301)—Kwang explicitly appeals to his constituents to privilege the experience of racial oppression as a basis for political and social alliance over shared language or country of origin. Again speaking to the group composed of Korean, Hispanic, and African American constituents, Kwang implores them:

> Think of yourselves, think of your close ones, whom no one else loves, and then you
> will be thinking of them, whom you believe to be the other, the enemy, the cause of
> the problems in your life. Those who are a different dark color. Who may seem
> strange. Who cannot speak your language just yet. Who cannot seem to understand
> the first thing about who you are. . . . I ask that you remember . . . that what we have
> in common, the sadness and pain and injustice, will always be stronger than our
> differences. (152–53)

Kwang lives out this philosophy, expanding the notion of the *ggeh*, the traditional "Korean money club," in order to provide a mode of shared capital to a whole range of new immigrants. As Henry notes: "My father would have thought him crazy to run a ggeh with people other than just our own. Spanish people? Indians? Vietnamese? How could you trust them? Then even if you could, why would you?" (280).

Henry's father, however, does see a point of intersection between Latinos and Asians in the United States; in his mind, this space is largely determined by the racialized conditions of the U.S. labor market—and, more broadly, by the binary structure of U.S. racial discourse itself. Henry explains that, when it came to hiring, his father preferred Puerto Ricans and Peruvians to African Americans: "The 'Spanish' ones were harder working, he said, because they didn't speak English too well, just like us. This became a kind of rule of thumb for him, to hire somebody if they couldn't speak English . . . because he figured they were new to the land and understood that no one would help them for nothing. The most important thing was that they hadn't been in America too long" (187). For Henry's father, then, it is a kind of distance from, or marginalization within, the dominant national culture, both linguistically and ideologically, that makes a "good" worker. It is only when one begins to make claims on the nation, to expect it to deliver on its promises, that one becomes less fit for the kind of dehumanizing labor that the market demands of so many immigrants. As You-me Park and Gayle Wald argue: "Asian Americans have come to occupy model minority status in part because of the belief that they are willing to work without demanding the civic reward for work—recognition as citizen-subjects."[14] It is the withholding of precisely this demand that Henry's father sees as linking him to other disenfranchised immigrant workers. Ultimately, however, the text will suggest that submission to capitalist imperatives on the part of immigrant subjects inhibits rather than enables the formation of interethnic and interracial alliances.

In addition to their mutually exploitable labor capacity, the only significant form of connection between Asians and Latinos that Henry's father can imagine hinges on their racial privilege relative to African Americans. He is careful, therefore, to mark his own distance from African Americans as greater than that from any other racialized immigrant group. Henry remembers that, when they were young, his father and other Korean American friends would "sometimes group up and play [soccer against] a team of Hispanic men. . . . [O]nce, they even played some black men, though my father pointed out to us in the car home that they were *African* blacks" (51). The passage registers Henry's father's calculus of his own ever-increasing distance from other ethnic and

ANDREA LEVINE

racial minorities in the United States, whereby he is closer to the Hispanic men than to the African blacks, whom he plays with only once, but whom he studiously distinguishes from African Americans. That Henry's father has come to believe that this stance will somehow protect him is clear when Henry adumbrates the list of behaviors that his parents practice to assure their own belonging in their affluent suburban neighborhood of "WASPs and Jews" (52). He chronicles their assiduous devotion to appearing as if they "believed in anything American, in impressing Americans, in making money, polishing apples in the dead of night, perfectly pressed pants, perfect credit, being perfect, shooting black people, watching our stores and offices burn down to the ground" (52–53). Like the gun that the military recruiter in *Drown* needs to support the vision of the American dream that he lives, the passage reveals the violent underside of Henry's immigrant parents' identification with an apparently benign vision of model "Americanness." Guaranteeing their own provisional acceptance requires that they adopt America's murderous racial ideologies and practices.

Henry remembers his father's characteristic relationships to the African American female customers who frequented his stores: "They fight like lovers, scarred, knowing. Their song circular and vicious. For she always comes back the next day, and so does he. It's like they are here to torture each other. He can't afford a store anywhere else but where she lives, and she has no other place to buy a good apple or a fresh loaf of bread" (186). Henry illuminates the class- and race-based imbrication of the two partners in this hateful "romance," their fury misdirected toward each other. As Lisa Lowe observes sharply about the riots in Los Angeles in the aftermath of the Rodney King verdict: "[T]he Los Angeles crisis, in which Korean Americans became the recipients of violent anger that might 'better' have been directed at white capital in other parts of the intensely spatially segregated city, illustrates precisely how a society 'structured in dominance' . . . can mask the interlocking functions of racism, patriarchy, and capitalism . . . by separating and dividing the objects of capitalist exploitation."[15] This is what has happened to Henry's father and his African American customers, of course, who have, in the face of their forced intimacy as well as of their compulsory separation from those most responsible for the oppressive conditions under which they live, learned to view each other as adversaries.

Both *Native Speaker* and *Drown* make clear, however, that these oppositional dynamics are not confined to the especially visible relationships between African Americans and Korean Americans. Both texts, in fact, portray a number of contested relationships between Asians and Latinos that circulate around questions of labor and ownership. In the final story of *Drown*, for instance, Yunior explains about his father's Puerto Rican friend: "[H]e didn't need to put a gate over his store. The local kids left him alone and instead terrorized a Pakistani family down the street. The family owned an Asian grocery store that looked like a holding cell" (189–90). Like the African Americans Lowe discusses, the Latino kids Díaz describes tend to see the Asian storeowners they torment both as external to their own community and as more economically advantaged than themselves. Toward the end of *Native Speaker*, however, Henry and his wife, Lelia, lean out their windows, watching the street: "[O]n the far corner is the all-night Korean deli; two workers, a Korean and a Hispanic, are sitting on crates and smoking cigarettes outside. . . . We listen to the earnest attempts of their talk, the bits of their stilted English" (337). The passage positions the workers in a moment of shared physical and rhetorical space, not configured by dominance or hierarchy, a moment that Henry valorizes. *Native Speaker*, then, suggests that, to the extent that Asians and Latinos position themselves as adversaries within a racist capitalist order, with only the shared possibility of profiting from their distance from the dominant racial binary (a distance that, of course, varies for each "group"), they are accepting the distortions of the capitalist imperative in the United States—and their relations with one another will be similarly distorted and politically unproductive. On the other hand, Henry first distinguishes himself in the Kwang campaign when he "mollifies a rowdy assemblage of twenty or so Peruvians who worked for Korean greengrocers" (85) and have come to Kwang's office to protest what they consider the Koreans' unfair labor practices. Eager to capture a "provocative scene" (86) of interethnic confrontation, the media is left to record the Peruvians' satisfied departure from the office, brandishing a collection of Kwang campaign materials.

It is exactly the "territorial" mode of establishing immigrant belonging, which is, the novel implies, a self-defeating version of "America," that Kwang attempts to contest in his political career. While he never collapses the historical circumstances of Asians, Latinos, and African Americans in the United States, he *does* strive to construct specific forms of personal and political alliances. Among a dedicated band of campaign workers, Kwang's favorite is a young Latino college student named Eduardo Fermin—like Yunior, a Dominican American. Their bond is a conventionally masculine one: both were once junior boxers, and Kwang loves to spar playfully with the much younger Eduardo. And, in a homosocial twist, Kwang sometimes procures sex partners for Eduardo at the Korean clubs that he and his staff frequent; at this point in the text, Kwang's prominence within the community easily affords him sexual access. This "straight" male camaraderie, however, enables an interethnic connection that would have been unimaginable for Henry's father. Eduardo works for Kwang for free, "except," Kwang says, "for what I might show him about our life, about what is possible for people like us" (311). Kwang here self-consciously enlarges what Henry depicts as the traditionally hermetic world of Korean immigrants like his parents, extending the phrase *people like us* to include Eduardo and, by implication, other Latinos.

When a bomb goes off in Kwang's campaign headquarters, Eduardo, working late, is killed; his death will begin the inexorable destruction of Kwang's political career—and, by extension, his claim to be a kind of "first citizen" (303). Revelations follow quickly from the bombing. Kwang tells Henry that he had discovered that Eduardo was betraying him, "betraying everything we were doing." Only Henry understands that Eduardo must have been working for Henry's own wealthy employers—and, therefore, at the behest of the U.S. government, which, Lee implies, is importantly invested not only in undermining Kwang's political success as a Korean American politician but also in disrupting the forms of interethnic alliance that propelled such success.

It takes a sex scandal to finish Kwang's career completely. Blind drunk one evening, in the wake of the revelations about Eduardo, Kwang crashes his car and critically injures his passenger, a sixteen-year-old Korean girl who is a waitress and sometime sex worker at a club Kwang frequents. Photographs of Kwang leaving the police station are splashed across the front pages of the New York tabloids: "They have him in the bricked alley behind the building, the shots dark and grainy. They have him walking away in half-profile, from the back, from the side, his suit jacket unfurled, suggesting flight. . . . The shots are nearly criminal" (321). In the past, Kwang's watchful staff orchestrated every camera angle for him, always turning the public view of their candidate to his advantage. Now, he has become the helpless object of the media gaze, caught in whatever position they choose.[16] Henry remarks: "[W]e pass by newsstands. He is papering their displays, their walls. . . . Will the people see just another politician in trouble, just another scandal? Will they see an American there?" (325). Lee suggests, however, with the "nearly criminal" photographs and the "indignant and righteous" (321) language of the accompanying articles, that the answer to this question is clear—that Kwang's self-created paradigm of citizenship has already cost him the masculine prerogative that would enable the public to "see an American" when they look at him. After the scandal, Henry returns to what was once the Kwangs' home and asks the real estate agent in charge of selling the house about its former residents; she tells him that they were "foreigners": "They went back to their country" (347). The failure of Kwang's effort to imagine America as "maybe even his" is complete, with the repudiation of his status as a U.S. national subject and his repositioning as external to the nation. While, in *Drown*, one may receive illicit sex from an Asian woman in a state-sanctioned context, that state sanction is violently withdrawn in *Native Speaker*, where its removal disciplines Kwang for his efforts to create multiethnic alliances and, finally, disaffiliates him from state power entirely.

In the face of Kwang's ubiquitous images after the accident, there are, strikingly, "no photos" of the girl. Not precisely misrepresented or vilified the way Kwang is, she instead remains *unrepresented*; at first, the police do not even know her name "because no one can read the ID card in her purse." Even after the language department at Columbia University comes back with a name, "no one where she works wants to talk, and everyone's English is poor." Official accounts reveal painfully little: "[T]hey know she is sixteen years old, born in Seoul. . . . [T]he police believe that she is a 'hospitality girl,' which the newspaper says is a type of Asian prostitute" (322). While they *know* her age and birthplace, Lee points out when he writes "the police believe" and "the newspaper says" that her sexuality is grounds for speculation, for interpretation. Naming and racializing her sexuality is something that they are authorized to do, in spite of the compulsory silence of their sources.

The "hospitality girl" injured in Kwang's car accident is only one of a series of voiceless Korean women in the text, as You-me Park and Gayle Wald suggest in their analysis of the figure of "Ah-ju-ma," the Korean woman who performs domestic labor in Henry's father's house after the death of his wife. Calling *Native Speaker* a text primarily concerned with "the legitimation of a male immigrant subject in the public sphere," Park and Wald write: " 'Ah-ju-ma' occupies a curious . . . mode of hyperprivatized existence in which she has

ANDREA LEVINE

no access to individualized subjectivity."[17] Even Henry's mother, to whose "smooth"-faced beauty he unfavorably compares the "pock-marked . . . thick ankle[d]" (62) Ah-ju-ma, goes largely unseen and unheard. Henry's father admitted him to his mother's hospital room immediately after her death; Henry reflects on that moment: "I don't now remember what I saw in her room, maybe I never actually looked at her, though I can still see so clearly the image of my father standing there in the hall when I came back out" (58–59). It is his father's response to his mother's death, not the figure of his mother herself, already silenced, that shapes the indelible tableau in Henry's mind.

Henry's wife, Lelia, who is white, discovers one summer that Henry doesn't actually know Ah-ju-ma's proper name; as Henry explains patiently, the title *Ah-ju-ma* is simply a "form of address . . . literally aunt, but more akin to ma'am, the customary address to an unrelated Korean woman. But in our context the title bore much less deference." Lelia is appalled at Henry's profound indifference to the woman who, in her words, "practically raised [him]" (69). She therefore determines to talk to Ah-ju-ma herself, with Henry as an interpreter, and, when Ah-ju-ma angrily refuses, telling Henry that "there is nothing for your American wife and me to talk about," Lelia attempts to join her in her domestic labors, trying to fold laundry alongside of her. Again, the woman bitterly resists Lelia's incursion into her only domain in the house, and Lelia must finally admit defeat. Lelia's futile efforts to name the woman, to encourage her to find her "voice" or to forge a personal connection with her through a moment of shared "women's work," seem to speak to the limitations of her Western feminist paradigm to redress—or even address—the multiple forms of inequity that structure the woman's life. As Park and Wald argue: "The issues raised by the main plot of the novel . . . have to be read against the backdrop of the numberless and nameless Ahjuhmas."[18] Lelia's effort to claim a more humane relationship to the woman who has been so relentlessly depersonalized by Henry's father, and even more so by Henry himself, may be fundamentally unequal to the woman's position, one determined far less by her "individual" circumstances than by her location within a series of collective, institutionalized oppressions.

Similarly, Yunior talks in the title story of *Drown* about his own mother's self-erasure: "[S]he has discovered the secret to silence: pouring cafe without a splash, walking between rooms as if gliding on a cushion of felt, crying without a sound" (94). As many critics of Latino literature and culture have discussed, this feminine submission, in conjunction with an aggressive culture of male dominance, or machismo, is, not simply a matter of transhistorical Latin American "cultural norms," but a profoundly overdetermined result of colonial violence within Latin America.[19] Lelia's horror at Henry's disclosure that he doesn't know Ah-ju-ma's name stems in part from her anxiety about its implications for their own relationship; she tells him: "It scares me. . . . I just think about you and me . . . what I am." "Don't be crazy," Henry replies (70). In a sense, Lelia *is* "being crazy" here because the concern that she articulates— that, as women, she and Ah-ju-ma could share a similarly functional status in Henry's life—elides the vast differences of race, class, and national origin that shape both their own lives and their places in Henry's estimation.

Unlike so many of the Asian and Asian American women in the text, that is, Lelia *does* have a name and a voice. The novel's first sentence, in fact, is dedicated to her power to name and to define. "The day my wife left," Henry tells us, "she gave me a list of who I was" (1). And the text's lyrical final sentence finds her calling out the names of her departing group of non-native-speaking students: "taking care of every last pitch and accent . . . calling all the difficult names of who we are" (349). Lelia's position in the text speaks to central questions about *Native Speaker*. While, in its portrait of the undoing of John Kwang, the text poses a powerful critique of the state and of the possibilities that it affords to immigrants and racial minorities to make claims on Americanness that resist hegemonic categories of racial and ethnic identity, Lee's depiction of Henry Park and his own claim to Americanness is a more equivocal one. The text chronicles, in part, Henry's relinquishing of his lifelong tendency to hide himself, to "celebrate every order of silence borne of the tongue and the heart and the mind" (171). By the end of the novel, Henry has given up his highly symbolic job as a spy, his complicity with his employers having resulted in the revelation of the "money club" that Kwang was running and the subsequent exposure and arrest of the dozens of undocumented immigrants who were among the club's participants. Instead of the betrayer of these immigrants, Henry imaginatively becomes their champion. When Henry and Lelia listen to the Korean and Hispanic workers at the all-night deli that they can see from their apartment, Henry muses: "I know I would have ridiculed them when I was young: I would cringe and grow ashamed and angry at those funny tones of my father and his workers. But now I think I would give most anything to hear my father's talk again. . . . I will listen for him forever in the streets of this city. I want to hear the rest of them, too, especially the disbelieving cries and shouts of those who were taken away" (337).

Henry's new appreciation for the speech of immigrants comes after a lifetime spent valorizing the kind of effortless, impeccable English possessed by Alice Eckels, the white girl who seemed to rule his elementary school class and whose parents Henry imagined must have spoken in the same "even, lowing rhythm of ennui and supremacy she lorded over us" (234). In many ways, then, Henry appears to have divested himself of the fear and furtiveness that have been so constitutive of his character. At the same time, however, the contested status of Henry's sexuality and its subsequent legitimation are critical to the confirmation of his legitimacy as a U.S. national subject. John Kwang himself trades on the popular conception of Asian American men as "sissies," as David Eng suggests. Reeling from the decline in his political fortunes after Eduardo's death, Kwang takes Henry to a Korean club he frequents, along with Sherrie Chin-Watt, a Chinese American staffer with whom he is having an affair. Kwang arranges for "an exceedingly pretty, exceedingly young" (306) Korean waitress to join them, presumably the same woman who is later critically injured in the passenger seat of Kwang's car. It is clear that she is intended to be Henry's willing partner. When Henry does not respond to her sexual advances, however, Kwang mocks him. "[T]he young man of integrity," he says. "Look at the clear principle, the control. He reminds me of another Asian figure in city politics we used to know and love. Where is he now? How I wish I could recall his name" (308). Kwang aligns Henry's sexual reserve and propriety with his own rectitude early in his political career, rectitude that has not yielded the dividends it ostensibly promised to pay. He suggests that, in playing the role of the "principled," disciplined Asian man, Henry is submitting to the expectations imposed by the dominant culture and intended to maintain white hegemony. Kwang, then, implies that only by asserting his masculinity—through seizing the chance to become the dominant male sexual agent, willing to exploit this young girl—can Henry refuse the politically accommodating position that Asian American men are expected to occupy. Meanwhile, when Henry does not take up the hostile homosocial challenge set forth, Kwang argues with Sherrie Chin-Watt and slaps her before she flees the room. Earlier, we have seen him scream at his silent wife; for Kwang, the subordination of Asian women functions as a last-ditch effort to demonstrate the masculine power of which he has himself been all but divested.

Although urging him to contain, rather than exercise, his sexuality, Henry's father nonetheless goads Henry just the way Kwang does: insinuating a direct link between the sexual "potency" of an Asian man and his secure claim to belonging in the United States. Henry remembers: "One of our worst nights of talk was when he suggested that the girl I was taking to the Eighth Grade Spring Dance didn't—or couldn't—find me attractive. . . . He laughed at me. You think she like your funny face? Funny eyes? You think she dream you at night?" (73). His father wants here to ensure that Henry does not see what appears to be nascent sexual opportunity as conferring other kinds of opportunity, that he understands his thoroughly compromised place in the eyes of white America: "You Korean man. So so different," he intones (74). He substitutes for the image of Henry as a sexually desirable object the specter of his own labor, which has secured Henry's residence in the "expensive area" (74) that is, he contends, the site of the eighth-grade girl's genuine interest. This effort to resituate Henry as a son, first and foremost, defined by his place in the Korean American nuclear family, also removes him from the heterosexual circuit. Ultimately, Henry's father reinscribes the popular notion of Asian American men as sexually insufficient while he positions the unavailability of white female sexuality as the sign or site of Henry's "unmanning."

Henry takes this lesson to heart, and Lee marks Henry's romance with Lelia's whiteness at several points in the text. Immediately on their first meeting, Henry comments: "I noticed she was very white, the skin of her shoulder almost blue, unbelievably pale considering where she lived." He imagines that her white boyfriend means to "make a gesture . . . let my Asian friend in the suit have a few moments with her" (9). As soon as Henry and Lelia kiss, he "ask[s] her if she has ever kissed an Asian before" (13). From the beginning, Lelia's body is valuable territory, Henry believes, meant to be unavailable to him, and her sexual desirability is always imbricated with her assured claim to American national identity. Their first intimate conversation is about Lelia's ability as a teacher of English to discern that Henry is "not a native speaker," his "perfect" accent a product of studied and "deliberate" effort (12), while she herself is "the standard-bearer" (12) of the language. Much later, Henry reflects about Stew, Lelia's "Groton, Princeton, Harvard Business School" father, that "what it was about Lelia that I desired and feared came partly through his bloodline. . . . [His] unmitigating stare of eyes and trim old body said it all over in simple, clear language: Chief Executive Officer. Do not fuck with this man" (119). Descended from this scion and guardian of WASP privilege, Lelia appears to offer Henry a kind of access to her lineage.

The totemic status of Lelia's whiteness reemerges when Henry and Lelia finally reconcile, after their marriage has been nearly sundered by the death of their young son. Henry narrates: "I kissed her again . . . and she craned so that the white skin inched up past the cover of her shirt fabric. Bone white. Purple white. I felt a heat anyway" (228). Later, Henry talks to the father of one of Lelia's students, a young Laotian boy. Once the father establishes that Henry is Korean American and that Lelia is Henry's wife, he seeks to be certain that Lelia herself is "purely" American. "No Korea!" "No Korea!" the father insists. And Henry agrees, noting: "My answer seemed to confirm something for him" (238). What Henry's marriage to a white woman appears to "confirm" for this immigrant father is, as the text suggests with his triumphant exclamations, the possibility of mobility, of securing full and legitimate citizenship.[20]

Both *Drown* and *Native Speaker*, I have suggested, posit a linkage between the process of becoming a U.S. national subject (an ideological process of interpellation, which I would distinguish from the legal process of becoming a *citizen*, although, of course, the two intersect) and the process of normative masculinization, which also entails the securing of heterosexuality, particularly in *Drown*. Both texts ultimately *critique* these operations, suggesting that one cost of the acquisition of masculine citizenship for their characters is the ability to imagine or to maintain alliances across lines of race and ethnicity, alliances that could enable the production of critical political subjectivities. The seductions of heterosexual masculinization, then, ultimately operate in the service of whiteness, as is evident in a long U.S. tradition of withholding or granting sexual agency to men on racialized grounds and offering that sexual agency as a substitution for full participation in the nation.

At the same time that *Drown* and *Native Speaker* indeed function as "critical acts" in terms of illuminating the political price of these processes for *men*, they also, in the end, tend to obscure the stories of those women of color who are so instrumental in the narrative of the male protagonist's quest for the recognition of his citizenship. Like the Filipino women in the pictures that Díaz's Yunior never sees, the silenced, invisible Korean girl in the hospital is the one who finally pays the price for John Kwang's audacious effort to renegotiate the terms of his place in the nation, while only the central white woman in *Native Speaker* is offered the opportunity to be a genuine narrative force. John Kwang's very failure to incorporate a gendered critique into his model of immigrant political subjectivity makes clear how profoundly difficult it is for "new Americans" to make claims on "Americanness" in ways that genuinely disrupt the dominant U.S. social formation. My analysis, then, begins to suggest the urgent need for both cultural productions and critical theory that work not only to examine but also consistently to challenge the imbrications between prevailing models of straight masculinity and ideologies of "Americanness" as they operate both within the United States and on the world stage.

## Notes

1. Díaz, *Drown*, 12. Page numbers for subsequent citations will be given parenthetically in the text.
2. For a discussion of the way that illusory "affective" structures—in this case *white manhood*—can work to foreclose the recognition of politically transformative alliances, see Nelson, *National Manhood*.
3. Eng, *Racial Castration*, 3.
4. Lowe, *Immigrant Acts*, 9.
5. Eng, *Racial Castration*, 111.
6. Chester, *Rag-Tags, Scum, Riff-Raff, and Commies*, 2.
7. Piedra, "Nationalizing Sissies," 370. Piedra (ibid., 375) actually works to demonstrate the potentially subversive or "rebellious" position of the figure of the sissy in the colonial dynamic, but his analysis of the gendered and eroticized dynamics of the colonial encounter nonetheless helps illuminate my less optimistic reading of the colonial politics in *Drown*.
8. My thanks to Nicholas De Genova for his insights into the reciprocal relations between the state and the family here.
9. Chester, *Rag-Tags, Scum, Riff-Raff, and Commies*, 272–74, 282.
10. Lee, *Native Speaker*, 139. Page numbers for subsequent citations will be given parenthetically in the text.
11. Lowe, *Immigrant Acts*, 6.
12. Ibid., 16.
13. Ibid., 16–17.
14. Park and Wald, "Native Daughters," 284.
15. Lowe, *Immigrant Acts*, 92–93.
16. Eng helpfully discusses the racializing—and queer—connotations for men who are on the receiving end of an objectifying gaze (see *Racial Castration*, 121–24).
17. Park and Wald, "Native Daughter," 265, 277.
18. Ibid., 278.
19. See, e.g., Burton, "Imperial-Patriarchal Unconscious," 36.
20. It is not only immigrants and men of color, of course, for whom sexual access appears to guarantee full status as a U.S. citizen. Bharati Mukherjee's short story "Loose Ends" (in *The Middleman and Other Stories*, 43–54 [New York: Grove Press, 1988]), e.g., also suggests the place of sexual domination in transforming the marginalized male subject into the subject of

ANDREA LEVINE

imperial America. In "Loose Ends," Jeb, a white Vietnam veteran, returns to the United States only to discover that the America he remembered has "gone down the rabbit hole" (48) in the wake of an influx of precisely the Asian immigrant populations against whom he believed he was fighting "to shut the back door" (48). Jeb learns that his tour in Southeast Asia has provided exemplary training for the work that he will find as a hit man for a Latino drug dealer, and he is certain that the "turbaned guy" (53) at the mall has fired Jeb's girlfriend in order to give work to newly arrived South Asian immigrants from his own family. Jeb's resentment toward the communal practices of some immigrant groups is magnified by his marginality within both the Florida town where he lives and the consumer economy that provides the only vision of salvation for his girlfriend. On the run after a botched drug hit, Jeb hitchhikes to a motel where the Indian American owners are holding a family reunion. The family's teenage daughter, showing Jeb to his room, asserts her own claim to American citizenship, informing him that she was born in "New Jersey" and not in "Bombay" (54), as he has presumed. Her rape and possible murder—Jeb has been taught by the U.S. government to leave "no traces" behind (47)—become almost foregone conclusions. Only the assertion of masculine domination over a woman of color can momentarily assure Jeb of the lost power of his whiteness in a multiethnic landscape. Straight male sexual privilege, then, can also offer disempowered white U.S. citizens an opportunity to identify with the reach of imperial America.

# 7 THE PASSION

*The Betrayals of Elián González and Wen Ho Lee*

Crystal Parikh

In April 2000, during the height of the media and political maelstrom surrounding the young Cuban boy rescued a little over four months earlier off the shores of Florida, the *Washington Post* ran a picture of Elián González hanging, arms akimbo, on a playground jungle gym, with a headline reading: "The Passion of Elian." The story's focus was on the local, religious significance that had been attributed to the plight of this "miracle boy." The image, headline, and story raised an alternate symbolics to the otherwise tiresome framing of the case in the national mainstream media as a matter of national political interests versus competing private rights. In highlighting a terrain of ethico-religious meaning, this text implicitly asked: Could this child indeed (potentially) provide some kind of collective redemption in a world fraught with postmodern identifications and loyalties? If so, whose redemption was it? Who were the Judases who betrayed this child-martyr? Did the betrayal make redemption possible?[1] With these questions in mind, this essay compares the case of Elián González with a contemporaneous case that also became figured on a national screen in terms of martyrdom, scapegoating, and betrayal, that of the Chinese American Los Alamos physicist accused of spying on the United States, Wen Ho Lee.

The questions that I want to ask of these two cases are meant to evoke some discomfort: What if Wen Ho Lee did, in fact, engage in espionage? What if we take seriously the traumas of Cuban exiles and their grievances against Castro's revolutionary government? To pose these questions in the context of minority politics and discourse is to follow Rey Chow's injunction that we accord to colonial and minority agents subjectivities as complex and contradictory as those we are willing to grant to white, Western subjects.[2] We need to be willing to forsake the victim-oppressor binary in order to chart the multiplicities of domination, desire, and agency. An ethically committed critique must, instead, rethink the framework of rightist and leftist politics. Such a critique must be willing to recognize that diaspora can constitute an "other" to the nation-state, an other whose desires the nation cannot resolve into its own narrative demands.³ The radical alterity of this otherness can produce loyalties and desires that must appear treasonous from inside the nation.

This then leaves us in a space that is fraught, where neither Right nor Left can claim a priori the higher or purer moral ground and betrayals loom in all directions. This is precisely the unstable and uncomfortable terrain from which new identifications and the possibility for ethico-political action emerge. This essay encompasses a twofold goal: (1) a disturbance of the categories (Right and Left, minority and dominant, domestic and diaspora) through which the González and Lee cases have been made intelligible to us and (2) a critique of the loyalties that drive the politics of racial representation, to the exclusion of desire and, perhaps, also *ethico*-political action. If, as Chow explains, "idealism is the kind of collective sentiment that demands the sacrifice of [observation of what is exploitative, coercive or manipulative in so-called 'oppositional' discourse]," ethico-political action involves "risk-taking" that puts into practice "a supplementing imperative—to follow, to supplement idealism doggedly with non-benevolent readings, in all the dangers that supplementarity entails."⁴ Thus, this is admittedly dangerous ground, no matter how cautiously or lightly one treads, because it takes to task the most impassioned forms of minority discourse, ones grounded in the civil rights of the citizen-subject. Yet it is ground that we must tread if we are to grapple with the discursive limits of minority formation and the ongoing possibility of radical critique that seeks to "do justice" to the other.

Understanding the passions that were aroused and the threat of betrayal that lurked in each of these highly sensationalized cases strikes me as central to questions of national and racial identification. *The passion* and *the betrayal* reference the irrational or the arational, desire and its fervent attachments, whose working is unpredictable and contingent and, therefore, difficult to account and adjudicate for. *The passion*, in particular, invokes the suffering, sacrifice, and redemption of Christ, made possible, paradoxically, through the betrayal of Judas. In the more concrete terms of these two cases, *the passion* suggests to me the type of intellectual and emotional commitment demanded by our political faiths. As I explain at length below, in the cases of Wen Ho Lee and Elián González, this means that commitment to minority politics and to leftist politics—which, I hope to show, have, in the past, mistakenly and too easily been conflated—can demand a closing off or shutting down of avenues of interrogation, avenues that desire, namely, diasporic desire, insists on breaking out into the open.

In order to trace the function of passion and betrayal in national and racial formation, I begin by arguing that the sensationalized visibility of these two cases was due to the fact that they secured a narrative of national belonging and formation under the "New World Order" of globalization and transnationalism. Yet, to the extent that diasporic desires on the part of "national others" threatened the self-image of the national subject, the narrative production in mainstream media and popular culture of Lee and González circulated around the possibility of betrayal. I then situate the communities involved in each case, Cuban Americans and Asian Americans, within the black-white poles that structure U.S. minority discourse and formation.[5] The model minority image, especially its construction against the cold war specter of communism, is particularly helpful in understanding the way in which cross-racial alliances were, or were not, forged in each instance. The third and fourth sections of this essay describe in detail the circuits of identification, desire, and betrayal at play in the production of the national subject and the disciplining of desire in each case. The discussion that follows, especially with respect to my comments on the economic privileges and political activities of each of these groups, is, thus, necessarily painted in the broad strokes of popular perception and representation rather than the specificity of lived experience.

What was it about these two cases that drew such heightened political and media attention to them? After all, neither the separation of families through immigration nor the racial profiling of Asians was an especially new or unique occurrence. The significance of the Lee and González cases resides instead, I argue, in the narrative of the nationalist subject that they bolstered. That is to say, each of these cases fashioned a narrative mode for the American subject by which to cope with the traumas of national deterritorialization and postmodern *dis*identification at the end of the twentieth century. As my discussion below will demonstrate, in each case the popular narratives that emerged attempted to reimagine America, to stabilize and smooth over the ruptures in national self-image wrought by the onset of transnationalism and global capitalism. For the United States, the nation-state most economically, politically, and militarily responsible for ushering in the New World Order, the integrity of such a developmental narrative was absolutely central to its self-image. In other words, the dominant narratives, and their staging of crises and resolutions, assured the national subject that globalization was, in fact, an "Americanization" that could subsume or obliterate otherness, and the desires of the other, into the here and now of an idealized America.

As narratives, both cases vividly engaged the national imagination with elements of sentimentality, intrigue, bombast, hubris, and repentance. The protagonists here were two very different people. Wen Ho Lee, a Taiwanese-born physicist, was fired on 8 March 1999 from his position at Los Alamos National Laboratories (LANL) for security breaches, after having been investigated for possibly having handed over secrets on U.S. nuclear technology and capability to the People's Republic of China (PRC). The Cox Committee report, the product of the House Select Committee investigation, found evidence of substantial advances in the PRC's nuclear sciences, which it linked to Chinese espionage and significant breaches of security during the previous four presidential administrations. At stake in Lee's case was the whereabouts of the "Legacy Files," the archival history of nuclear warhead development and testing that had, reportedly, been leaked to the PRC.

Lee was arrested on 10 December 1999 and, in a fifty-nine-count indictment, charged with compromising U.S. security, under the terms of the federal Espionage Act and the Atomic Energy Act. Although the investigation of Lee focused on him as a potential spy, he was not charged with passing nuclear secrets, but the indictment indicated that the security breaches had been committed in order to "secure an advantage to a foreign nation." He was denied bail after the prosecution argued that, if released, Lee posed a formidable threat to national security because he could surreptitiously signal to another PRC agent the whereabouts of the missing tapes or other directives regarding them. After Lee spent eight months in solitary confinement, an expert witness for the defense argued in a second bail hearing that the prosecution had overstated the secrecy and significance of the missing files. Lee was subsequently released on bail, under the conditions of house incarceration, at the beginning of September 2000. Shortly thereafter, Lee and the prosecution reached a plea bargain agreement. Lee pled guilty to only one of the charges, was sentenced to time already served, made himself available for questioning, and agreed to drop any counter-charges that he was being prosecuted because of his Chinese ethnicity.

Only two weeks prior to Lee's arrest, fishermen had found Elián González clinging to an inner tube three miles off the coast of Fort Lauderdale, Florida, on Thanksgiving Day, 25 November 1999. The five-year-old child had left Cuba in a small aluminum boat carrying fourteen people, including his mother, Elizabeth Brotons, and her boyfriend, Lázaro Munero. Brotons had left Cuba for the United States with Munero and her son, unbeknownst to Juan Miguel González, Elián's father. Elián was one of only three passengers who survived after the boat began taking on water and broke apart. Both Brotons and Munero drowned, and their bodies were never recovered. The child was placed in the care of a great-uncle, Lázaro González, and a cousin, Marisleysis González, both relatives of the child's father, living in the Little Havana section of Miami.

In January 2000, the Immigration and Naturalization Service ruled that Elián should be returned to Cuba, but the child's U.S. relatives sued the Justice Department to keep him in the United States and asked a Florida court to grant them custody. Mass protests in support of the Miami family on the part of Cuban Americans living in south Florida accompanied the ensuing custody struggle for Elián. In late March of that year, the Justice Department asked Lázaro González to sign a pledge to surrender the child if he lost the court battle; he refused the request. Federal agents seized Elián from Lázaro González's home on 22 April in a widely publicized armed raid and returned the child to his father, who had arrived from Cuba to reclaim his son. In May, a federal appeals court conceded the right of Elián's father to speak for the child and, ultimately, the right of custody over him. Elián returned with Juan González in June 2000 to Cuba, where he has since remained, for the most part, out of the media spotlight.

The release of Lee and the return of González to his Cuban father may have been the best, or, as some legal experts who saw both cases as cut-and-dried all along contended, the only solutions available under the formal and reductive categories of criminal law and immigration law, respectively. In fact, for many Americans, in both the Wen Ho Lee and the Elián González cases, justice was eventually served, if unfortunately deferred for a spell. In placing these two narratives in conversation with one another, I am not necessarily arguing that they should have been resolved differently. Indeed, in describing them as narratives and approaching them from the perspective of a literary critic, I would like us, instead, to return to the scenes of crisis in order to defer these endings so that we might consider alternative ways, as the *Washington Post* article did, of staging the crises themselves. The popular narrativization of these two cases reduced the complexities of desire to the binaristic categories of innocence and guilt, national security and individual freedom, politics and family. In generating desires that move across the boundaries of these categories, the other of the nation-state undermined our sense of the national self. The narrative representations of these cases accordingly enacted an epistemic violence that marked the nation's inability to account for the other and its desires. To return to and restage the crises, then, affords the possibility for ethically committed critiques and agency that take these desires seriously.

Lee and González functioned as symbols under the New World Order, but they also threatened to reveal its fissures. As national others in these narratives, they attracted most attention precisely when their suffering and redemption were most visible. Like the paradigmatic figure of Christ, whose Passion constituted a renunciation of all individual desires except for the singular mission of sacrifice for the collective good of humanity, the others of these narratives provided sacrificial examples of model Americanness under the New World Order. As Judith Butler writes in a different context:

> This reference to the figure of Christ becomes embodied, but does so only to be sacrificed or returned to the unchangeable world from which it came. As a model for the sacred life, Christ is understood as an embodiment which is continually in the mode of giving thanks. In its desire and in its work, this embodied consciousness seeks to give thanks for its own life, capacities, faculties, abilities. These are given to it; its life is experienced as a gift; and it lives out its life in the mode of gratefulness.[6]

In contrast, the moments of Judas-like betrayal in each case, which I discuss at length below, represented failures in the functioning of the model minority construct and the idealized image of the nation that it upholds. Public attention wavered at these points because they marked the failure of the totalizing nationalist fantasy, threateningly suggesting that globalization is, indeed, *not* synonymous with Americanization.

In a world where the specter of communism has been killed off, the fullness of the American promise—that one can somehow have both the traditional values of hierarchy secured by the family romance and the idealized equities of democratic modernism—is affirmed and managed by the private-public split. The familial and the national not only served as analogies for one another but also intervened and disrupted one another, and, when they did, they threatened profound failures of recognition between the self and its others. Indeed, they threatened a dissolution of the self. In other words, the triumph of the traditional in the González case required that the conflicts of the domestic and the global, or the national and the diasporic, be completely elided. This was possible because, as the Lee case demonstrated, we (are to) believe that we now live in a globalized world *without borders and without history*. The narrativization of the Wen Ho Lee and Elián González cases functioned to cover over diasporic desire, that is, a desire that the American dream could not fulfill. In so doing, the nation simultaneously constructed a progressive historical narrative about the relation between the modernity of the nation-state and the postmodernity of transnational capitalism.

By placing the United States at the center of this historical narrative, whereby the American ideal comes to encompass, through cultural and economic penetration, every corner of the globe, the narrative defused the threats that borderlessness, fragmentation, and fluidity—all hallmarks of postmodernity—posed to a unified national image. There is no space in this American imaginary for diasporic desire, rooted in lack and otherness; such desire, and its complex passions, cannot be countenanced and must be cleared away. Chinese Americans and Cuban Americans emerged, not as unruly, productive agents of new terrains for imagining self and other, but as national objects, gratefully "liberated" or disciplined into model Americanness. The readings that I forward below thus attempt to tease out the presence of diasporic desire in order to elucidate the temporal and spatial unevenness of social and cultural existence under the New World Order.

Taken together, the national discord surrounding González and Lee revealed the anxieties over racial, ethnic, and diasporic differences that plague the American subject. Both these instances, especially when examined through the theme and tropes of betrayal and treason, offer insight into the meaning of belonging and exclusion not only for minorities but also for a more generic sense of the nation. The political strategies adopted by activists and communities in each of these cases, and the public responses that they elicited, differed from one another in many ways. Yet, insofar as both cases presented the nation with revivals of the specter of communism in a post–cold war or New World Order, the two groups shared the same ground in the complex terrain of racial and national formation at the beginning of the twenty-first century.[7]

I want to begin this section, then, with the fairly obvious claim that both

CRYSTAL PARIKH

Chinese American and Cuban American communities, separately, constitute model minorities. The widely familiar construct of the model minority has usually been ascribed to those of Asian descent within the United States, but it is important to the meaning of Cuban American identity as well. The pages of an array of publications in the United States during the second half of the twentieth century attest that the Cuban exiles, who fled their island nation after Fidel Castro's defeat of the Batista government in 1959 and the installation of a socialist political order there, have been welcomed into this nation as paragons of the economic, political, religious, and familial values that the nation attributes to itself.[8] As such, the stories of the remarkable economic and social rise of Cubans in the United States have long captivated politicians, journalists, and public commentators.[9] Cuban Americans, like Asian Americans, are easily held out to other minority groups, namely, African Americans and *other* Latino/as (especially those of Mexican or Puerto Rican descent), as examples that the nation can and does live up to its promise of economic, social, and political fulfillment. David Palumbo-Liu's description of the function of the Asian American model minority in the cold war context—"Asian Americans serve both to prove the rightness of American democracy as a *worldwide* model and to remind Americans of the traditional values it had cast aside in its rush to modernization"—thus seems equally applicable to the plight of Cuban Americans.[10] Asian and Cuban Americans serve as models both domestically, to Anglos and to other people of color, and internationally, as the idealized ethos of democratic capitalism and American exceptionalism.[11]

This construction of Cuban American model minoritarianism against the specter of communism is in place not only for right-wing politics. Leftists project ideological value onto the "Miami Mafia" as well. Consider, for example, a particularly acerbic, if not uncharacteristic, attack on Miami's Cuban exile population:

> The monopoly on information concerning Cuba, which up until now has largely consisted of prime pickings from the ideological refuse heap of information conjured by the Miami exile community and supported by the United Stated [*sic*] government—always eager to reinvest in the Cold War—is bent on the continual demonization of Fidel Castro and the hellification of that prickly anticapitalist state so close to our sovereign shore. The anti-Castro cultists seek their salvation in the capitalist market doctrine and their undiminished and militant faith in the frictionless character of its market laws. Such a position removes the inconvenience of having to

undress such laws so as to reveal their inner workings and to evaluate the consequences of such laws in the lives of millions of poor and suffering children.[12]

Leftist support of Cuba's revolutionary government thus also needs *the same
image* of the Cuban American, as fanatically anti-Castro and staunch supporters
of U.S. capitalism, Christianity, and traditional family and social values, against
which it can define itself.[13]

There are, however, also striking differences between Cuban American
model minoritarianism and Asian American model minoritarianism that became especially prominent in the Elián González case. The most important, I
believe, is that, because of their numbers, concentration, and location in the
electorally key state of Florida, Cuban Americans have managed, unlike Asian
Americans, to amass considerable and, some argue, disproportionate political
strength on the national stage. The visibility and clout of Cuban Americans on
the political scene is in dramatic contrast to the position of Asian Americans.[14]
For the latter, an important aspect of their model minority status has been
precisely their economic success combined with a political *invisibility*, and this
is, perhaps, nowhere better illustrated than in the case of the Lee family itself.
Lee's daughter, Alberta, who became an outspoken advocate for her father's
release, described Lee as "clueless" about American law and government, despite being involved in some of its most highly classified matters of national
security. Alberta Lee herself had, prior to her father's arrest, distanced herself
from Asian American studies and political activities as an undergraduate at the
University of California, Los Angeles, because, she stated, "I thought it was
whining."[15]

In the early months of the year 2000, during the midst of both cases, few
writers compared the two communities' politics of representation. Among
those who did, like the legal and political commentators Phil Nash and Albert
Yee, there was a decided sense that the Cuban American community had been
much more successful at garnering support for its cause than Asian Americans
had.[16] While Lee wasted away in solitary confinement, Elián had become a
diminutive star. In retrospect, then, each case was poised for a dramatic "reversal of fortune." At the beginning of the year, it seemed quite likely that Cuban
Americans would succeed in their protests to retain Elián in the United States
and that the Justice Department would successfully try and convict Wen Ho
Lee. Of course, as it turned out, neither of these conclusions was foregone.
Thus, the raid on Elián's Miami family's home, the forcible removal of the child

CRYSTAL PARIKH

from the care of his great-uncle and cousin, and the child's return to his father stand in stark contrast to the dismissal of the majority of charges, and all the serious ones, against Lee, an unprecedented apology from the judge in the case, and Lee's release from prison.

In part, the representation of race and ethnicity was responsible for these dramatic shifts, especially in public perception. In the case of Wen Ho Lee, as articulated first by Asian American activists but eventually, if slowly and at some times reluctantly, by the news and popular media, the question of martyrdom and betrayal came to be seen as straightforward. Lee became figured as a scapegoat, a citizen profoundly betrayed by the state, through a violation of one of the most sacred principles of the nation, abstract equality before the law and the right to a fair trial. The federal government—in the figures of the FBI, the Department of Energy, and the Justice Department—seemed clearly to have violated Lee's rights. Even if the mainstream media were slow to adopt this point of view, they did so ultimately—most famously in the *New York Times* mea culpa of sorts after the Justice Department and Lee struck a plea bargain agreement in September 2000.[17] That this particular narrative—that Lee was a scapegoat—could become so prevalent was due to the history of minority discourse and its successful rereading of racial injustice in the past. Invoking what has broadly come to be known as *racial profiling*, this narrative produced an analogy that sought to unify incidents as disparate as Japanese American internment during World War II, "driving while black," and, in Lee's termination, "downloading while Asian."[18]

The charges of racial profiling made against the federal government gained strength when the former head of counterintelligence at LANL publicly announced that there was no evidence that Lee had passed along atomic secrets to the PRC and concluded that Lee had been singled out because of his ethnicity.[19] Subsequent testimony during the trial by expert witnesses suggested that the importance and level of secrecy of the files that Lee had been accused of mishandling had been overstated. This further weakened the claims of the FBI and Energy Department enough that Judge James Parker ordered the government to produce evidence of ethnic profiling, including a classified report of computer security violations at LANL. A survey by the Committee of 100 and the Anti-Defamation League concluded that a substantial number, one out of every four, Americans held strong anti-Chinese attitudes, further affirming for many Asian Americans that Lee had been a victim of pervasive racist sentiment in the United States.[20] Thus, *racial profiling* provided a narrative mode for cross-racial alliances between Asian Americans and other people of color, especially African Americans, in the Lee case.

When cross-racial comparisons were made over the course of the Elián case, it was also primarily to black Americans. But these comparisons drew on the racial and ethnic *tensions* between African Americans and Cuban Americans in Miami and the differing impact of U.S. immigration policy on Cubans and Haitians (the other primary group of asylum seekers in Florida). That is to say, whereas the activists involved in the Lee case allied themselves with other communities of color by embracing the dominant terms of minority discourse, the discursive history of racial hierarchy and model minoritarianism in Miami made such alliances virtually impossible.[21]

Both the Lee and the González cases were staged against the black/white poles of America's racial terrain. Both were haunted by the specter of communism and its construction of the model American minority subject. Yet the strategies of maneuver in each instance articulated racial, ethnic, and national belonging to strikingly different effects, calling attention to the question of ambivalence that characterizes betrayal, an ambivalence that rests, here, on the contradictions of national, racial, and ethnic belonging. The following two sections, then, examine the circuits of identification, betrayal, and desire at work in the narrative modes of each case.

Much consternation was directed at the use of Elián as a "political football." Commentators expressed concern that both the Cuban American exile community and elected officials had delivered the child into a symbolic realm at the expense of the "real" considerations of his developmental needs and familial attachments. In contrast, I am arguing that the narrative production of Elián González, on the part of both liberals and conservatives, took place in the realm of the imaginary. Although each side argued for different outcomes, both vied for a narrative that fully subsumed and assimilated the other, without any stain of excess or desire left over. "Having Elian" was effectively a disciplining that at once protected and masked the *dis*order of national existence under a globalized and multiculturalist New World Order. Ultimately, it anchored a developmental narrative of global relations that swept away the remnants and memory of the cold war and, with it, the necessary objects of Cuban exile passion.

For Cuban Americans, then, the narrative of Elián was a tragedy, a grave betrayal of democratic rights. The movement to posit Elián as a savior or redeemer of the Cuban people laid bare the desire for the "arrival" of an imagined Cuba that organizes Cuban diasporic nationalism, an arrival that Castro's rule seems to perpetually render impossible.[22] This aspect of the Cuban American response to domestic and international politics has been widely reported on in the American media. Cuban Americans' hard-line leadership has long labeled as sellouts those (Cubans and non-Cubans alike) who hold out the possibility of any engagement with or appeasement of Castro. This particular discursive trajectory stretches back to the first arrivals of political exiles from the island—key political leaders in Batista's regime and economic elites who fled the Revolution and the subsequent nationalization of property by the revolutionary government. It has found an organizational face in institutions such as the Cuban American National Foundation, established in the early 1980s as part of the Reagan administration's cold war strategies. As Jesús Arboleya explains:

> The Cuban American National Foundation was never representative of the entire community, even though it tries to present itself as such. What it does reflect is the degree of domination the ultraright sector of Cuban American businessmen has managed to impose on the rest of the community. That control is based on the predominantly conservative ideology of Cuban émigrés and on the marginal benefits that the new counterrevolutionary upsurge has brought to a part of the community. That control has also been exercised through the application of all kinds of coercive measures against those who have dared to defy it.[23]

In addition to the Cuban American National Foundation, the politics and exploits of Jorge Mas Canosa, the longtime leader of exile activists, and paramilitary groups who were held responsible for bombings and other acts of intimidation (including a role in the scandal of the Watergate burglary during Richard Nixon's reelection campaign) have all been explained as protests against "Castro appeasers."[24] Thus, while Cuban Americans served a key function in cold war politics, anchored in good part by the community's embodiment of an American imaginary, the group's position within the United States was simultaneously shot through with ambivalence. As Agustin Tamargo wrote in 1989, during the Reagan-Bush administration, of the Cuban "sufferers in exile" who refuse assimilation: "Some [Cuban Americans] can exchange what is their own for something borrowed, others cannot. Some can frivolously enjoy the freedom and prosperity they did not produce themselves. Others believe this enjoyment, as it is not a product of the Cuban people, is a subtle form of betrayal."[25]

Perhaps the most vivid illustration of this political mode in the Elián González case can be located in the anxieties about Cuban "spies" whom many protestors believed had infiltrated their ranks.[26] Mainstream journalists suggested that, in branding as spies those who wished to advocate for Elián's return and declaring that " 'Elian's street' is sacred ground," where such opinions were unwelcome, Cuban protestors exhibited a "one-sided" notion of free speech.[27] While many observers believed that a younger generation of U.S.-born Cuban Americans had become distanced from these forms of exile politics, the Elián case saw an upsurge of political and personal interest among Cuban Americans that crossed generational, gender, racial, and class lines.[28] Figured as the child-savior—in some versions he was compared to Jesus, in others to Moses—Elián González embodied the hope and desire of Cuban exiles for a restoration to and with an imagined Cuba.[29]

Since Elián himself had lost his mother—a loss that was easily laid at the feet of Castro's repressive regime as well—the child's own lack, recent, raw, and nakedly visible, materialized the passionate desires of Cuban emigrants. The understanding of Elián as savior and as symbol, rather than as a "real" child, was further overdetermined by the exile activists' arguments that Castro's regime had effectively vitiated the familial rights due to any child, such that Juan González's paternal claims to Elián were farcical.[30] Consequently, the demand to retain Elián in the United States was a matter of "stopping up" losses at two levels. For the Cuban exile subject, Elián as savior held out the promise of spatial and temporal restoration of an imagined Cuba, and this restoration would also symmetrically save Elián from his own loss, recuperating him to wholeness by supplying him with a "mother Cuba." As one commentator wrote of the child: "Elián represents the salvation of a people, the slandered and unseen exile, the homeland in chains, and in the purest sense, our condition as human beings who find ourselves in another's land."[31]

Thus, the betrayal of Elián, the symbolic body of Cuban diasporic desire, signified a betrayal by the American democratic state of the entire Cuban community. The United States, as harbinger of democracy, failed to make good on its promise of rights and freedom. The Cuban American community's traumatic sense of betrayal at Elián's return rested in its perception that the American federal government, which had been previously pictured as a kindly Uncle Sam, had collaborated with the Castro government and, subsequently, extended the reach of Castro's authority. Thus, when Cuban exiles later compared the loss of Elián to the terrorist attacks of 11 September 2001, as some did, the language of catastrophe was hardly far-fetched.[32] The trauma for the Cuban community was on the level of a castration. It revealed the impossibility of its imagined self; its phallicity as the "true Cuba" had been uncloaked as a fiction.[33]

What remains underarticulated in the narrative logic of this version of the Elián case is that Elián himself had turned traitor. In other words, Elián's transformation from savior to a desiring other has remained, for the most part, undiscussed by both Cuban American leadership and mainstream American observers. The child's father, Juan González, was consistently portrayed as a handmaiden to Castro.[34] For this reason, the child, who in his reunion was happy, smiling, and affectionate with his father, became a "deserter" of Cuban Americans, gone over to the other side. His happy return to his "home" thus played an important ideological function for politically committed leftist scholars and activists, who have long been unable to tolerate much, if any, criticism of the revolutionary government. Leftists have long been enamored with the "New Man" ideal of the Revolution, identified with Castro and, perhaps to an even greater extent, with the late Ernesto "Che" Guevara. As Irving Horowitz suggests:

> To this day, Castro esteems the purity of self-sacrifice, and almost (but not quite) to the point of the Christian notion of sainthood. The party cadre may not always be sanctified, since sometimes they are called upon to engage in violent acts. But in their devotion to party, state, and nation, the Communist Party member is the apotheosis of what the Cuban society as a whole was to become under socialism. Cuba was to be the showpiece for the hemisphere and ultimately for all of the developing world. Indeed, many claims to leadership in the Third World came to rest on this quite special concept of moral man.[35]

While Horowitz's own commentary, in the González case and elsewhere, aligns itself with hard-line anti-Castro invective, his characterization of leftists and Cuban Communists does offer a helpful sense of the ideological mirroring between the Left and the Right in Cuban nationalist discourse. The desire embodied in this leftist ideal requires an impassioned fervor not dissimilar in intensity and structure to the zeal of Cuban diasporic nationalism.[36]

Elián's return marked a triumph for both Communist Cuba and sympathetic leftists. In the David and Goliath story of revolutionary Cuba and its tenacity against international hostilities, spearheaded by U.S. foreign policy, the restoration of Elián to the island provided a key victory for the Castro government.[37] Mass emigrations during the past three decades, including the Freedom Flights of 1965–73, the Mariel Boatlift of 1980, and the *balseros* crisis in the summer of 1994 (when a record number of Cuban "rafters" sought to flee the economic fallout in Cuba of the collapse of the Soviet Union) had proved an embarrassment to the revolutionary government. The jubilant return of Elián, as well as Juan González's complete lack of interest in defecting to the United States, signaled the continuing vitality of the dream of a socialist democracy. But, as Slavoj Žižek points out, this type of fantasy on the Left entails an idealization of "the People" that parallels the ideological fantasies of the Right: "[T]hose who work against [the Party's] rule are automatically excluded from the People; they became the 'enemies of the People.' . . . [T]he People always support the Party because any member of the People who opposes Party rule automatically excludes himself from the People."[38] *The People* thus serves the leftist as a fetish, a mode to sanctify a fantasy of an idealized other, pure, complete, and positive, the loss of which would enact a dissolution of the self.[39]

However, the case of Elián González was meaningful not just for Cuban nationalisms—whether anti- or pro-Castro—and their identification with an idealized Cuba. I believe that possibly its most long-term, resonant, and subtle significance might very well have been for the self-image of the United States and the ideological ruptures of that self-image that it threatened. The Elián case represented an attempt to restore an imagined Cuba "here" rather than "there." Thus, at the same time, it obviated the American fantasy, which, ironically, is at once the Cuban dream and the dream of capitalist "freedom." The "betrayal of Elián" threatened to uncover the fiction of unified national formation, for *both* U.S. and Cuban nationalisms. But equally important for this analysis is that the betrayal of Elián González worked through the *antagonistic* exchanges of the two nationalisms, consequently laying bare a certain *intolerability* between these competing claims. The security of American self-image, the ideal of the American dream, necessitated the disciplining of Cuban nationalism. For this reason, the state could justify its own dealings with its avowed cold war foe at the expense of Cuban American demands even though those demands seemed to accord more fully with the policy and political positions repeatedly adopted by the United States during the cold war.

The alignment of sympathies in the Elián González case was rooted in the Cuban American model minority status, which rests on the double, and what, in the end, we can see as the contradictory, qualities that Palumbo-Liu describes: the domestic versus the international *and* the traditional versus the modernist. Cubans were model minorities because of the fact that they were exiles, because they held Castro's Cuba in contempt and found salvation in the United States *and* because of an ethic of hard work, God, and the family. As a model minority, the Cuban exile reflected back to the normative America its own idealized construction, its own impossible desire that it had resolved through the model minority. The model minority was, therefore, also a kind of fetish by which the United States convinced itself that the Cuban was fully American and that neither the Cuban American nor America itself suffered any kind of lack. On the other hand, and at the same time, the model minority was a diasporic group of exiles always looking to a return, for whom American democratic capitalism was (only) a proxy for Cuban democratic capitalism.[40] In other words, as Palumbo-Liu has made clear, not only is model minority status founded on these contradictions but it also evokes a strong ambivalence on the part of the nation in response to them.

If the Cuban exiles and their Republican supporters saw Elián's residency in the United States as a triumph of modern democracy—best demonstrated in Senator Connie Mack's introduction of a bill to grant Elián citizenship—they ran up against the other premise of model Americanness, that the private sphere of the family is off-limits to the state, except to protect its integrity and sanctity. There was no way to predict beforehand that, in this showdown, the traditional would trump the modernist, the rights of the family would subsume those of the individual. But central to this reversal of fortune was the national desire on the part of Americans for Cubans to "give up the ghost," as it were, to kill off not only the specter of communism but that of Cuba itself, and, thus, ultimately, of diasporic desire. The cold war narrative of national formation needed the Cuban to function as a model minority, to play the part of the displaced exile raging against the ills of Communist totalitarianism. However, under the New World Order, the Cuban American—the exile—proved disruptive to the reimagining of the national self under globalization.

David Leiwei Li explains that the model minority is an "abjection" by the national body politic, a "bodily scheme" and a "border-setting mechanism" whereby *proximity* to the center marks the minority as the *abject*, that which is not radically alien enough to be entirely excluded but is, nevertheless, marked by difference. The model minority therefore "must be kept at a respectable distance."[41] The disciplining of the Cuban American evidenced the nation's horror at what Žižek describes as the "intrusive *over*proximity" of the beloved other. A "gap" between the subject and the other, who, the subject believes, holds onto the "fantasmatic kernel of the subject's being," is necessary for the subject's imaginary and symbolic identifications.[42] Žižek describes the movement between longing for the other, on the one hand, and "feeling estranged and repelled by her proximity," on the other, as, consequently, "constitutive of human desire," such that "the true enigma is rather how a 'normal' subject succeeds in covering it up and negotiating a fragile balance between the sublime image of the beloved and her real presence."[43] Certainly the containment of Cuban American passion offered a case study in just such a process.

Many outsiders trivialized the Cuban community's preoccupation with Castro and Communist Cuba as an outdated preoccupation on the part of an exile community, what one writer described as the "Cold Spat" between "Cuba and Cuba," two "palmy, balmy banana republics" that trafficked in "active discontent."[44] From this perspective, the Cuban community was, finally, called to account, forced to forgo its "banana republic" political modes and live within the laws of the nation. As a result, Anglo-Americans and black Americans found Cubans' ties to the United States insufficient and lacking, as was demonstrated in the opinions of *black and white* non-Latinos, who strongly favored González's return to Cuba, wishes that were widely disparate from those of the majority of Cuban Americans.[45] In fact, as polls demonstrated, as a group, black Americans favored even more strongly than whites the child's return and objected more strongly to the rhetoric used by Miami-Dade County Mayor Alex Penelas suggesting that he would refuse to uphold the law if the federal government attempted to remove Elián forcibly.[46] There would be little forging of cross-ethnic alliances in this case because the diasporic desire that it unleashed overdetermined the local economic and political hierarchies already in place in south Florida. Americans, both black and white, found this intolerable. As an editor at the *Miami Herald* observed: "Every single argument about why Elian should stay begins and ends with Fidel Castro. . . . There is no sympathy and not much empathy for that position."[47]

It seems telling, then, that, in the aftermath of the decision to return Elián, the impact of the case on the Cuban American community was described in terms of the group's tarnished *image*: "The Elian Gonzalez custody struggle united and invigorated anti-Castro Cuban exiles in Miami, but their campaign to keep the boy in this country hurt their image and may have helped those who favor easing the U.S. economic embargo on Cuba."[48] In particular, the "anti-patriotic actions" of Cuban protestors were objects of negative attention. José Cárdenas, the current head of the Cuban American National Foundation, put it even more bluntly when he explained, "I think that the American people sort of began to resent it being forced into their living rooms every night. . . . They just wanted all those shouting people out of their living room."[49] The impassioned demands of Cuban American protestors that Cárdenas describes reflected, I suggest, not just a defective image *of* Cuban Americans *to* non-Latinos in the United States. Rather, because of the fetishistic role performed by the Cuban American model minority, what the American subject wanted banished most of all was this gaping confrontation with alienation and loss, a seemingly uncontainable diasporic desire that betrayed the American dream.

Critics thus derided Cuban Americans for being unable to build alliances with other minority racial and ethnic groups in their protests over Elián's plight. In Lee's case, such alliances proved crucial to the significant reversal of fortune, but they depended, as I argue here, on a domestically contained discourse of civil rights against charges of diasporic and national difference. Such alliances probably could never have occurred in the Cuban situation because the passions of the Cuban American protest threatened to break out of the national frame of minority discourse. In both cases, the Republican Party seemed to come out the loser, as its support of Cuban exile politics and Asian baiting eventually fell flat before a larger American public. But an ideological critique of the Wen Ho Lee case—and the mode by which model Americanness was secured there—presses us to consider the ethico-political implications of these conclusions.

The protest on the part of Lee's advocates was, it seems to me, *against the possibility of diaspora*: that one might have an intimate and enduring desire *for some thing and some where other than the self-presence, the here and now, that the nation demands*. Racial and ethnic difference could never have been inserted to the advantage of the Cuban exile community as a civil rights concern, precisely because Cuban Americans did not just stoke and keep alive the disruptive desire of diasporic longing but paraded it on the streets and broadcast it to the entire country. It was a desire, rooted in the traumas and life of exile, that the nation could not countenance and that the state had to discipline at the risk of betraying the nation's own claim to democratic exceptionalism. In contrast, Lee's advocates seemed to act on the principle that one rouses oneself to political activism *only* in order to dispel the charge of diasporic desire and prove one's loyalty to the nation. The *content* of desire, then, ultimately matters much less to understanding either case than does the *structure* of belonging, belonging that excludes altogether the possibility that the national other has desires that do not reflect the nation's image back to itself but are aimed at some other time and place.

As numerous observers were quick to point out, it made little sense that Lee, a Taiwanese-born Chinese immigrant, would spy for the PRC, especially out of any ideological commitment. This explains the recourse to the neo-Confucianism underlying the federal government's perspective in "Operation Kindred Spirit," as the investigation into Lee's "Chinese connection" was named. That is, the government argued that, rather than depending on any loyalty to the Communist state, the PRC regularly played on a more deeply rooted sense of "Chineseness" to recruit overseas Chinese as intelligence agents, an appeal that, according to federal agents, might have found its mark in Lee. The FBI saw the PRC's hospitable treatment of Lee and his wife on their visits to China as "standard PRC intelligence tradecraft" to "encourage Chinese living abroad to visit ancestral villages and family members as a way of trying to dilute loyalty and encouraging solidarity with the authorities in Beijing."[50]

The state's case resorted to overtly Orientalist stereotypes where the homeland exerts a mystical hold over its diasporic subjects and overrides the professed loyalties of U.S. citizenship. While I do not wish to credit such reductive and essentializing constructions of Asian difference, I also do not want to dismiss the complex and competing forms of the subject's desires. My discussion therefore asks about how the *possibility* of diasporic desire, in this case for Chineseness, might disrupt minority discourse and politics in the United States. In so doing, I am not positing an inherent form of true Chineseness. Rather, I take it as a *structure* of belonging or feeling that cannot be reconciled to the demands of loyalty made by the United States. As a "structure of feeling," diasporic belonging offers a mechanism by which the subject makes meaning of his or her position(s) in the world, the "logics and practices . . . produced within particular structures of meaning about family, gender, nationality, class mobility, and social power."[51] The narrative production of Wen Ho Lee, I suggest, covered over the potential contradictions of belonging, thus bolstering a narrow conception of social formation with a totalizing vision of Americanization.

Alberta Lee's role in the protests emblematized the model minoritarian—and, I should say, quite successful—mode of political action. Her presence figured the moral sentimentality necessarily attributed to Lee's victimhood: "She became the human figure in the story, the alter ego of her dad, who was silent behind bars. The news media needed her to bring life to their stories, and she was willing."[52] As her father's face, Alberta secured a sense of his innocence by projecting her own political innocence. She had no *desire* to be thrust into the role of the outspoken, disagreeable minority American. In fact, she claimed an ignorance of the legal and cultural histories of racial exclusion in the United States, an ignorance that had been ruptured, not by any willfulness on her part or her father's, but by the failure of the state. As the national other, the Lees' *only desire* was to fulfill the desire of the American subject.

As he has been popularly imagined, Wen Ho Lee fulfilled this role as redeemer quite successfully. His betrayal was followed by redemption, a saving face as it were, not just for himself, but for the entire minority collective that saw itself embodied in his plight—and, because of the broad appeal of the discourse of racial profiling, this extended well beyond the Asian American model minority to people of color from other racial and ethnic groups. If Elián alienated Cubans from other Americans, Lee's case symbolically articulated the concerns of a broad range of subjects. Yet, if we take seriously the other interpretive possibility, grounded in a haunting "what if," Lee also threatened a much broader range of peoples, "duped" into good-faith advocacy by a duplicitous agent whose desires ran elsewhere than their own. I am not arguing for the truth of the claim that Lee was actually a spy but, rather, calling attention to the structural possibility of such a critical truth. Certain questions haunted the narrative of scapegoated victim. As a former counterintelligence officer argued:

Lee's guilty plea to a single count of mishandling national security information means that there will be no dramatic day in court to judge what really happened. However, under the terms of his deal with the government, he must explain his conduct to FBI debriefers, and those explanations will be put to the test of the polygraph. Some of the questions that most certainly will be posed are:

Why did you transfer 410,000 pages of sensitive information from the classified directory of your computer to the unclassified directory? This deliberate effort required you to defeat multiple security mechanisms in the Los Alamos system.

Why did you copy this information to tapes, and later make copies of these tapes? What did you do with these tapes?

What legitimate work purpose did you fulfill by making these tapes? The data on these tapes represented the most sensitive information in the Los Alamos computer system. Your colleagues and superiors affirm that your particular job did not require you to aggregate and use such files.

After you were barred in late December 1998 from entering the "X Division" secure offices, why did you make 18 attempts to enter this area, including one attempt at 3:30 a.m. on Christmas Eve?

Why, between Jan. 20 and Feb. 10, 2000, when the FBI was interviewing and polygraphing you, did you bypass security mechanisms to electronically access your secure computer in the "X Division" and delete hundreds of classified files that you had previously declassified and moved into the computer's unclassified directory?

During an FBI-administered polygraph examination, why did the results indicate deception when you were asked (1) "Have you ever given codes to unauthorized persons?" and (2) "Have you ever given W-88 (warhead) information to unauthorized persons?"

Have you ever provided classified nuclear weapons information to an unauthorized party?

If, as you have contended, your file transfers, downloading and other risky security practices were common to many of your co-workers, why is it that FBI investigators failed to locate a single other employee in your work area who had engaged in such actions? Who are these co-workers?

Please explain why the search of your office and home resulted in the recovery of classified documents that you had "declassified" by either cutting off the classification markings or by masking the classification markings before making copies of them.[53]

Some of Lee's advocates hedged on the question of Lee's innocence, especially prior to the plea bargain agreement, arguing that they were primarily calling for due process and a fair trial. Of course, this was not the case for his daughter or for Cecilia Chang, a longtime friend of Lee's who started up the Wen Ho Lee Defense Fund, for whom the personal ties of friendship and family meant that loyalty could be rendered manifest only by insisting on Lee's innocence.

CRYSTAL PARIKH

One could further argue that the strategy adopted by Asian American activists precluded the possibility of Lee's guilt as well. Such a possibility would have been devastating to the Asian American community, even for those who were less closely associated with Lee than were Alberta Lee or Cecilia Chang but who had invested so much significance in Lee's status as *scapegoated American*, a national citizen whose *only* crime was being of Asian birth. For example, many activists called attention to the fact that the then-CIA director, John Deutch, was not prosecuted for the security breaches, which were similar in nature to Lee's, that he committed.[54] This argument delimited Lee's violations to acts of carelessness, not treason, for, if Lee had, in fact, provided the PRC with the computer codes, it would be a moot defense. The possibility of Lee's guilt further made the actions of the many local Chinese Americans living in Los Alamos who distanced themselves altogether from Lee intelligible. Some recalled that, during the cold war, Taiwanese intelligence agencies branded critics of the Kuomintang in the United States as Communist sympathizers. Moreover, because federal agents cited, as reasons for their suspicion of Lee, his socializing with PRC officials when they visited LANL and when he visited Beijing—a common practice among many Chinese American scientists— many also worried about being fingered as well.[55] In either case, Lee's guilt would symbolically imperil this broader range of people.

The fact that, after Lee's release from jail, his defense team managed to have certain documents remain sealed, in the face of demands by Asian American activists who wanted all evidence of racial profiling in Energy Department investigations to be made public, is telling. Moreover, those documents that were unsealed revealed that Lee had actually made many more copies of the tapes than had previously been known. According to the documents, both Lee's attorneys and prosecution lawyers learned of the existence of these tapes after negotiations were drawing near a close, and the revelation almost entirely undermined the plea bargain agreement itself.[56] Relatively little attention was given to these incidents by either the press or the Asian American activists. In calling attention to these matters and, more generally, hypothesizing that Lee was, indeed, a spy—and, I stress, I am *only hypothesizing*, in the manner that literary speculation allows—I am *not* suggesting that there is necessarily some evidence damning to Lee in those documents.[57] Indeed, Lee has addressed many of the questions concerning his violation of security measures and downloading of sensitive materials at LANL, although there remains disagreement as to how satisfactory his explanations are.[58] Rather, I want to argue that Lee's desires (those of the other in the national narrative here) are probably multiple and, thus, do not always align with those of the activists who were making the demands in his name. As a symbolic body, Lee secured an idealized fantasy that Asian Americans, and minority Americans more generally, needed to uphold their image of themselves as fully deserving of citizenship rights and trust.[59] This imaginative production of Lee left no space for other desires, for desires that did not reflect back to the minority subject an idealized image of itself.

The banality of *professional* desire, the explanation that Lee downloaded the files as part of a job search to make himself a more attractive candidate, "a kind of immigrant striver with an international portfolio—a job seeker rather than a spy," in the end rationalized his actions and put to rest most of the troubling questions of his case.[60] It also defused the possibility of the more insidious or explosive cold war narrative of diasporic desire, largely because it did not necessarily run into irreconcilable contradictions with the nationalist narrative. As many commentators at the time observed, the stories surrounding Lee's arrest and also the politics of the Republican-backed Cox Committee report itself, which precipitated the investigation of Lee in the first place, depicted a cloak-and-dagger world of espionage and intrigue, worthy, as one diplomat suggested, of the spy novels of John Le Carré.[61] Prosecutors argued that Lee should be denied bail because he had information "so valuable that a hostile nation could conceivably plan a Ninja-style commando raid and airlift him out of the country" and because the data and codes were sensitive enough to "upset the 'global strategic balance.' " This narrative could not play easily alongside the transnationalist trends, endorsed by multinational corporations and political liberals and centrists, that sought to curry favor with the PRC. But, rather than settling the issue, I contend, this tension raises even more questions regarding the ethics of political action in the Lee case.

The question of professional desire received attention for the most part indirectly, with respect to the impact of the case on the position of Asian Americans in the nuclear labs particularly and in the sciences more broadly. The Lee case revealed as much about professional allegiances and conventions of belonging and exclusion as it did about race and ethnicity. It exposed the extent to which the daily life of nuclear weapons labs was imbricated in the antagonisms between state mandates for secrecy and the scientific community's demands for open inquiry and exchange. In fact, Wen Ho Lee's defense team's key expert witness, John Richter, testified that, precisely because of these

CRYSTAL PARIKH

tensions, the data that Lee was accused of stealing was not as sensitive as the prosecution had portrayed. Richter saw his participation in the trial as an attempt to rein in the actions of federal agents, who had, he felt, long acted like "thugs" toward scientists.[62]

Thus, questions of espionage aside altogether, Lee's betrayal could be said to have definitively occurred at this other level, the level of the "priesthood" of nuclear scientists, centered in the close-knit world of Los Alamos. That is, Lee broke the "fundamental trust" that underlies the world of nuclear weapons research and, in the process, eroded the nation's confidence in its security. His security breaches revealed to a national audience the laxity of security arrangements at LANL. The kinds of security measures—for example, polygraphs of the lab scientists—that had been unnecessary under the "sacred trust" of the profession were now justified. Lee's "down-partitioning" of the classified codes from classified to unclassified directories was, therefore, a "mortal sin," regardless of his motives, against the normative assumptions of the vocation.[63] In testifying for the defense, Richter aligned himself with Lee, but Lee's own actions threw the sense of professional trust *among* scientists into disarray. Many of Lee's coworkers and friends from the scientific community thus found *both* Lee's actions *and* the government's arguments and tactics in the bail hearing to be highly troubling.[64]

More important, Lee's case revealed a tightly spun web between the professional production of knowledge and the legal and military conventions of national formation. The indictment of Lee relied heavily on the Atomic Energy Act of 1946, under which an entire body of knowledge was classified, named at its very origin as secret, its security deemed to be in the supreme national interest. Under the terms of this law, the simple "mishandling" of nuclear secrets, let alone their disclosure, constituted crimes with serious penalties, including life imprisonment.[65] As Virginia Carmichael explains:

> Crucial to the development of the cold war . . . were the ways in which the cluster of ideas around that of atomic warfare was manipulated and imaginatively displaced, through mobilization of fears and anxieties, into ideas of ownership, secrecy, and defensive aggression. . . . The idea of national security was certainly not new, but with the development and use of electronic technology and atomic weapons it had become a qualitatively different idea. Even more than other ideas, that of national security was actively driven by its opposites: breach, espionage, betrayal, treason, aggression, take-over, overthrow, revolution.[66]

In this context, the dual meaning of *intelligence* found itself further embodied in the figure of the scientist-spy of the cold war world. The CIA often recruited foreign students in the sciences as spies, waiting for them to return home and move through the professional ranks of their native countries until they had access to sensitive information to return as intelligence.[67] Moreover, in 1987, the Department of Energy created its own counterintelligence organizations, which promoted exchanges between foreign and American scientists, favoring collection of intelligence in this manner (often to the chagrin of other federal agencies like the FBI).[68] The use of this type of open "scientific intelligence" had become such a routine matter that it was known as ASKINT, "ask intelligence," intelligence derived from open visits, conversations, and observations between U.S. and foreign scientists. In the case of China, much of this information was made available by PRC officials themselves as a way of delivering a political message to the United States about Chinese capabilities.[69]

Thus, despite any claims of the profession about the political and ethical neutrality of scientific knowledge, from the very beginnings of the national security state and the military-industrial complex at the end of World War II, through their full-scale operation beginning in the late 1950s after the decline of McCarthyist anticommunism, and until the fall of the Eastern bloc in the early 1990s, scientific knowledge did not just play a role in the production of cold war bilateralism; it was the very discursive and material universe that constituted it.[70] It was repeatedly lamented that U.S. national security had long depended on attracting "the best brains the world has to offer us" and that a drop-off in Asian American scientists applying for appointments at nuclear labs would have a long-term impact on U.S. military dominance. Anxiety over the state of the security and the future of nuclear research further increased when the Association for Asian American Studies and Asian Pacific Americans in Higher Education endorsed a call by Ling-Chi Wang, the chair of the Ethnic Studies Department at the University of California, Berkeley, for Asian Americans to boycott labs.[71]

This discourse, especially when adopted by Asian Americans themselves, was firmly rooted in the model minority image and the fantasy of the American dream that the image secured. For example, Xiao-huang Yin, chair of the American Studies Program at Occidental College, wrote in the *Los Angeles Times*:

CRYSTAL PARIKH

To many aspiring Asian Americans, particularly immigrants, a career as a research scientist means guaranteed freedom and employment security, awe-inspiring enough to symbolize the realization of their American Dreams. It is no accident, then, that Asian American contributions to science have been singular. There have been six Chinese American Nobel Laureates, five in physics and one in chemistry. As they earn distinction in science, Asian Americans are lauded by the mass media as the latest success story of the American Dream. In fact, it is mainly their accomplishments in science and academe that have made Asians the "model minority" in U.S. society.[72]

In explaining his own role as a member of the "nuclear brotherhood," Lee has invoked the political neutrality that science affords him: "I had never had much interest in politics. . . . I stuck to science and math, which are much more fascinating to me and have a clear benefit to humanity. They are also far less volatile than politics"(24–25). He has also portrayed himself as a good citizen: "My research on the numerical modeling of nuclear reactors and reactions has been used in many countries, and I was proud that my work contributed to America's safety and to global nuclear security. I . . . took [my research] very seriously—if I didn't do my job well, the consequences could be dire" (19).[73] The decrease in applications by persons of Asian descent to national defense laboratories after Lee's termination and indictment only further highlighted that Asian Americans have long been implicated in the construction of national security.[74]

The good faith of Asian American activists' efforts notwithstanding, the fight to clear Wen Ho Lee's name was, in effect, a struggle to clear the road for a person of color to participate in the development of weapons of mass destruction and the ongoing military and economic dominance of the United States on the global stage.[75] This is a critical truth that might be so obvious that it would not need mentioning were it not so readily elided by the entrenched domestic boundaries of civil rights discourse, through which legal and political critics examined the Wen Ho Lee case. I am neither dismissing the veracity of racial profiling as one of the most potent technologies for the surveillance and disenfranchisement of people of color nor faulting those who have insisted on juridical and legal redress in this arena. I am, however, arguing that we must also begin accounting for the *other* stakes and that at stake are the *others of the nation-state*, in our political modes of minority representation, without which we will fail to understand the heavy historical weight of the ethico-political decisions we face.

The "betrayals" of Wen Ho Lee and Elián González functioned to forestall the possibility of the desiring other and to secure a developmental narrative about global relations under the New World Order. This thesis accounts, then, not just for the visibility of Lee and González on the national screen. It also helps explain the relative *invisibility* of the feminine, which so often conventionally figures otherness in the familial narrative of subject formation. Many questions have been raised, and, for the most part, left unanswered, about the roles of Lee's wife, Sylvia, and Elián's mother, Elizabeth Brotons: Why did Brotons leave Cuba with Elián, and what was the nature of her relationship with her boyfriend, Lázaro Munero, and of her relationship with Elián's father? To what extent did Sylvia Lee know about her husband's suspicious activities, did she engage in any of her own separately from him, and what was the state of their marital affairs? There have certainly been attempts to map these women's own interests onto the binaries of the dominant narratives, but these accounts leave numerous gaps and openings for contestation.[76] Very little is known about Brotons; in the scores of pages written about Elián in the nation's papers, for example, only a handful even mention her by name. The mystery surrounding Brotons is almost matched by Sylvia Lee's near silence in public on her husband's case.

In the midst of both cases, it was quite easy to lose track of Elizabeth Brotons and Sylvia Lee. This was especially true because more unambiguous figures of feminine loyalty captured public attention. Elián's cousin Marisleysis González and Wen Ho Lee's daughter, Alberta Lee, were much more readily integrated into the narrative demands of the nation. In response to the question, "What did she want," the figures of Sylvia Lee and Elizabeth Brotons offer little clearcut evidence. These subjects resist symbolization. Their loyalties are questionable, their investments and sacrifices of self—were they selfish? were they selfless?—not easily discerned. As others, they remained resolutely inaccessible, unimaginable even, and they failed to bolster the totalized signification that each narrative sought.

In contrast, Elián González and Wen Ho Lee offered to the nation an otherness that it could incorporate, or expel, from the body politic at will, too easily covering over the uneven and shifting modalities of history and historically conditioned agency, so as to secure a smooth integration of the national and the transnational. If the narrative imperatives of national formation reduced Lee and González to the demands of "Americanization," it remains the

CRYSTAL PARIKH

task of the ethically committed cultural critic to seek openings in such narratives where we might countenance the desiring other who refuses to shore up the national imaginary of citizenhood. Such readings might be politically risky gestures, as the other demands that we forgo the idealized selves that drive our impassioned commitments. But they are necessary risks if we are to shift our attention to the imagined spaces to which these others lead us, spaces where the citizen's discourse of rights and law will not suffice in meeting the demands articulated there.

## Notes

I would like to thank Corrinne Harol, Vincent Cheng, and Nicholas De Genova for their helpful comments on this essay. Unless otherwise noted, Christopher Sánchez provided all translations; I am grateful for his contributions to this essay as well.
1. Gene Weingarten, "The Passion of Elian: Spirited Away from a Dictator's Land, a Child Surfaces among Those Who See in Him Their Salvation," *Washington Post*, 7 April 2000, CI. The article details the adoration and symbolization of Elián González both in Cuba and in Miami's Cuban exile community. Weingarten explains that Elián's school desk in Havana had been turned into a shrine and that, in Miami, many Cubans identified him with the baby Jesus. Further, he describes reports that circulated among Cuban Americans protesting the possibility of Elián's return to Cuba. According to these reports, Fidel Castro, rumored to be a practitioner of the Afro-Cuban religion of Santería, wished to have Elián returned to Cuba because he believed that the saint Eleggua inhabited Elián's body. It was further rumored that Castro intended to sacrifice Elián. As Weingarten writes: "It does not take an expert in geopolitics to understand that the saga of Elian Gonzalez . . . is not merely about the fate of a little boy whose mother drowned and whose father wants him back. That would be clean, and easy. This is not easy. Or clean."
2. Chow, "Leading Questions."
3. I borrow this formulation of diaspora as the other of the nation-state from Khachig Tölölyan, who explains that analyses from the diasporic perspective can provide insight into the way that "real yet imagined communities . . . are fabulated, brought into being, made and unmade, in culture and politics, both on land people call their own and in exile" (Tölölyan, "The Nation-State and Its Others," 3). Homi Bhabha has, in *Location of Culture* and *Nation and Narration*, best described the concept of *narrating the nation*.
4. Chow, *Ethics after Idealism*, xxii.
5. The Lee case itself specifically invoked anti-Chinese rhetoric and anxieties about Communist China. At the same time, however, it was distinguished by the prevalence of images —e.g., those of the treacherous "forever foreign" Asian and the model minority—that have historically been broadly attributed to Asian Americans of other ethnicities. The case thus raised questions about national belonging for Asians from a range of ethnic backgrounds and mobilized, not just Chinese American activists (although this group did generally spearhead the effort), but a broader range of Asian American activists as well.
6. Butler, *Psychic Life of Power*, 48–49.

7. Both these cases further evocatively recall the trial and execution of Julius and Ethel Rosenberg for espionage in the 1950s and the Rosenbergs' significance for Jewish national belonging as it played out through and against the threat of communism. The Rosenberg trial provides an important point of reference in the genealogy of American anticommunism and the terms of loyalty and treason (although, like Wen Ho Lee, the Rosenbergs were tried, not for treason, but for espionage) in the construction of the national security state. As Virginia Carmichael explains: "[T]he Rosenberg story can be read either, in mythic terms, as a story of the betrayal of the patriarchal father (the nation-state, or perhaps civil society at large) by the children . . . or as a story of the patriarchal father's allaying of family guilt, shame, and fear of retribution through the ritual of scapegoating sacrifice" (*Framing History*, xv). As such, the Rosenberg case provides what Carmichael calls a *frame story*, within which both the experience of Cuban American nationalism and the investigation and indictment of Wen Ho Lee were articulated. (For example, during one of the interrogation sessions that Lee underwent, a federal agent pressured him by explicitly alluding to the Rosenberg case, threatening: "Do you know who the Rosenbergs are? . . . The Rosenbergs are the only people that never cooperated with the federal government in an espionage case. You know what happened to them? They electrocuted them, Wen Ho" [Stober and Hoffman, *Convenient Spy*, 15].)

As Deborah Dash Moore has written about the impact of the Rosenberg trial: "For second-generation Jews, especially for those born and bred in New York City, the trial of the Rosenbergs became a definitional ceremony in which opposing versions of American Jewish identity competed for ascendancy. At stake was an understanding of what was required of a Jew in America." While the Rosenbergs might have felt their Communist loyalties, patriotism to a democratic America, and Jewish heritage to be in line with one another, their trial and execution (an "all-Jewish drama" where the defendants, prosecutor, and judge identified as Jewish) were seen by many, including the judge who handed down the sentence, as an act of atonement to the nation: "Thus, the Rosenbergs' execution cleansed American Jewry of the taint of betrayal. Their death represented a symbolic atonement demanded to signify the loyalty of American Jews to the United States and its ideals" ("Reconsidering the Rosenbergs," 21–22, 33–34; see also Horwitz, "Jews and McCarthyism").

Thus, in the symbolic absolutism regarding Jewish and American identity that pervaded the trial and later public debate, the Rosenberg case provides many of the terms through which national loyalty and treason have been framed for racial and ethnic minorities. Yet, as I am arguing in this essay, to the extent that such bilateralism has been relegated to anachronism in contemporary liberal discourse, these terms have also been remarkably rearticulated in the Lee and González cases. Moreover, although suspicion of Jewish American loyalties continues to emerge in nativist rhetoric (illustrated, e.g., in the case of Jonathon Pollard), for the most part, as Andrew Ross ("Work of the State") argues, Jewish American identity has become increasingly assimilated to the national interests of the United States, displaced in particular by fears of Muslims and Arab Americans in the United States.

8. For examples on a national scale, see Edward J. Linehan, "Cuba's Exiles Bring New Life to Miami," *National Geographic Magazine*, July 1973, 68–95; and Tom Alexander, "Those Amazing Cuban Emigres," *Fortune*, October 1966, 144–49. A Heritage Foundation Report, "The Cuban Refugee Problem in Perspective: 1959–1980," which unequivocally celebrated the economic and social successes of Cuban exiles, was presented to the U.S.

Congress and recorded in full in the *Congressional Record* as a means to stem anti-Cuban fears following the Mariel Boatlift of 1980 (see "The Cuban Success Story: Let Us Tell It," *Congressional Record*, 96th Cong., 2nd sess., 1980, 126, pt. 16:21159–66). As might be expected, the *Miami Herald* has also extensively chronicled the social and economic experiences of Cuban exiles and their descendants in the United States over the past four decades. For analysis of the representation of Cuban Americans as a model minority, see Boswell and Curtis, *Cuban-American Experience*; and Croucher, *Imagining Miami*, 102–41.

9. This does not mean, however, that Cuban exiles did not encounter significant hostility as well. Especially in local political and social responses beginning in the 1960s and lasting well into the 1980s, both African Americans and Anglo-Americans in the Miami area voiced strong concerns, and, in numerous cases, outright antipathy, in response to the influx of Cubans into the region. These complaints centered on the job displacement and economic burdens that "native" south Floridians feared would result from Cuban immigration. Cultural xenophobia, especially concerning language issues, also played a central role (see Croucher, *Imagining Miami*; Masud-Piloto, *Cuban Migration to the U.S.*; and García, *Havana USA*).

10. Palumbo-Liu, *Asian/American*, 156. The bulk of Cuban emigrants from 1959 to the early 1980s (until just after the Mariel Boatlift of April 1980) were allowed to enter the United States under the special status afforded to refugees. It is important to note, however, that not all these emigrants can be said to conform to the definition of *refugee* as defined by the 1949 UN Convention Relating to the Status of Refugees. As Jesús Arboleya writes: "Although there are some exceptions, from that perspective Cuban emigration doesn't have a political nature, since the vast majority of those people haven't left the country because they were persecuted for their political ideas. Many of them—especially in the most recent generations of émigrés—have left without any substantial conflicts with the revolutionary process. But, even if this weren't so, political nonconformity doesn't determine status as a political refugee" (*Havana-Miami*, 10). Furthermore, as Boswell and Curtis point out: "There is . . . considerable evidence that the motivation for migrating from Cuba to the United States has changed over time. During the early 1960s it was clear that most were emigrating for political, social, and religious reasons. These persons were clearly refugees and therefore were accorded special immigration status upon entry into the United States. This expedited their processing by American immigration authorities and made it easier for them to receive financial and social assistance. By the 1970s, however, it began to become apparent that economic motives were beginning to replace those of political and religious persecution. As a result, the United States government enacted the 1980 Refugee Act which severely limits the number of Cubans allowed to legally enter this country" (*Cuban-American Experience*, 57).

11. I am describing here the ideological function of the model minority construct, not its truth value. Several studies have suggested that the socioeconomic situation of the majority of Cuban Americans is more tenuous than the model minority image suggests (see, e.g., Croucher, *Imagining Miami*, 125–26). It is also important to consider the extensive legislative and economic assistance provided in all aspects of Cuban refugee resettlement. Most significantly, the Cuban Adjustment Act, passed in 1966, allowed for Cuban refugees to apply for permanent status if their asylum claim had not been acted on in a year and a day. In contrast, other groups, such as Haitians, have faced much longer waiting periods and received much less assistance as immigrants.

12. McLaren and Pinkney-Pastrana, "Cult of Elián González," 206.

13. This characterization grossly oversimplifies the political affinities of those Cuban exiles who arrived during the early 1960s as "wealthy extremists with Fascist leanings who only wanted to recoup the property and social position they had lost as a result of Castro's revolution." According to various surveys from the early 1960s, a majority of Cuban Americans had, in fact, favored the downfall of Batista's regime, and somewhere between one-third to half of the exiles at one time supported Castro's Revolution. Contemporary Cuban American testimonies also eloquently record that exiles held a spectrum of political views toward the Castro government in the early days of the Cuban Revolution (Boswell and Curtis, *Cuban-American Experience*, 170). Herrera, ed., *ReMembering Cuba*, offers an ambitiously wide range of autobiographical essays, many of which address this issue.

14. Lee's arrest followed on the 1996 Clinton-Gore campaign fund-raising scandals, which focused on two Asian Americans, John Huang and Charlie Yahn-lin Trie. Huang and Trie, both naturalized U.S. citizens, were accused of raising money from illegal foreign sources, fueling suspicions of a plot by foreign Chinese to gain influence over U.S. politics. Many Asian Americans saw the actions of Bill Richardson and Janet Reno in the Lee case as an attempt to counter Republican criticism that the Clinton administration had been "soft" on China. For a discussion of the racial politics in the campaign finance scandal, see Volpp, " 'Obnoxious to Their Very Nature.' "

15. Vanessa Hua, "A Daughter's Struggle: Fighting to Free Her Father, Charged with Violating National Security," *San Francisco Examiner*, 11 June 2000, D1.

16. Albert H. Yee, "Elian Gonzalez and Wen Ho Lee: No Racial Profiling?" *Asian Reporter*, 14 February 2000, 7; Phil Tajitsu Nash, "Washington Journal: Elian Gonzalez and the Context of History," *Asian Week*, 3 May 2000, 12.

17. In an editors' note, the paper both defended, but also remarkably described, some of the flaws in its coverage of the Wen Ho Lee case that began in March 1999, when it first reported that the PRC had made advances in its nuclear weapons program via access to U.S. defense secrets and that the FBI had concentrated its investigation on a Chinese American scientist: "[L]ooking back, we also found some things we wish we had done differently in the course of the coverage to give Dr. Lee the full benefit of the doubt. In those months, we could have pushed harder to uncover weaknesses in the F.B.I. case against Dr. Lee. Our coverage would have been strengthened had we moved faster to assess the scientific, technical and investigative assumptions that led the F.B.I. and the Department of Energy to connect Dr. Lee to what is still widely acknowledged to have been a major security breach. . . . Passages of some articles also posed a problem of tone. In place of a tone of journalistic detachment from our sources, we occasionally used language that adopted the sense of alarm that was contained in official reports and was being voiced to us by investigators, members of Congress and administration officials with knowledge of the case. . . . There are articles we should have assigned but did not. We never prepared a full-scale profile of Dr. Lee, which might have humanized him and provided some balance. Some other stories we wish we had assigned in those early months include a more thorough look at the political context of the Chinese weapons debate, in which Republicans were eager to score points against the White House on China; an examination of how Dr. Lee's handling of classified information compared with the usual practices in the laboratories; a closer look at Notra Trulock, the intelligence official at the Department of Energy who sounded some of the loudest alarms about Chinese espionage; and an exploration of the various suspects and

leads that federal investigators passed up in favor of Dr. Lee" ("*The Times* and Wen Ho Lee," *New York Times*, 26 September 2000, A2).

18. See, e.g., Pam Adams, "No Insulation from Racial Discrimination," Copley News Service, 27 September 2000, LEXIS-NEXIS, Academic Universe. The Coalition against Racial Scapegoating was organized as a result of the Lee case. The coalition, which began with the interest of a number of Asian American organizations such as the National Asian Pacific American Bar Association and the Committee of 1000, eventually appealed to a broad array of minority and civil rights advocacy groups, including the American Civil Liberties Union of northern California, the National Lawyers Guild, the National Association for the Advancement of Colored People, the Mexican American Legal Defense Fund, and the Anti-Defamation League (Hua, "A Daughter's Struggle" [n. 15 above], D1; see also James Sterngold, "Asian Americans Outraged about Arrest of Scientist," *Austin American-Statesman*, 13 December 1999, A11).

19. William Wong, "DOE, FBI, Wen Ho Lee and the 'China Card,'" *Seattle Post-Intelligencer*, 10 May 2000, A17. For a detailed list of the evidence that the FBI and Department of Energy investigations engaged in racial profiling, see "Update: The Wen Ho Lee Case," *Chinese American Forum*, July 2000, 40.

20. Florangela Davila, "What It Feels Like Being on the 'Outside': Asian Americans Gather for Meeting," *Seattle Times*, 26 July 2001, B1.

21. For extended discussions of Miami's multiracial history, including the numerous conflicts between Anglo-American, Cuban American, Afro-Caribbean, and African American residents, see Croucher, *Imagining Miami*; and Portes and Stepick, *City on the Edge*. This is not to suggest that there were *no* attempts made to articulate Elián's case—and that of the Cuban exiles—rhetorically in the terms of minority discourse. Augustin Tamargo ("La honra en el estrado," *Nuevo Herald*, 4 June 2000, 30A), e.g., argues for an "honorable" decision on the part of the federal appeals court that heard the González case, using Martin Luther King Jr.'s activism and Lyndon Johnson's signing of the Civil Rights Act as examples of such "honor" and the Japanese internment as an instance of "dishonor."

22. As Augustin Tamargo writes about the Cuban "sufferers in exile": "Cubans will remain, many Cubans, as witnesses to that hour of return, which historically is bound to arrive. Even if there are not many, it does not matter. To step on the native soil, upon the rubble of despotism, only one exile is enough, he who shouts out on that day, 'Cuba, we will not fail you!'" ("Los enfermos del exilio," *Nuevo Herald*, 1 October 1989; see also José Sánchez-Boudy, "El exilio histórico: Compendio de una Cuba eterna," *Diario las Américas*, 3 January 1990). The religious interpretation of Elián's story for the most part unfolded according to the symbols and iconography of Cuban Catholicism. Elián's rescue by fishermen recalls the recovery of the image of la Caridad del Cobre, the patron saint of Cuba. Protestors also drew out the Christ allegory further, with signs in Spanish that demanded "Do not deliver Elian to the Romans" and "Elian is Christ. Reno is Lucifer. Castro is Satan." Clergy also explained: "Jesus was saved by his mother and foster father who took him away from Herod's murderous grasp, just as Elian was saved by his mother and stepfather who took him away from Castro to make him safe." As one priest bluntly put it: "These religious connections to Elian are a way for people to channel their grief and anger over 41 years of revolution. This child is a way for them to envision resurrection for Cuba" (Meg Laughlin, "Prayer Vigil Lifts Elian Fervor to New High," *Miami Herald*, 31 March 2000, 1B). José Sánchez-Boudy ("Como Herodes en Madrugada," *Diario las Américas*, 25 April

2000) compares the early morning raid on Lázaro González's home with Herod's seizing of Jesus.

Although much of the religiously inflected rhetoric in the case was posed in opposition to Santería (an opposition whose roots in the racist demonization of the Afro-Cuban tradition were only thinly, if at all, veiled), because of the pervasiveness of Santería in both Cuban and Cuban American culture, it was never entirely or exclusively demonized. Rather, appeals were made to Santería saints to protect Elián as well. Cuban Americans involved with Santería cast Elián as a "son" of Eleggua, "who has a boyish mischievous manifestations [sic] not unlike Elian." They were also often likely to cite the story regarding Castro's belief that Elián was either favored or inhabited by Eleggua and destined to bring about the demise of Castro's regime (Tom Carter, "Santeria Ceremony Held to Guard Boy," *Washington Times*, 3 April 2000, A10). For further detail on the rumors regarding Castro's belief that Elián was an incarnation of Eleggua, see Guillermo Cabrera Infante, "El niño prodigo," *Nuevo Herald*, 24 February 2000, 17A.

23. Arboleya, *Havana-Miami*, 31–32.

24. For an example of such a critique of "Castro appeasing" in the case of Elián González, see Irving Louis Horowitz, "Los dos Cubas de Elián González," *Nuevo Herald*, 16 April 2000, 127.

25. Tamargo, "Los enfermos del exilio" (n. 22 above).

26. The more extreme versions of this rhetoric in the González case accused the American press of being influenced or infiltrated by Cuban communism and, thus, unable to report the truth about Castro's regime: "The American press has demonstrated that it is subsidized by the murderer of more than 140,000 Cubans, Fidel Castro Ruiz, by its constant attacks against the combatant Cubans in exile, and by their silence regarding the misery, corruption, deaths, and imprisonments that occur daily on the enslaved Cuban island" (Aurelio Torrente Iglesias, "El vir del castrismo en la prensa Norteamericana," *Diario las Américas*, 20 April 2000).

27. See Alan Clendenning, "Free Speech a One-Sided Notion on Elian's Street," Associated Press State and Local Wire, 21 April 2000, LEXIS-NEXIS, Academic Universe. Weingarten further explains: "The leaders of Cuban Miami rose to power and held it by marshaling the passion of a single political ideology: Communism is evil; Castro is the enemy, and he must be punished through relentless economic sanctions until he is overthrown. It has been said that the mayoralty of Miami is the only municipal position in America that requires a foreign policy" ("The Passion of Elian" [n. 1 above], C1).

28. It is also important to consider, as Croucher contends, that the emergence of interest in domestic politics and issues beyond Cuba, Castro, and communism on the part of Cuban Americans (especially second-generation, U.S.-born Cuban Americans) does not necessarily mean that exile politics have been altogether displaced. Cuban American deployment of a more traditional immigrant narrative of Americanization "does not simply represent a desire or willingness among Cubans to assimilate into the American mainstream. . . . [A]n increased focus on the 'new land' does not signal a disinterest in the 'homeland.' Instead, the shift away from exile politics is more accurately interpreted as an alternative discursive strategy consistent with an altered set of social, political and economic circumstances" (*Imagining Miami*, 135).

29. Julio Estorino contends that Cuban Americans can "avoid the irreverence of comparing [Elián] with Christ, by turning instead to the human model of Jose Martí." Moreover,

writing on the anniversary of Martí's birth, Estorino insists on the need for unity among Cubans: "Today we must again ask all those who squander their energies in fratricidal and stupid enmity against those, who consider their ideological or political adversaries to be in the ranks of the exile or of the internal dissidence, that they stop for a moment this twenty-eighth of January and reconsider their course in light of the ideal and the commonality of practical experience" ("Los tres niños y el milagro posible," *Diario las Américas*, 28 January 2000).

30. Elián's arrival in the United States as a "virtual orphan" recalls the mass emigration of children in the early 1960s as part of Operation Peter Pan, emigration sparked by rumors that the revolutionary government of Cuba would be eliminating parental rights. An estimated fourteen thousand children arrived in the United States as part of Operation Peter Pan. For detailed discussions of the operation, see Conde, *Operation Pedro Pan*; and Triay, *Fleeing Castro*. One Cuban American commentator, Ramon Ferreira, writes: "¿Quién es el padre de Moisés?" (Who is the father of Moses?). Ferreira further presses the question of the child's role in the community by arguing that, for those destined to be great leaders, the identity—and the claims—of the father is insignificant. History recalls only the great leader himself, and, in Elián, the author locates the possibility of another such preordained history ("¿Quién es el padre de Moisés?" *Nuevo Herald*, 28 March 2000, 10A; see also Ramon Ferreira, "Elián: Derecho o maniobra política?" *Nuevo Herald*, 16 June 2000, 23A).

31. Belkin Cuza Male, "Es Elián un angel?" *Nuevo Herald*, 28 January 2000, 14A.

32. See Miranda Leitsinger, "Elian's Fla. Home Opens as a Shrine," *The Record*, 22 October 2001, A10. Others have also likened the conditions on the island under Castro's government and of exile displacement to the Holocaust (see, e.g., Néstor Díaz de Villegas, "Elián y el sistema americano," *Nuevo Herald*, 18 April 2000, 11A). José Sánchez-Boudy ("Una decisión desacertada," *Diario las Américas*, 22 August 2000) portrays the decision to return Elián to Cuba as the infliction of "a wound in the collective soul of a people [that] will never disappear even with the passing of centuries."

33. The symbolization of Elián further follows Žižek's argument regarding the role of "error" in the function of ideological fantasy. For Žižek, the central problem with materialist theories of ideology is in their insistence, to some degree or other, that ideology is a kind of false consciousness, an error. As he writes: "[T]he illusion is not on the side of knowledge, it is already on the side of reality itself, of what the people are doing. What they do not know is that their social reality itself, their activity, is guided by an illusion, by a fetishistic inversion. What they overlook, what they misrecognize, is not the reality but the illusion which is structuring their reality, their real social activity. They know very well how things really are, but still they are doing it as if they did not know. The illusion is therefore double: it consists in overlooking the illusion which is structuring our real, effective relationship to reality. And this overlooked, unconscious illusion is what may be called the *ideological fantasy*. . . . The fundamental level of ideology, however, is not of an illusion masking the real state of things but that of an (unconscious) fantasy structuring our social reality itself" (*Sublime Object of Ideology*, 32–33). In other words, the important question is not whether Cuban exiles *knew* or *believed* that there was something magical or redemptive about this particular "miracle child." In their *behaving* as if there were, the fantasy produces a bearable "reality," where " 'Reality' is a fantasy-construction which enables us to mask the Real of our desire": "Ideology is not a dreamlike illusion that we build to escape the insupportable reality; in its basic dimension it is a fantasy-construction which serves as a support for our

'reality' itself: an 'illusion' which structures our effective, real social relations and thereby masks some insupportable, real, impossible kernel. . . . The function of ideology is not to offer us a point of escape from our reality but to offer us the social reality itself as an escape from some traumatic, real kernel" (45).

34. See, e.g., "Elián: El hijo de los delfines," *Voz Libre*, 21 January 2000.

35. Horowitz, *Conscience of Worms*, 71.

36. Indeed, in Cuba, Elián had been likened to a "new Che" (see Laughlin, "Prayer Vigil" [n. 22 above]). As one Havana resident predicted Elián's position in Cuban society on his return: "He is going to be written into Cuban history. He is going to have to live up to the image of himself with Fidel's arm around him—when that happens—forever." Another added: "The party is going to be telling us that this is one of the triumphs of the revolution" ("Havana Residents Wait, Wondering What's Next," *Miami Herald*, 31 March 2000, 19A).

37. See Markovits, "The Enemy Makes the Man."

38. Žižek, *Sublime Object of Ideology*, 147.

39. As Chow further elaborates: "The ingenuity of Žižek's critique lies in the way it speaks equally compellingly to the operational fantasies of communist regimes as it does to that of 'democratic' ones. . . . Typical of totalitarian rule's self-representation and self-legitimation is a kind of language, verbal or visual, which proclaims/presents a noble, respectable idea/ image of 'the people.' The point of this kind of language is to seduce—to divert attention away from the rulers' violence and aggressivity at the same time that sympathy/empathy with the good idea/image is aroused. Totalitarianism thus exemplifies the problematic of privileging imaginary identification that for Žižek lies at the heart of idealism" (Chow, *Ethics after Idealism*, 42–43).

40. In 1974, the *Miami News* reported that, despite increasing numbers of Cuban refugees who were becoming U.S. citizens, many regarded naturalization as a "convenience," rather than a committed choice, and many others refrained from naturalizing as they considered this (or thought that others would see it as) an act of betrayal to their country (Humberto Cruz, "Some Cubans Feel U.S. Citizenship Just 'Convenience,' " *Miami News*, 1 July 1974). In 1990, amid optimism that events in Eastern Europe forebode the end of Communism in Cuba, a survey of Cuban adults in Dade County found that one of every five claimed that he or she would return to Cuba if Castro's government were to fail. While this number had fallen greatly since the 1970s, that 20 percent of the Cuban American population lived with the hope of returning, coupled with the survey's finding that 54 percent favored a U.S. invasion of Cuba, seems to drive the sense on the part of non-Latinos that the community's national loyalties remain divided. This perception in turn influenced much of the coverage and discourse surrounding the Elián González case (Ronnie Ramos, " 1 in 5 Dade Cubans Would Go Back," *Miami Herald*, 20 February 1990, 1).

41. Li, *Imagining the Nation*, 10.

42. Žižek, "Love Thy Neighbor?" 161. Žižek writes: "It is never possible for me fully to assume (in the sense of symbolic integration) the fantasmatic kernel of my being. When I approach it too much, when I come too close to it, what occurs is the *aphanisis* of my subjectivity: I lose my symbolic consistency; it disintegrates. Perhaps in this way, the forced actualization in social reality of the fantasmatic kernel of my being is the worst and most humiliating type of violence because it undermines the very basis of my identity—my 'self-image' " (ibid.).

43. Ibid., 163–64.

CRYSTAL PARIKH

44. Hendrik Hertzberg, "A Tale of Two Cubas," *New Yorker*, 17 April 2000, 33.

45. A national Gallup poll conducted in February 2000 found that 67 percent of Americans supported the return of Elián to his father in Cuba, marking a steady increase in support for the federal government's position since December 1999, when public opinion was more evenly split between allowing Elián to stay and returning him to Cuba (Carol Rosenberg, "National Polls Steadily Support Return of Elian," *Miami Herald*, 23 February 2000, 3B). An April 2000 poll of Miami-Dade County residents found deep divisions based on ethnicity: 92 percent of non-Hispanic blacks and 76 percent of non-Hispanic whites favored the child's return to Cuba, whereas 83 percent of Cuban Americans believed that he should remain in the United States. Interestingly, the poll also found that the majority (55 percent) of other non-Cuban Latinos agreed with the majority of Cuban Americans (Andres Viglucci and Diana Marrero, "Poll Reveals Widening Split over Elian," *Miami Herald*, 9 April 2000, 1A). As one news story explained: "The least sympathetic [to the Cuban Americans' position on the Elián case] was Miami's black community, whose own long-standing civil rights issues don't command equal attention from Cuban-American political leaders. American and Haitian-born blacks can only dream of the political clout and media-drawing powers of the Cuban Americans." Cuban Americans certainly did not help their own cause here when they insisted on presenting themselves as model minorities in the face of such hostility: "We've been around here for 41 years and have learned how the system works. . . . Other groups can do the same thing we do" (Bill Douthat, "Miami's Cuban Community Strengthens Its Position," Cox News Service, 15 April 2000, LEXIS-NEXIS, Academic Universe).

46. In March 2000, Alex Penelas stated that he would refuse to allow county police to aid federal agents if they attempted to remove Elián from his Miami relatives' home and that Attorney General Reno and President Clinton would be to blame if any violence ensued from such a course of action. A poll showed that 90 percent of blacks and 80 percent of white non-Hispanics disapproved of these statements. Penelas later argued that his statements had been misconstrued and that police would, indeed, be available to maintain order and protect agents (Viglucci and Marrero, "Poll Reveals Widening Split" [n. 45 above]).

47. Moreover, Cuban Americans were perceived by non-Latinos as "using Elian for purely political reasons while ignoring the father's rights to claim his own child" (Douthat, "Miami's Cuban Community Strengthens Its Position" [n. 45 above]). *Time* magazine construed the conflicts surrounding the Elián case in terms of a "we," i.e., a reasonable, paternal America, and its Cuban others: "We sympathize with his father, who wants Elián returned home to Cuba. But then we remember that Elián's mother drowned trying to get him to freedom. And we're disgusted with both Castro and the anti-Castro zealots in Miami who are shamelessly using Elián and his father as fresh draftees in their tiresome feud" (Joshua Cooper Ramo, "The Odyssey of Elián González: A Big Battle for a Little Boy," *Time*, 17 January 2000, 60; see also Robert Steinback, "Cuban Exiles in Need of Allies," *Miami Herald*, 6 January 2000, 1B).

48. Alex Veiga, "Elian Saga United Cuban Exiles, but Hurt Image, Political Clout," Associated Press State and Local Wire, 28 June 2000, LEXIS-NEXIS, Academic Universe. See also Peter Katel, "Buscan reparar la afectada imagen de los Cubanoamericanos," *Nuevo Herald*, 27 April 2000, 4A.

49. Veiga, "Elian Saga United Cuban Exiles" (n. 48 above).

50. Eileen Welsome, "Spies, Lies and Portable Tapes," *Denver Westword*, 20 April 2000.

51. Ong, *Flexible Citizenship*, 6.

52. Stober and Hoffman, *Convenient Spy*, 312.

53. Stuart Herrington, "Is Wen Ho Lee a Tarnished Martyr?" *San Diego Union-Tribune*, 6 October 2000.

54. For a comparison of Deutch's and Lee's security violations, see Tzy C. Peng, "The Tragic Case of Wen Ho Lee," *Chinese American Forum*, October 2000, 26.

55. Stober and Hoffman, *Convenient Spy*, 206.

56. Heather Clark, "Unsealed Documents Shed Light on Wen Ho Lee Plea Deal Talks," Associated Press State and Local Wire, 5 October 2001, LEXIS-NEXIS, Academic Universe.

57. Frank H. Wu has also asked this question, about the possibility of Lee's guilt, but toward a different and important end. Wu argues that, with respect to legal strategy and principle, a defense of Lee must subordinate entirely and as a premise the likelihood of Lee's guilt or innocence to the issue of civil rights. Indeed, the defense must, he suggests, be willing even to concede the probability of guilt in order to get to the principle of racial profiling. As Wu contends, against the utilitarianism of "rational discrimination": "If an anti-discrimination principle has any meaning at all, it must be at its most effective when it is least attractive" ("Profiling Principle," 53).

58. For Lee's explanation of his actions, see Lee and Zia, *My Country versus Me*. For a discussion of the questions that remain unanswered in his account, see Pat Holt, "It Takes Two Books to Untangle Story of Accused Spy," *Pittsburgh Post-Gazette*, 3 March 2002, E9.

59. One of the nearly catastrophic traumas facing Asian Americanists just prior to the Wen Ho Lee case was the now-infamous controversy of the awarding and rescinding of a literary prize by the Association for Asian American Studies (AAAS) to Lois-Ann Yamanaka's novel *Blu's Hanging* (1997) in 1998. This widely publicized controversy—focused on the novel's representation of a Filipino man as rapist—has been described according to the terms of a number of different political and critical discourses. It has been characterized as indicative of the tensions between "freedom of speech" and ("politically correct") censorship, ethnic studies and literary production and reception, the academic and the community, the privileged Japanese American and the disenfranchised Filipino American, and mainland, pan-ethnic Asian Americanism and postcolonial Hawaii. In light of the political havoc that the controversy wreaked in the self-image of Asian American studies, one might say that the Wen Ho Lee case offered an ameliorative for ideologically committed Asian American activists and intellectuals, an opportunity to cover over the painful conflicts and contradictions that the controversy had revealed. For discussions of the significance of the controversy that followed on the AAAS decision to rescind the award, see So, "Crisis of Representation in Asian American Studies"; and Fujikane, "Sweeping Racism under the Rug," 158–94.

60. Stober and Hoffman, *Convenient Spy*, 310.

61. Lewis Dolinsky, "A Chinese Spy Mystery Remains Just That," *San Francisco Chronicle*, 18 March 2001, WB1.

62. Stober and Hoffman, *Convenient Spy*, 316–17.

63. Ibid., 262–64.

64. Ibid., 259

65. Ibid., 245.

66. Carmichael, *Framing History*, 11.

67. Stober and Hoffman, *Convenient Spy*, 72.

68. Ibid., 77.

CRYSTAL PARIKH

69. Ibid., 92.

70. To argue that the development of the security state has been imbricated in the disciplinary and epistemological formation of the physical sciences is, however, to imply neither that this was an inevitable state of affairs nor that this mutual dependency was advocated by all or even most scientists. As Jessica Wang explains in impressive detail, during the postwar period between 1945 and 1950, the relationship between the military, the government, and the sciences was a highly contested one. Many of the scientific elite, who espoused what Wang calls a "progressive left politics," promoted civilian oversight of and international cooperation in research in nuclear energy and weapons in order to prevent the proliferation of an arms race. Further, many strongly objected to the underlying assumptions that shaped the Atomic Energy Act, arguing that the scientific knowledge could not be conceived of as a "secret" over which the state needed to maintain a monopoly. One theoretical physicist who became a Senate adviser predicted: "Having created an air of suspicion and mistrust, there will be persons among us who think other nations can know nothing except what is learned by espionage. So, when other countries make atom bombs, these persons will cry 'treason' at our scientists, or they will find it inconceivable that another country could make a bomb in any other way except by aid from Americans" (*American Science*, 17–25). The warning proved prescient for the Lee case, four decades later, where it remains yet unclear whether advances in the PRC nuclear capability were even in fact a result of espionage at all or rather advances made by Chinese scientists over the past decade.

71. "The Disappearing Asian Scientist," *San Francisco Examiner*, 18 July 2000, A18. See also Stober and Hoffman, *Convenient Spy*, 304–5.

72. Xiao-huang Yin, "The Lee Case Shakes Asian Americans' Faith in Justice System," *Los Angeles Times*, 24 September 2000, M1.

73. Lee and Zia, *My Country versus Me*, 19–25.

74. "The Disappearing Asian Scientist" (n. 71 above), A18.

75. For a historical overview of the military-scientific-industrial complex through which the national security state was organized and of the revitalization of cold war militarism and science under the conditions of globalization, see McLauchlan and Hooks, "Last of the Dinosaurs?"

76. There have been two versions of Brotons's actions. On the one hand, it is stipulated that her own dream for capitalist freedom—not only or even primarily for herself, but for her son—led her to make the heroic voyage. On the other hand, Brotons is blamed for making the decision to leave Cuba in order to accompany her boyfriend. Hardly the self-sacrificing mother in this latter version, she recklessly endangered her son's life because of her own illicit passions or because she was unable to stand up to Munero, who was described by some as physically and verbally abusive toward her. Likewise, Lee's wife played a central but in many ways unintelligible role in his story. In the summer of 1998, when the two-year investigation of Lee had produced little evidence against him, the FBI mounted a "false flag" operation, in which an FBI agent pretending to be a foreign operative contacted Lee in order to maneuver him into saying or doing something incriminating. While, during the undercover agent's first phone call, Lee initially seemed interested in meeting him, he backed out because, the FBI presumed, his wife had cautioned him against the meeting. Furthermore, while Lee did not report the incident to the lab's counterintelligence staff, Sylvia Lee did so through a friend's husband working at the lab: "The FBI didn't know what to make of the situation. Wen Ho Lee had not reported an obvious approach by a foreign intelligence

service, but his wife arguably had—apparently without his knowledge" (Stober and Hoff-man, *Convenient Spy*, 159–61). Moreover, Sylvia Lee worked as an informant for the FBI and the CIA from 1985 to 1991. Socializing with delegations of Chinese scientists, she served as a translator and, eventually, supplied both agencies with intelligence on correspondence, even as agents from the FBI investigated her husband. In fact, her work as an informant jeopardized her position as a data analyst at LANL, as it took her away from her assigned job duties. Her supervisors described her as difficult to work with, partly because they believed that she used her ethnic difference, including language difficulties, as a ruse for getting out of work she found overly menial. When Sylvia Lee committed a major security violation in what appeared to be a retributive gesture, her supervisor, Harold Sullivan, found himself unable to terminate her. While the human resources division of the lab cited numerous problems, including domestic problems with her husband, for her poor job performance, Sullivan denounced the decision as an example of political correctness: "She was a woman, she was a TEC [a job defined as requiring minimal experience and involving fairly simple tasks under direct supervision], she was ethnic, and she had some connection with the laboratory director." Sylvia Lee was never charged with any crimes, but it was clear that the FBI considered her central to their investigation of Lee as a potential spy, in part because of her "aggressive" involvement with the visiting Chinese. Agents involved in Lee's investigation overlooked that she had been recruited by other agents for this very purpose (Stober and Hoffman, *Convenient Spy*, 69–81).

# Bibliography

Acuña, Rodolfo. *Anything but Mexican: Chicanos in Contemporary Los Angeles*. New York: Verso, 1996.

——. *Occupied America: A History of Chicanos*. 5th ed. New York: Pearson Longman, 2004.

Almaguer, Tomás. *Racial Fault Lines: The Historical Origins of White Supremacy in California*. Berkeley and Los Angeles: University of California Press, 1994.

Alvarez, Robert R. "National Politics and Local Responses: The Nation's First Successful School Desegregation Court Case." In *School and Society: Learning Content through Culture*, ed. Henry T. Trueba and Concha Delgado-Gaitan, 37–52. New York: Praeger, 1988.

Ancheta, Angelo N. *Race, Rights, and the Asian American Experience*. New Brunswick: Rutgers University Press, 1998.

Arboleya, Jesús. *Havana-Miami: The US-Cuba Migration Conflict*. Translated by Mary Todd. Melbourne: Ocean, 1996.

Arriola, Christopher. "Knocking on the Schoolhouse Door: *Mendez v. Westminster*, Equal Protection, Public Education, and Mexican Americans in the 1940s." *La Raza Law Journal* 8, no. 2 (1995): 166–207.

Avila, Eric. *Popular Culture in the Age of White Flight: Fear and Fantasy in Suburban Los Angeles*. Berkeley and Los Angeles: University of California Press, 2004.

Bailey, Thomas A., and David M. Kennedy, eds. *The American Spirit: United States History as Seen by Contemporaries*. 2 vols. Lexington: D. C. Heath, 1984.

Balderrama, Francisco. *In Defense of La Raza: The Los Angeles Mexican Consulate and the Mexican Community, 1929–1936*. Tucson: University of Arizona Press, 1982.

Balderrama, Francisco E., and Raymond Rodríguez. *Decade of Betrayal: Mexican Repatriation in the 1930's*. Albuquerque: University of New Mexico Press, 1995.

Barrows, David P. "The Negrito and Allied Types in the Philippines." *American Anthropologist* 12, no. 3 (July–September 1910): 358–76.

Bean, Robert Bennett. "Philippine Types." *American Anthropologist* 12, no. 3 (July–September 1910): 376–89.

——. *The Racial Anatomy of the Philippine Islanders*. Philadelphia: J. B. Lippincott, 1910.

——. "Types of Negritos in the Philippine Islands." *American Anthropologist* 12, no. 2 (April–June 1910): 220–36.

Bederman, Gail. *Manliness and Civilization: A Cultural History of Gender and Race in the United States, 1880–1917*. Chicago: University of Chicago Press, 1995.

Beisner, Robert L. *Twelve against Empire: The Anti-Imperialists, 1898–1900*. New York: McGraw-Hill, 1971.

Berkhofer, Robert F., Jr. *The White Man's Indian: Images of the American Indian from Columbus to the Present*. New York: Vintage/Random House, 1978.

Bhabha, Homi K., ed. *Nation and Narration*. London: Routledge, 1990.

——. *The Location of Culture*. London: Routledge, 1994.

Blauner, Robert. *Racial Oppression in America*. New York: Harper and Row, 1972.

Boas, Franz, and Clark Wissler. *Statistics of Growth*. Washington: U.S. Government Printing Office, 1905.

Boswell, Thomas D., and James R. Curtis. *The Cuban-American Experience: Culture, Images, and Perspectives*. Totawa, N.J.: Rowman and Allanheld, 1984.

Brinkley, Alan. *American History: A Survey*. New York: McGraw-Hill, 1995.

Brinton, Daniel G. *Races and Peoples: Lectures on the Science of Ethnography*. New York: N. D. C. Hodges, 1890.

———. "The Peoples of the Philippines." *American Anthropologist* 11, no. 10 (October 1898): 292–307.

Browning, Rufus P., Dale Rogers Marshall, and David H. Tabb. *Protest Is Not Enough*. Berkeley and Los Angeles: University of California Press, 1985.

Burnight, Ralph. "The Japanese in Rural California." *Sociological Monograph* no. 16, 1920 (University of Southern California).

Burton, Julianne. "Don (Juanito) Duck and the Imperial-Patriarchal Unconscious: Disney Studios, the Good Neighbor Policy, and the Packaging of Latin America." In *Nationalisms and Sexualities*, ed. Andrew Parker, Mary Russo, Doris Sommer, and Patricia Yaeger. New York: Routledge, 1992.

Butler, Judith. *The Psychic Life of Power: Theories in Subjection*. Stanford: Stanford University Press, 1997.

Cabán, Pedro A. *Constructing a Colonial People: Puerto Rico and the United States, 1898–1932*. Boulder: Westview, 1999.

Camarillo, Albert. *Chicanos in a Changing Society: From Mexican Pueblos to American Barrios in Santa Barbara and Southern California*. Cambridge: Harvard University Press, 1979.

Carmichael, Virginia. *Framing History: The Rosenberg Story and the Cold War*. Minneapolis: University of Minnesota Press, 1993.

Carr, Henry. *Los Angeles: City of Dreams*. New York: Appleton-Century, 1935.

Carroll, Henry K. *Report on the Industrial and Commercial Condition of Porto Rico*. Washington: U.S. Government Printing Office, 1899.

Chan, Sucheng, ed. *Entry Denied: Exclusion and the Chinese Community in America, 1882–1943*. Philadelphia: Temple University Press, 1991.

Chang, Robert S. *Disoriented: Asian Americans, Law, and the Nation-State*. New York: New York University Press, 1999.

Channing, Walter, and Clark Wissler. *The Hard Palate in Normal and Feeble-Minded Individuals*. New York: Trustees of the American Museum of Natural History, 1908.

Chester, Eric Thomas. *Rag-Tags, Scum, Riff-Raff, and Commies: The US Intervention in the Dominican Republic, 1965–66*. New York: Monthly Review Press, 2001.

Chow, Rey. *Ethics after Idealism: Theory-Culture-Ethnicity-Reading*. Bloomington: Indiana University Press, 1998.

———. "Leading Questions." In *Orientations: Mapping Studies in the Asian Diaspora*, ed. Kandice Chuh and Karen Shimakawa. Durham: Duke University Press, 2001.

Chuman, Frank. *The Bamboo People: The Law and Japanese Americans*. Del Mar, Calif.: Del Mar, 1976.

Chun, Gloria Heyun. *Of Orphans and Warriors: Inventing Chinese American Culture and Identity*. New Brunswick: Rutgers University Press, 2000.

Churchill, Ward. *Fantasies of the Master Race: Literature, Cinema, and the Colonization of American Indians*. Monroe, Maine: Common Courage, 1992.

Cohn, Bernard S. *An Anthropologist among the Historians and Other Essays*. Delhi: Oxford University Press, 1987.

Conde, Yvonne M. *Operation Pedro Pan: The Untold Exodus of 14,048 Cuban Children.* New York: Routledge, 1999.

Cressey, Paul G. *The Taxi-Dance Hall: A Sociological Study in Commercialized Recreation and City Life.* 1932. Reprint, Montclair, N.J.: Patterson Smith, 1969.

Croucher, Sheila. *Imagining Miami: Ethnic Politics in a Postmodern World.* Charlottesville: University of Virginia Press, 1997.

Daniels, Roger. "The Bureau of the Census and the Relocation of the Japanese Americans: A Note and a Document." *Amerasia Journal* 9, no. 1 (1982): 101–5.

Davidson, Chandler, and Bernard Grofman, eds. *Quiet Revolution in the South: The Impact of the Voting Rights Act, 1965–1990.* Princeton: Princeton University Press, 1994.

De Genova, Nicholas. "Migrant 'Illegality' and Deportability in Everyday Life." *Annual Review of Anthropology* 31 (2002): 419–47.

——. "The Legal Production of Mexican/Migrant 'Illegality.' " *Latino Studies* 2, no. 2 (2004): 160–85.

——. *Working the Boundaries: Race, Space, and "Illegality" in Mexican Chicago.* Durham: Duke University Press, 2005.

De Genova, Nicholas, and Ana Y. Ramos-Zayas. "Latino Racial Formations: An Introduction." *Journal of Latin American Anthropology* 8, no. 2 (2003): 2–16.

Delgado, Richard, and Vicky Palacios. "Mexican Americans as a Legally Cognizable Class under Rule 23 and the Equal Protection Clause." *Notre Dame Law Review* 50 (1975): 393–418.

Deloria, Vine, Jr., and David E. Wilkins. *Tribes, Treaties, and Constitutional Tribulations.* Austin: University of Texas Press, 1999.

Deverell, William. "Plague in Los Angeles, 1924: Ethnicity and Typicality." In *Over the Edge: Remapping the American West,* ed. Valerie Matsumoto and Blake Allmendinger. Berkeley and Los Angeles: University of California Press, 1999.

——. *Whitewashed Adobe: The Rise of Los Angeles and the Remaking of Its Mexican Past.* Berkeley and Los Angeles: University of California Press, 2004.

Díaz, Junot. *Drown.* New York: Riverhead, 1996.

Dinwiddie, William. *Puerto Rico: Its Conditions and Possibilities.* New York: Harper and Bros., 1899.

Dower, John W. *War without Mercy: Race and Power in the Pacific War.* New York: Pantheon/Random House, 1986.

Drinnon, Richard. *Facing West: The Metaphysics of Indian-Hating and Empire-Building.* Norman: University of Oklahoma Press, 1980.

Edwards, Elizabeth, ed. *Anthropology and Photography, 1860–1920.* New Haven: Yale University Press, 1992.

Eng, David L. *Racial Castration: Managing Masculinity in Asian America.* Durham: Duke University Press, 2001.

Escobar, Edward J. *Race, Police, and the Making of a Political Identity: Mexican Americans and the Los Angeles Police Department, 1900–1945.* Berkeley and Los Angeles: University of California Press, 1999.

Fairchild, Amy. *Science at the Borders: Immigrant Medical Inspection and the Shaping of the Modern Industrial Labor Force.* Baltimore: Johns Hopkins University Press, 2003.

Ferg-Cadima, James A. 2004 "Black, White, and Brown: Latino School Desegregation

Efforts in the Pre- and Post-*Brown v. Board of Education* Era." Mexican American Legal Defense and Education Fund, May 2004. Available at http://www.maldef.org.

Fernandez, Ronald. *The Disenchanted Island: Puerto Rico and the United States in the Twentieth Century*. Westport, Conn.: Praeger, 1996.

Foley, Neil. *The White Scourge: Mexicans, Blacks and Poor Whites in Texas Cotton Culture*. Berkeley and Los Angeles: University of California Press, 1997.

——. "Becoming Hispanic: Mexican Americans and the Faustian Pact with Whiteness." In *Reflexiones 1997: New Directions in Mexican American Studies*, ed. Neil Foley, 53–70. Austin: Center for Mexican American Studies Books/University of Texas Press, 1998.

——. "Partly Colored or Other White: Mexican Americans and Their Problem with the Color Line." Lecture delivered at the Labor and Working Class Historians luncheon at the meeting of the Organization of American Historians, St. Louis, MO, 1 April 2000. Available at http://www.lawcha.org.

Foner, Philip. *The Spanish-Cuban-American War and the Birth of American Imperialism, 1895–1902*. 2 vols. New York: Monthly Review Press, 1972.

Foreman, John. *The Philippine Islands: A Political, Geographical, Ethnographical, Social and Commercial History of the Philippine Archipelago*. New York: Scribner's, 1899.

Fujikane, Candace. "Sweeping Racism under the Rug of 'Censorship': The Controversy over Lois-Ann Yamanaka's *Blu's Hanging*." *Amerasia Journal* 26 (2000): 158–94.

García, María Cristina. *Havana USA: Cuban Exiles and Cuban Americans in South Florida, 1959–1994*. Berkeley and Los Angeles: University of California Press, 1996.

García, Mario. "Americans All: The Mexican American Generation and the Politics of Wartime Los Angeles, 1941–45." *Social Science Quarterly* 65, no. 2 (1984): 278–89.

García, Matt. *A World of Their Own: Race, Labor, and Citrus in the Making of Greater Los Angeles, 1900–1970*. Chapel Hill: University of North Carolina Press, 2001.

Gartner, Alan. "Redrawing the Lines: Redistricting and the Politics of Racial Succession in New York." Typescript, City University of New York, Graduate School and University Center, 1993.

González, Gilbert G. *Chicano Education in the Era of Segregation*. Philadelphia: Black Institute Press, 1990.

——. *Labor and Community: Mexican Citrus Worker Villages in a Southern California County, 1900–1950*. Urbana: University of Illinois Press, 1994.

——. *Mexican Consuls and Labor Organizing: Imperial Politics in the American Southwest*. Austin: University of Texas Press, 1999.

Grant, David M., Melvin L. Oliver, and Angela D. James. "African Americans: Social and Economic Bifurcation." In *Ethnic Los Angeles*, ed. Roger Waldinger and Mehdi Bozorgmehr, 379–411. New York: Russell Sage, 1996.

Grant, Madison. *The Passing of the Great Race*. Reprint, New York: Arno, 1970.

Greenfield, Gary A., and Don B. Kates Jr. "Mexican Americans, Racial Discrimination, and the Civil Rights Act of 1866." *California Law Review* 63 (1975): 662–731.

Guerin-Gonzales, Camille. *Mexican Workers and American Dreams: Immigration, Repatriation, and California Farm Labor, 1900–1939*. New Brunswick: Rutgers University Press, 1994.

Guglielmo, Thomas A. *White on Arrival: Italians, Race, Color, and Power in Chicago, 1890–1945*. New York: Oxford University Press, 2003.

Guinier, Lani. *The Tyranny of the Majority: Fundamental Fairness in Representative Democracy*. New York: Free Press, 1994.

Gutiérrez, David. *Walls and Mirrors: Mexican Americans, Mexican Immigrants, and the Politics of Ethnicity*. Berkeley and Los Angeles: University of California Press, 1995.

Hall, Stuart. "Introduction: Who Needs Identity?" In *Questions of Cultural Identity*, ed. Stuart Hall and Paul du Guy. London: Sage, 1996.

Haney López, Ian. *White by Law: The Legal Construction of Race*. New York: New York University Press, 1996.

Henry, W. O., M.D. "The Prevention of the Diseases of Women." *Southern California Medical Practitioner* 35, no. 6 (1920): 71–77.

Hero, Rodney, and Caroline J. Tolbert. "Latinos and Substantive Representation in the U.S. House of Representatives: Direct, Indirect, or Nonexistent?" *American Journal of Political Science* 39, no. 3 (1995): 640–52.

Herrera, Andrea O'Reilly, ed. *ReMembering Cuba: Legacy of a Diaspora*. Austin: University of Texas Press, 2001.

Hietala, Thomas. *Manifest Design: Anxious Aggrandizement in Late Jacksonian America*. Ithaca: Cornell University Press, 1985.

Higham, John. *Strangers in the Land: Patterns of American Nativism, 1860–1925*. New York: Atheneum, 1965.

Hing, Bill Ong. *Making and Remaking Asian America through Immigration Policy, 1850–1990*. Stanford: Stanford University Press, 1993.

Hoffman, Abraham. *Unwanted Mexican Americans in the Great Depression: Repatriation Pressures, 1926–1939*. Tucson: University of Arizona Press, 1974.

Hofstadter, Richard, ed. *Great Issues in American History: From the Revolution to the Civil War, 1765–1865*. New York: Vintage/Random House, 1958.

Hoganson, Kristin L. *Fighting for American Manhood: How Gender Politics Provoked the Spanish-American and Philippine-American Wars*. New Haven: Yale University Press, 1998.

Holt, Elizabeth Mary. *Colonizing Filipinas: Nineteenth-Century Representations of the Philippines in Western Historiography*. Manila: Ateneo de Manila University Press, 2002.

Honig, Bonnie. "Immigrant America? How Foreignness 'Solves' Democracy's Problems." *Social Text* 56 (1998): 1–27.

——. *Democracy and the Foreigner*. Princeton: Princeton University Press, 2001.

Horowitz, Irving Louis. *The Conscience of Worms and the Cowardice of Lions: Cuban Politics and Culture in an American Context*. New Brunswick: Transaction, 1993.

Horsman, Reginald. *Race and Manifest Destiny: The Origins of American Racial Anglo-Saxonism*. Cambridge: Harvard University Press, 1981.

Horwitz, Morton J. "Jews and McCarthyism: A View from the Bronx." In *Secret Agents: The Rosenberg Case, McCarthyism, and Fifties America*, ed. Marjorie Garber and Rebecca L. Walkowitz, 257–63. New York: Routledge, 1995.

Hosokawa, Bill. *JACL in Search of Justice*. New York: Morrow, 1982.

Hoxie, Frederick E. *A Final Promise: The Campaign to Assimilate the Indians, 1880–1920*. Lincoln: University of Nebraska Press, 2001.

Hutterer, Karl L. "Dean C. Worcester and Philippine Anthropology." *Philippine Quarterly of Culture and Society* 6, no. 3 (1978): 125–29.

Ichioka, Yuji. "The Japanese Immigrant Response to the 1920 Alien Land Law." *Agricultural History* 43, no. 2 (April 1984): 157–78.

Ignatiev, Noel. *How the Irish Became White*. New York: Routledge, 1995.

Jacobson, Matthew Frye. *Special Sorrows: The Diasporic Imagination of Irish, Polish, and Jewish Immigrants in the United States*. Cambridge: Harvard University Press, 1995.

——. *Whiteness of a Different Color: European Immigrants and the Alchemy of Race*. Cambridge: Harvard University Press, 1999.

——. *Barbarian Virtues: The United States Encounters Foreign Peoples at Home and Abroad 1876–1917*. New York: Hill and Wang, 2000.

Jordan, Winthrop. *White over Black: American Attitudes toward the Negro, 1550–1812*. Chapel Hill: University of North Carolina Press, 1968.

Kim, Claire Jean. *Bitter Fruit: The Politics of Black-Korean Conflict in New York City*. New Haven: Yale University Press, 2000.

Kim, Hyung-chan. *A Legal History of Asian Americans, 1790–1990*. Westport: Greenwood, 1994.

Kitano, Harry H. L. *Japanese Americans: The Evolution of a Subculture*. Englewood Cliffs, N.J.: Prentice-Hall, 1969.

Kluger, Richard. *Simple Justice:* Brown v. Board of Education *and Black America's Struggle for Equality*. New York: Vintage, 1975.

Koos, Cheryl. "Engendering Reaction: The Politics of Pronatalism and the Family in France, 1919–1944." Ph.D. diss., University of Southern California, 1996.

Kousser, J. Morgan. *Colorblind Injustice: Minority Voting Rights and the Undoing of the Second Reconstruction*. Chapel Hill: University of North Carolina Press, 1999.

Kraut, Alan. *Silent Travelers: Germs, Genes, and the "Immigrant Menace."* New York: Basic, 1994.

Kroeber, A. L. "Measurements of Igorotes." *American Anthropologist* 8, no. 1 (January–March 1906): 194–95.

Kurashige, Lon. *Japanese American Celebration and Conflict: A History of Ethnic Identity and Festival in Los Angeles, 1934–1990*. Berkeley and Los Angeles: University of California Press, 2002.

Kurashige, Scott Tadao. "Transforming Los Angeles: Black and Japanese American Struggles for Racial Equality in the 20th Century." Ph.D. diss., Department of History, University of California, Los Angeles, 2000.

Lee, Chang-rae. *Native Speaker*. New York: Riverhead, 1995.

Lee, Erika. *At America's Gates: Chinese Immigration during the Exclusion Era, 1882–1943*. Chapel Hill: University of North Carolina Press, 2003.

Lee, Wen Ho, and Helen Zia. *My Country versus Me*. New York: Hyperion, 2001.

Leonard, Kevin Allen. "Brothers under the Skin? African Americans, Mexican Americans, and World War II in California." In *The Way We Really Were: The Golden State in the Second Great War*, ed. Roger W. Lotchin. Urbana: University of Illinois Press, 2000.

——. " 'In the Interest of All Races': African Americans and Interracial Cooperation in Los Angeles during and after World War II." In *Seeking El Dorado: African Americans in California*, ed. Lawrence B. De Graaf, Kevin Mulroy, and Quintard Taylor. Los Angeles: Autry Museum of Western Heritage; Seattle: University of Washington Press, 2001.

Li, David Leiwei. *Imagining the Nation: Asian American Literature and Cultural Consent*. Stanford: Stanford University Press, 1998.

Lieberson, Stanley. *A Piece of the Pie: Blacks and White Immigrants since 1880*. Berkeley and Los Angeles: University of California Press, 1980.

Lipsitz, George. *The Possessive Investment in Whiteness: How White People Benefit from Identity Politics*. Philadelphia: Temple University Press, 1998.

Lowe, Lisa. *Immigrant Acts: On Asian American Cultural Politics*. Durham: Duke University Press, 1996.

Lubiano, Wahneema. "Black Nationalism and Black Common Sense: Policing Ourselves and Others." In *The House That Race Built: Black Americans, U.S. Terrain*, ed. Wahneema Lubiano, 232–52. New York: Pantheon/Random House, 1997.

Markovits, Elizabeth Katharyn. "The Enemy Makes the Man: U.S. Foreign Policy, Cuban Nationalism, and Regime Survival." *Problems of Post-Communism* 48 (2001): 31–42.

Martínez-Alier, Verena. *Marriage, Class, and Colour in Nineteenth-Century Cuba: A Study of Racial Attitudes and Sexual Values in a Slave Society*. London: Cambridge University Press, 1974.

Mason, William, and John McKinstry. *The Japanese of Los Angeles*. Los Angeles: Los Angeles County Museum of Natural History, History Division, 1969.

Masud-Piloto, Felix Roberto. *From Welcomed Exiles to Illegal Immigrants: Cuban Migration to the U.S., 1959–1995*. Lanham, Md.: Rowman and Little, 1996.

Matsumoto, Valerie. *Farming the Home Place: A Japanese American Community in California*. Ithaca: Cornell University Press, 1993.

Mauro, Frank J., ed. *Restructuring the New York City Government: The Emergence of Municipal Reform*. New York: Academy of Political Science, 1989.

Mazón, Mauricio. *The Zoot Suit Riots: The Psychology of Symbolic Annihilation*. Austin: University of Texas Press, 1984.

McClain, Charles. *In Search of Equality: The Chinese Struggle against Discrimination in Nineteenth Century America*. Berkeley and Los Angeles: University of California Press, 1994.

McCormick, Joseph, and Charles E. Jones. "The Conceptualization of Deracialization: Thinking through the Dilemma." In *Dilemmas of Black Politics: Issues of Leadership and Strategy*, ed. Georgia Persons, 66–84. New York: Harper Collins, 1993.

McLaren, Peter, and Jill Pinkney-Pastrana. "Cuba, Yanquización, and the Cult of Elián González: A View from the 'Enlightened' States." *International Journal of Qualitative Studies in Education* 14, no. 2 (2001): 201–19.

McLauchlan, Gregory, and Gregory Hooks. "Last of the Dinosaurs? Big Weapons, Big Science, and the American State from Hiroshima to the End of the Cold War." *Sociological Quarterly* 36 (1995): 749–76.

McWilliams, Carey. "Is Your Name Gonzales?" *The Nation* no. 164, 15 March 1947, 302–04.

———. *Brothers under the Skin*. 2nd ed. Boston: Little, Brown, 1964.

———. *North from Mexico: The Spanish-Speaking People of the United States*. 1949. Reprint, New York: Greenwood, 1968.

Meckel, Richard. *Save the Babies: American Public Health Reform and the Prevention of Infant Mortality*. Baltimore: Johns Hopkins University Press, 1990.

Meier, Matt S., and Feliciano Rivero, eds. *Readings on La Raza: The Twentieth Century*. New York: Hill and Wang, 1974.

Miller, Stuart Creighton. *"Benevolent Assimilation": The American Conquest of the Philippines, 1899–1903*. New Haven: Yale University Press, 1982.

Mintz, Sidney W. "North American Anthropological Contributions to Caribbean Studies." *Boletín de Estudios Latinoamericanos y del Caribe* 22 (1977): 68–82.

Modell, John. *The Economics and Politics of Racial Accommodation: The Japanese of Los Angeles, 1900–1942*. Urbana: University of Illinois Press, 1977.

Molina, Natalia. *Fit to Be Citizens: Public Health and Race in Los Angeles, 1879–1939*. Berkeley and Los Angeles: University of California Press, in press.

Mollenkopf, John H. *A Phoenix in the Ashes: The Rise and Fall of the Koch Coalition in New York City Politics*. Princeton: Princeton University Press, 1992.

Moore, Deborah Dash. "Reconsidering the Rosenbergs: Symbol and Substance in Second Generation American Jewish Consciousness." *Journal of American Ethnic History* 8 (1988): 21–37.

Mukherjee, Bharati. "Loose Ends." In *The Middleman and Other Stories*, 43–54. New York: Grove Press, 1988.

Muncy, Robin. *Creating a Female Dominion in American Reform, 1890–1935*. New York: Oxford University Press, 1991.

Nakashima, Cynthia L. "An Invisible Monster: The Creation and Denial of Mixed-Race People in America." In *Racially Mixed People in America*, ed. Maria P. P. Root, 162–78. Newbury Park: Sage, 1992.

Nelson, Dana D. *National Manhood: Capitalist Citizenship and the Imagined Fraternity of White Men*. Durham: Duke University Press, 1998.

Ngai, Mae M. "From Colonial Subject to Undesirable Alien: Filipino Migration, Exclusion, and Repatriation, 1920–1940." In *Re / Collecting Early Asian America: Essays in Cultural History*, ed. Josephine Lee, Imogene L. Lim, and Yuko Matsukawa, 111–26. Philadelphia: Temple University Press, 2002.

———. *Impossible Subjects: Illegal Aliens and the Making of Modern America*. Princeton: Princeton University Press, 2004.

Nobles, Gregory. *American Frontiers: Cultural Encounters and Continental Conquest*. New York: Hill and Wang, 1997.

Ober, Frederick A. *Puerto Rico and Its Resources*. New York: D. Appleton, 1898.

Okamura, Raymond. "The Myth of Census Confidentiality." *Amerasia Journal* 8, no. 2 (1981): 111–120.

Okihiro, Gary Y. *Margins and Mainstreams: Asians in American History and Culture*. Seattle: University of Washington Press, 1994.

———. *Common Ground: Reimagining American History*. Princeton: Princeton University Press, 2001.

Omi, Michael, and Howard Winant. *Racial Formation in the United States: From the 1960s to the 1980s*. 1986. Rev. ed., New York: Routledge, 1994.

Ong, Aihwa. *Flexible Citizenship: The Cultural Logics of Transnationality*. Durham: Duke University Press, 1999.

Ong, Paul, and Don T. Nakanishi. "Becoming Citizens, Becoming Voters: The Naturalization and Political Participation of Asian Pacific Immigrants." In *The State of Asian Pacific America: Reframing the Immigration Debate*, ed. Bill Ong Hing and Ronald Lee, 275–305. Los Angeles: Leadership Education for Asian Pacifics, Asian Pacific American Public Policy Institute / University of California, Los Angeles, Asian American Studies Center, 1996.

Palumbo-Liu, David. *Asian / American: Historical Crossings of a Racial Frontier*. Stanford: Stanford University Press, 1999.

Park, You-me, and Gayle Wald. "Native Daughters in the Promised Land: Gender, Race, and the Question of Separate Spheres." In *No More Separate Spheres!* ed. Cathy Davidson and Jessamyn Hatcher. Durham: Duke University Press, 2002.

Parrington, Vernon Louis. *Main Currents in American Thought: An Interpretation of American Literature from the Beginnings to 1920*. Vol. 3. New York: Harcourt, Brace, 1930.

Pascoe, Peggy. *Relations of Rescue: The Search for Female Moral Authority in the American West, 1874–1939*. New York: Oxford University Press, 1990.

Patterson, Orlando. *Slavery and Social Death: A Comparative Study.* Cambridge: Harvard University Press, 1982.

Pernick, Martin. "Eugenics and Public Health in American History." *American Journal of Public Health* 87, no. 11 (1997): 1767–72.

Perrett, Geoffrey. *Days of Sadness, Years of Triumph.* Baltimore: Penguin, 1974.

Piedra, José. "Nationalizing Sissies." In *Entiendes? Queer Readings, Hispanic Writings,* ed. Emilie L. Bergmann and Paul Julian Smith, 370–409. Durham: Duke University Press, 1995.

Pitkin, Hanna Fenichel. *The Concept of Representation.* Berkeley and Los Angeles: University of California Press, 1967.

Pomeroy, John. "The Japanese Evil in California." Lecture prepared for the San Dimas Church, n.d. Department of Health Services Library, Los Angeles.

Portes, Alejandro, and Alex Stepick. *City on the Edge: The Transformation of Miami.* Berkeley and Los Angeles: University of California Press, 1993.

Quinsaat, Jesse, ed. *Letters in Exile: An Introductory Reader on the History of Pilipinos in America.* Los Angeles: University of California, Los Angeles, Asian American Studies Center, 1976.

Rafael, Vicente. "White Love: Surveillance and Nationalist Resistance in the U.S. Colonization of the Philippines." In *Cultures of United States Imperialism,* ed. Amy Kaplan and Donald E. Pease, 188–204. Durham: Duke University Press, 1993.

Reid, Whitelaw. *Problems of Expansion.* New York: Century, 1900.

Robbie, Sandra. *Méndez v. Westminster: For All the Children, Para Todos los Niños.* Real Orange Films, 2002.

Robinson, Greg. *By Order of the President: FDR and the Internment of Japanese Americans.* Cambridge: Harvard University Press, 2001.

Robinson, Greg, and Toni Robinson. "*Korematsu* and Beyond: Japanese Americans and the Origins of Strict Scrutiny." *Law and Contemporary Problems* 68, no. 2: 31–58.

Roediger, David R. *The Wages of Whiteness: Race and the Making of the American Working Class.* New York: Verso, 1991.

———. *Towards the Abolition of Whiteness: Essays on Race, Politics, and Working Class History.* New York: Verso, 1994.

Romo, Ricardo. *East Los Angeles: History of a Barrio.* Austin: University of Texas Press, 1983.

Rosaldo, Renato. *Culture and Truth: The Remaking of Social Analysis.* Boston: Beacon, 1989.

Ross, Andrew. "The Work of the State." In *Secret Agents: The Rosenberg Case, McCarthyism, and Fifties America,* ed. Marjorie Garber and Rebecca L. Walkowitz, 291–99. New York: Routledge, 1995.

*Rudyard Kipling's Verse, 1885–1926.* Garden City, N.Y.: Doubleday, Page, 1927.

Ruiz, Vicki L. "We Always Tell Our Children That They Are Americans: *Méndez v. Westminster* and the California Road to *Brown v. Board of Education.*" *College Board Review,* no. 200 (fall 2003): 21–27.

Ruppel, Kristin Tanner. "Nations Undivided, Indian Land Unearthed: The Dis-Owning of the U.S. Federal Indian Trust." Ph.D. diss., Department of Anthropology, Columbia University, 2003.

Rydell, Robert W. *All the World's a Fair: Visions of Empire at American International Expositions, 1876–1916.* Chicago: University of Chicago Press, 1984.

Saito, Leland T. "Beyond Numbers: Asian American and Latino Politics in Los Angeles'
San Gabriel Valley." In *Racial and Ethnic Politics in California*, ed. Michael B. Preston,
Bruce E. Cain, and Sandra Bass, 45–72. Berkeley: University of California, Berkeley,
Institute of Governmental Studies Press, 1998.

———. "Asian Americans and Multiracial Political Coalitions: New York City's Chinatown
and Redistricting, 1990–1991." In *Asian Americans and Politics: An Exploration*, ed.
Gordon Chang, 383–408. Stanford: Stanford University Press, 2001.

———. "The Sedimentation of Political Inequality: Charter Revision and Redistricting in
New York City's Chinatown, 1989–1991." *UCLA Asian Pacific American Law Journal* 8,
no. 1 (2002): 123–45.

Salyer, Lucy E. *Laws Harsh as Tigers: Chinese Immigrants and the Shaping of Modern
Immigration Law*. Chapel Hill: University of North Carolina Press, 1995.

Sánchez, George. " 'Go after the Women': Americanization and the Mexican Immigrant
Woman, 1915–1929." In *A Multi-Cultural Reader in US Women's History*, ed. Ellen
DuBois and Vicki Ruiz. New York: Routledge, 1990.

———. *Becoming Mexican American: Ethnicity, Culture, and Identity in Chicano Los Angeles,
1900–1945*. New York: Oxford University Press, 1993.

San Miguel, Guadalupe, Jr. "The Struggle against Separate and Unequal Schools: Middle
Class Mexican Americans and the Desegregation Campaign in Texas, 1929–1957."
*History of Education Quarterly* 23 (1983): 343–59.

Santiago, John, ed. *Redistricting, Race and Ethnicity in New York City: The Gartner Report and
Its Critics*. New York: Institute for Puerto Rican Policy, n.d.

Santiago-Valles, Kelvin A. *"Subject People" and Colonial Discourses: Economic Transformation and
Social Disorder in Puerto Rico, 1898–1947*. Albany: State University of New York Press, 1994.

Saxton, Alexander. *The Indispensable Enemy: Labor and the Anti-Chinese Movement in
California*. Berkeley: University of California Press, 1971.

———. *The Rise and Fall of the White Republic: Class Politics and Mass Culture in Nineteenth-
Century America*. New York: Verso, 1990.

Shah, Nayan. *Contagious Divides: Epidemics and Race in San Francisco's Chinatown*. Berkeley
and Los Angeles: University of California Press, 2001.

Smedley, Audrey. *Race in North America: Origin and Evolution of a Worldview*. Boulder:
Westview, 1993.

Smith, Neil. *American Empire: Roosevelt's Geographer and the Prelude to Globalization*.
Berkeley and Los Angeles: University of California Press, 2003.

Smith, Rogers M. *Civic Ideals: Conflicting Visions of Citizenship in U.S. History*. New
Haven: Yale University Press, 1997.

So, Christine. "Reading *Blu's Hanging* and the Crisis of Representation in Asian American
Studies." Paper presented at the annual meeting of the Modern Language Association,
Washington, 2000.

Sonenshein, Raphael J. *Politics in Black and White: Race and Power in Los Angeles*. Princeton:
Princeton University Press, 1993.

Spengler, Oswald. *The Decline of the West: Form and Actuality*. New York: Knopf, 1926.

State of California. *The Statutes of California*. Sacramento: Superintendent of State
Printing, 1913.

———. *The Statutes of California: Measures Submitted to Electors California*. Sacramento:
Superintendent of State Printing, 1921.

Steinberg, Stephen. *The Ethnic Myth: Race, Ethnicity, and Class in America.* 1981. Updated and expanded ed., Boston: Beacon, 1989.

Stober, Dan, and Ian Hoffman. *A Convenient Spy: Wen Ho Lee and the Politics of Nuclear Espionage.* New York: Simon and Schuster, 2001.

Stoddard, Lothrop. *The Rising Tide of Color against White World-Supremacy.* New York: Scribner's, 1920.

Suárez Findlay, Eileen J. *Imposing Decency: The Politics of Sexuality and Race in Puerto Rico, 1870–1920.* Durham: Duke University Press, 1999.

Takaki, Ronald. *Iron Cages: Race and Culture in 19th-Century America.* New York: Oxford University Press, 1979.

———. *Double Victory: A Multicultural History of America in World War II.* Boston: Little, Brown, 2000.

Thompson, Lanny. *Nuestra isla y su gente: La construcción del "otro" puertorriqueño en "Our Islands and Their People."* Recinto de Río Piedras: Centro de Investigaciones Sociales y Departamento de Historia de la Universidad de Puerto Rico, 1995.

———. "The Imperial Republic: A Comparison of the Insular Territories under U.S. Dominion after 1898." *Pacific Historical Review* 71, no. 4 (2002): 535–74.

———. "Representation and Rule in the Imperial Archipelago: Cuba, Puerto Rico, Hawaii, and the Philippines under U.S. Dominion after 1898." *American Studies Asia* 1, no. 1 (2002): 3–39.

Tocqueville, Alexis de. *Democracy in America,* ed. J. P. Mayer, trans. George Lawrence, 1966. Reissue ed., New York: Harper and Row, 1988.

Tölölyan, Khachig. "The Nation-State and Its Others: In Lieu of a Preface." *Diaspora* 1, no. 1 (1991): 1–7.

Triay, Victor Andres. *Fleeing Castro: Operation Pedro Pan and the Cuban Children's Program.* Gainesville: University of Florida Press, 1998.

Turner, Frederick Jackson. *The Frontier in American History.* New York: Henry Holt, 1920.

Underwood, Katherine. "Process and Politics: Multiracial Electoral Coalition Building and Representation in Los Angeles' Ninth District, 1949–1962." Ph.D. diss., University of California, San Diego, 1992.

Urciuoli, Bonnie. *Exposing Prejudice: Puerto Rican Experiences of Language, Race, and Class.* Boulder: Westview, 1996.

U.S. Immigration Commission. *Reports of the Immigration Commission.* 41 vols. Washington: U.S. Government Printing Office, 1911.

U.S. War Department. Division of Customs and Insular Affairs. *Puerto Rico, Embracing the Reports of Brig. Gen. Geo. W. David, Military Governor. . . .* Washington: U.S. Government Printing Office, 1900.

Vaughan, Christopher A. "Ogling Igorots: The Politics and Commerce of Exhibiting Cultural Otherness, 1898–1913." In *Freakery: Cultural Spectacles of the Extraordinary Body,* ed. Rosemarie Garland Thomson. New York: New York University Press, 1996.

Vergara, Benito M., Jr. *Displaying Filipinos: Photography and Colonialism in Early 20th Century Philippines.* Quezon City: University of the Philippines Press, 1995.

Volpp, Leti. " 'Obnoxious to Their Very Nature': Asian Americans and Constitutional Citizenship." *Asian Law Journal* 8 (2001): 71–87.

Wang, Jessica. *American Science in an Age of Anxiety: Scientists, Anticommunism, and the Cold War.* Chapel Hill: University of North Carolina Press, 1999.

Williams, Walter L. "United States Indian Policy and the Debate over Philippine Annexation: Implications for the Origins of American Imperialism." *Journal of American History* 66, no. 4 (1980): 810–31.

Williams, William Appleman. "The Frontier Thesis and American Foreign Policy." *Pacific Historical Review* 24 (November 1955): 379–95.

———. *Empire as a Way of Life*. New York: Oxford University Press, 1980.

Wilson, Steven H. "*Brown* over 'Other White': Mexican Americans' Legal Arguments and Litigation Strategy in School Desegregation Lawsuits." *Law and History Review* (Spring 2003). Online. http://www.historycooperative.org/journals/lhr/21.1.

Wissler, Clark. *Measurements of Dakota Children*. New York: New York Academy of Sciences, 1910.

———. *Changes in Population Profiles among the Northern Plains Indians*. New York: American Museum of Natural History, 1936.

———. *Population Changes among the Northern Plains Indians*. New Haven: Yale University Press, 1936.

Wollenberg, Charles. "*Mendez v. Westminster*: Race, Nationality and Segregation in California Schools." *California Historical Quarterly* 53 (1974): 317–32.

———. *All Deliberate Speed: Segregation and Exclusion in California Schools, 1855–1973*. Berkeley: University of California Press, 1976.

Wong, K. Scott, and Sucheng Chan, eds. *Claiming America: Constructing Chinese American Identities during the Exclusion Era*. Philadelphia: Temple University Press, 1998.

Woofter, T. J., Jr. "The Status of Racial and Ethnic Groups." In *Recent Social Trends in the United States: Report of the President's Research Committee on Social Trends*. New York: McGraw-Hill, 1933.

Worcester, Dean C. *The Philippine Islands and Their People*. New York: Macmillan, 1898.

———. "The Non-Christian Peoples of the Philippines: With an Account of What Has Been Done for Them under American Rule." *National Geographic* 24, no. 11 (November 1913): 1157–1256.

Wu, Cheng-Tsu, ed. *"Chink!" A Documentary History of Anti-Chinese Prejudice in America*. New York: World, 1972.

Wu, Frank H. "Profiling Principle: The Prosecution of Wen Ho Lee and the Defense of Asian Americans." *UCLA Asian Pacific American Law Journal* 7 (2001): 52–56.

Yu, Henry. *Thinking Orientals: Migration, Contact, and Exoticism in Modern America*. New York: Oxford University Press, 2001.

Yung, Judy. *Unbound Feet: A Social History of Chinese Women in San Francisco*. Berkeley and Los Angeles: University of California Press, 1995.

Žižek, Slavoj. *The Sublime Object of Ideology*. London: Verso, 1989.

———. "Love Thy Neighbor? No Thanks." In *The Psychoanalysis of Race*, ed. Christopher Lane, 154–75. New York: Columbia University Press, 1998.

# Contributors

NICHOLAS DE GENOVA is an assistant professor of anthropology and Latino studies at Columbia University. He is the author of *Working the Boundaries: Race, Space, and "Illegality" in Mexican Chicago* (Duke University Press, 2005) and the coauthor (with Ana Y. Ramos-Zayas) of *Latino Crossings: Mexicans, Puerto Ricans, and the Politics of Race and Citizenship* (Routledge, 2003). He has coedited and contributed to "Latino Racial Formations in the United States," a special thematic issue of the *Journal of Latin American Anthropology* (2003), and has previously published articles in *Latino Studies*, the *Annual Review of Anthropology*, *Latin American Perspectives*, *Estudios Migratorios Latinoamericanos*, *Anthropology and Humanism*, *Public Culture*, *Transition*, and *Social Text*.

VICTOR JEW has taught Asian American history and U.S. legal and constitutional history at Michigan State University, the University of Wisconsin, Madison, and Cornell University. He has published on anti-Chinese violence in the U.S. Midwest in the *Journal of Social History* (2003), and his forthcoming book on the social, legal, and cultural history of arson in the United States will be published by the University of Pennsylvania Press.

ANDREA LEVINE is an assistant professor of English at George Washington University. She has published articles on race and masculinity in *MELUS* (2003) and *American Literature* (2001). Her forthcoming *Bodies on the Line: Writing Sex and Nation after the 1960s* examines the role of sexuality in contemporary literary and cultural constructions of U.S. citizenship.

NATALIA MOLINA is an assistant professor of ethnic studies at the University of California, San Diego. She has previously published on medicalized representations of Mexican communities in *Aztlán: A Journal of Chicano Studies* (2003). She is also the author of the forthcoming *Fit to Be Citizens? Public Health and Race in Los Angeles, 1879–1939* (University of California Press).

GARY Y. OKIHIRO is a professor of international and public affairs and the director of the Center for the Study of Ethnicity and Race at Columbia University. He is the author of eight books, including, most recently, *Common Ground: Reimagining American History* (Princeton University Press, 2001) and *The Columbia Guide to Asian American History* (Columbia University Press, 2001). He is a recipient of the Lifetime Achievement Award from the American Studies Association and is a past president of the Association for Asian American Studies.

CRYSTAL PARIKH is an assistant professor of English and American studies at New York University. She has published articles in *Modern Fiction Studies* (2002), *Contemporary Literature* (2002), and the *Journal of Asian American Studies* (2002). She is writing a book on the ethics of betrayal, which will examine the themes and tropes of betrayal for racial and national formation in Asian American and Latino literary and cultural narratives.

GREG ROBINSON is an assistant professor of history at the Université du Québec, Montréal. He is the author of *By Order of the President: FDR and the Internment of Japanese Americans* (Harvard University Press, 2001), an associate editor of *The Encyclopedia of African American Culture and History* (Gale/Macmillan, 1995–2001), a coeditor of and contributor to the Miné Okubo memorial tribute in the *Amerasia Journal* (2004), and a coauthor of the afterword to *Ayako Ishigaki, Restless Wave* (Feminist Press, 2004). He has also published numerous articles and chapters of anthologies.

TONI ROBINSON (1942–2002) received her B.A. from the City College of New York at age nineteen. After raising a family, she earned her J.D. from Brooklyn Law School in 1974. She was a practicing attorney for over twenty-five years in the New York State and federal courts, primarily in the fields of corporate and commercial litigation and family law. Following her retirement, she devoted her energies to researching and writing a legal history of postwar African American–Nisei encounters, in collaboration with Greg Robinson. Their essay in this collection was the first of three essay-length manuscripts from this project accepted for publication. The second, on the origins of the Supreme Court's doctrine of strict scrutiny, was published in 2005 in *Law and Contemporary Problems*.

LELAND T. SAITO is an associate professor of sociology and of American studies and ethnicity at the University of Southern California. He is currently the chair of the board of directors of the Southwest Center for Asian Pacific American Law and was formerly the vice chair of the San Diego City Council Redistricting Commission (2000). He is the author of *Race and Politics: Asian Americans, Latinos, and Whites in a Los Angeles Suburb* (University of Illinois Press, 1998). His articles have appeared in *Remapping Asian American History* (Altamira Press, 2004), *Asian Americans and Politics: An Exploration* (Stanford University Press, 2001), and *The State of Asian Pacific Americans: Transforming Race Relations* (LEAP/UCLA Asian Pacific American Public Policy Institute, 2000) as well as the *Journal of San Diego History* (2003) and the *UCLA Asian Pacific American Law Journal* (2002).

# Index

Asians (*cont.*)
197n.5; and national self-image, 172; and racialization, 11–12, 41. *See also* Asian, as racial category; Asian Americans; Chinese; Chinese Americans; Filipinos; Japanese; Japanese Americans; Korean Americans
Asiatic, as racial category, 14
Association for Asian American Studies, 194, 206n.58
Atomic Energy Act (1946), 173, 193, 207n.70
Ayres, Edward D., 9, 77–82, 84, 85, 89–90n.33
Aztecs, 9, 77, 80, 82. *See also* Mexicans

Baca, Lee, 136
Bagobo "savages," 34. *See also* Filipinos
Balderrama, Francisco, 12
*Balseros* crisis (1994), 184
Barret, Wayne, 125
Barrows, David P., 31
Batista, Fulgencio, 177, 200n.13
Battery Park City (New York), 122
Bederman, Gail, 26
Beijing, China, 191
Benedict, Ruth, 81
Benevolent assimilation, idea of, 34
Bennett, Charles, 56
Berkeley, California. *See* University of California, Berkeley
Berman, Howard, 132
Betrayal, concept of, 171–72, 175, 180–84, 189, 193, 196. *See also* Lee, Wen Ho
Beveridge, Albert, 6
Biologism, 81–83
Black Americans. *See* African Americans
Black nationalism, 18n.13
Blackness, 1–5, 10–11, 15–16; as distinctive racial condition of African Americans, 11; "driving while Black," 179; as encompassing all nonwhites, 8. *See also* African Americans; whiteness
Black-white binary, 1–17, 36, 44, 47, 63, 83, 180
Blumentritt, Ferdinand, 30

*Blu's Hanging*, 206n.58
Boas, Franz, 66–69
Bogardus, Emory, 81
*Bolling v. Sharpe*, 112
Boswell, Thomas D., 199n.10
Boyle Heights (Los Angeles), 85
Braceros, 115n.22
Braverman, Harry, 80
Briggs, Herman, 47
Brotons, Elizabeth, 174, 196, 207n.76
Brown, as racial category, 5, 12, 33
*Brown v. Board of Education*, 93–94, 104, 110–113
Bureau of Education (U.S.), 67
Butler, Judith, 175

Calderon, Ruben A., 84
California, 8, 41, 120; Alien Land Acts of, 42, 53; anthropometry of Chinatown, 65–74; Chicano crisis in Los Angeles, 76–77, 82, 85; and Japanese, 42, 45, 47–50; and Mexicans, 42, 43, 46–49, 63, 76–80, 86–87; public health in Los Angeles, 47–58; and redistricting, 126–39; school segregation in, 93–94, 95–97
California Education Code, 105, 107, 114n.4
*California Journal*, 129
California State Assembly, 126
California State Emergency Relief Administration (SERA), 66, 69–70, 72, 86
California State Senate, 126
California Supreme Court, 8
*Cano v. Davis*, 131,132
Canosa, Jorge Mas, 181
Cárdenas, José, 187
Carmichael, Virginia, 193, 198n.7
Carrol, Henry K., 27–29
Carter, Robert, 109
Castro, Fidel, 177, 181–183
Caucasian, as racial category, 69, 78
Caucasoid, as racial category, 111
Census, U.S. Bureau of, 6, 133
Central Intelligence Agency (CIA), 191, 194, 208n.76
Chaining, concept of, 64

Chan, Elaine, 122, 123
Chang, Cecilia, 190–91
*Changes in the Bodily Forms of Descendents of Immigrants*, 67
*Changes in Population Profiles among the Northern Plains Indians*, 67
Chávez, César, 113
*Cherokee Nation v. Georgia*, 18n.11
Chester, Eric T., 153
Chicago, Illinois, 24–26
Chicano crisis (1942–44), 76–77, 82, 85, 86
Chicanos, 78, 83, 113. *See also* Mexican Americans; Mexicans
Chin, Margaret, 122, 124–26, 135, 138
China, 25–26, 188. *See also* People's Republic of China (PRC)
Chinatown (New York), 138, 139; and redistricting, 120–27, 133, 139. *See also* Chinese; Chinese Americans
Chinatown (San Francisco), 62–65, 68–75. *See also* Chinese; Chinese Americans
Chinatown Planning Council (New York), 125
Chinatown Voter Education Alliance (New York), 133
Chinese, 8, 11, 14, 53–54, 62–74; and anthropometry, 63–74, 86; as "niggers," 10; and San Francisco, 62–63, 69; and social surveillance, 68–69; as "unsanitary," 53–54; as "yellow," 72. *See also* Chinese Americans
Chinese, as racial category, 11–12
Chinese Americans, 62, 87, 136, 170; and anthropometry, 63–74, 86; as model minority, 177–78; as national objects, 176; and Wen Ho Lee trial, 191. *See also* Chinese
"Chinese Colony," 86
Chinese Exclusion Act (1882), 14, 24, 39n.41, 44
"Chinese"-ness, 11–12; and neo-Confucianism, 188
Chippewa Indians, 19n.33
Chow, Rey, 170–171, 204n.39
Christ, figure of, 171, 175, 182, 197n.1, 201n.22, 202n.29
Chu, Judy, 130, 136

Chuman, Frank, 112
Churchill, Ward, 2
Citizenship (U.S.), 5, 13–14, 42, 185, 188; and deportation of Mexican Americans, 12; and Japanese Americans, 42, 80, 94–99. *See also* Fourteenth Amendment; Naturalization Act
City Hall (New York), 122
Clinton administration, 200n.13, 205n.46
Coalition Against Racial Scapegoating, 201n.22
Coalition of Asian Pacific Americans for Fair Redistricting, 129, 134
Cold war, 152, 177, 180, 181, 184, 185, 191, 192, 194
Colombia, 6
Colonialism (U.S.), 1–17, 23–37. *See also* Imperialism (U.S.)
Colony, as racialized term, 84–85, 90n.49. *See also* Mexican Americans; Mexicans
Columbia University, 162
"Column Left," 82
Committee of 100, 179, 201n.18
Communism, 175–77, 180, 184–85, 198n.7
Community Service Society, 123
Compton, California, 127
Confucius Plaza (Chinatown, New York), 125
Congress of Industrial Organizations (CIO), 112
Constitution (U.S.), 121
Coordinating Council for Latin American Youth, 100–101
Corona, Bert, 80
Cox Committee, 173, 192
Crossover voting, 136
Cuba, 6, 7, 10, 174, 181, 185; as imagined, 182; U.S. embargo of, 187
Cuban Adjustment Act (1966), 199n.11
Cuban American National Foundation, 181, 187
Cuban Americans, 172, 174, 176–78, 180–87; as "banana republic," 186; and cold war politics, 181, 186; ethnic tensions with African Americans, 180; and Elián

Gender, 23, 28; and Filipina/os, 34–35; and "New Woman," 26; and Puerto Ricans, 29–30, 37. *See also* Masculinity

General Allotment (Dawes) Act (1887), 5

Genocide, 7

Gentleman's Agreement (1907–8), 14, 48

Gentrification, 125

"Ggeh," 157–158; as "money club," 164

Globalization: and Americanization, 172–73, 175, 176, 185

González, Elián, case of, 170, 171, 172, 173–87, 189, 196. *See also* Cuban Americans; Cubans

González, Juan M., 174, 182, 183, 184

González, Lázaro, 174

González, Marisleysis, 174, 196

Gook, as racial epithet, 19n.33

Gramsci, Antonio, 87

Grant, Madison, 48

Great Depression, 62–63, 68–69

*Grizzly Bear*, 50

Guam, 6, 10

Guevara, Ernesto "Che," 183

Gu-Gu, as racial epithet, 35

Guzman, William, 102

Haiti, 6, 7

Haitians, 19n.33, 180

Hall, Stuart, 64

Hanna, Philip C., 27

*Hard Palate in Normal and Feeble-Minded Individuals*, 67

Hawaii, 6

Hawaiians, 19n.33

Hay, John, 25

Haymarket Square bombing, 24–25

Henderson, Harry, 80

Henry, W. O., 52

*Hernández v. State of Texas*, 112–13

Heteronormativity, 17, 167

Hispanic, as racial category, 14–15

Hispanics, 156. *See also* Latinos

"Homeland Security," 16

Honduras, 6

Hoover, Herbert, 85

Hoover elementary (Westminster, California), 102

Horowitz, Irving, 183

Huang, John, 200n.13

Huerta, Dolores, 132

Hull House, 26

*Hurd v. Hodge*, 112

Identity, 64

Igorots, 33–37. *See also* Filipinos

"Immigration," discourse of, 13

Immigration Act of 1917, 14

Immigration Act of 1924, 58, 94

Immigration and Naturalization Service (INS), 174

Immigration law (U.S.), 13–14

*Impact of Redistricting in Your Community*, 129

Imperialism (Japanese), 156

Imperialism (U.S.), 6–7, 10–13, 16–17, 156–57, 195; and the Dominican Republic, 151–54. *See also* Colonialism (U.S.)

Indian, as racial category, 4–5, 18n.9. *See also* Native American, as racial category; Native Americans

Infant mortality rates (IMRs), 55–56

Internment (of Japanese), 9, 97–98, 133, 149, 179, 201n.21

Inui, K. S., 42

Iraq, 19n.33

Issei, 44, 80, 94–95, 97–98; as "enemy aliens," 98; and U.S. citizenship, 42. *See also* Japanese; Japanese Americans; Nisei

Jacobson, Matthew F., 19n.22

Japan, 9, 94

Japanese, 9, 40–54, 58, 78; internment of, 9, 97–98, 133, 149, 179, 201n.21; prohibition of labor migration of, 14, 48. *See also* Issei; Japanese Americans; Nikkei; Nisei

Japanese American Citizens League (JACL), 93–96, 107–10, 112–13; and Americanization, 98–99; and interracial alliances, 100–101

Paonessa, Alfred E., 100–101
Park, Robert, 90n.48
Park, You-me, 158, 162–63
Parker, James, 179
*Passing of the Great Race, The*, 49
Passion, concept of, 171–72, 175, 180, 187.
    *See also* González, Elián, case of
Patterson, Orlando, 4
Pearl Harbor, 9, 18n.20, 97
Penelas, Alex, 186, 205n.46
People of color, 127, 135, 139, 147, 152,
    177, 180, 189, 195; and U.S. imperialism,
    195
People's Republic of China (PRC), 173,
    179, 188, 191, 192, 194. *See also* China
*People v. Hall*, 8, 9
Peruvians, 158, 160
Phelan, James, 42, 50
*Philippine Islands and Their People*, 32
Philippines, 6, 10, 19n.33; colonization of,
    6, 10, 23–25; national liberation struggle
    in, 6, 7; and racialization, 23, 30–35; as
    racial terra incognita, 31; as "tribal," 31,
    38n.25. *See also* Filipinos
Philology, 8
Piedra, José, 152, 168n.7
*Plessy v. Ferguson*, 103, 107–10
Pomeroy, John L., 47, 50–54, 58
*Population Changes among the Northern Plains
    Indians*, 67
Postmodernity, 176
Public health, and racial discourse, 40–41,
    42, 44–58 passim
Public-private split, 175, 185
Puerto Rican Legal Defense and Education
    Fund, 123
Puerto Ricans, 158, 177; as "docile," 28; as
    enemy, 27; ethnography of, 29, 36–37; as
    feminized, 29–30; and labor, 28, 37; as
    "Moorish," 29; and racialization, 26–30;
    as racially mixed, 27, 29, 36; as sexually
    promiscuous, 29–30; as a social problem,
    24. *See also* Puerto Rico
Puerto Rico, 6, 7, 10, 124; and racializa-
    tion, 23
*Puerto Rico: Its Conditions and Possibilities*, 28

Quevedo, Eduardo, 80

Race, 15, 64, 72, 122, 134, 179, 192; al-
    liances, 167; and anthropometry, 63; and
    Chicanos, 83; as gendered, 41; immu-
    tability, 79; and redistricting, 120, 127–
    28, 131, 133, 138–39; and segregation,
    106, 109, 111; and voting patterns, 136–
    37. *See also* Asian, as racial category;
    Blackness; Latino, as racial category; Ra-
    cial formation; Racialization; Whiteness
*Race, Police, and the Making of a Political Iden-
    tity*, 75
*Racial Castration*, 148
Racial formation, 10–17
Racial hierarchy, 41–42, 49, 58, 139, 180
Racialization, 1–17, 41, 45; as gendering,
    37, 41
Racial minorities, 137, 138, 159–60; and
    "American"-ness, 2–3, 16–17, 155–57,
    164, 168
Racial ordering, concept of, 41
Racial profiling, 179, 180, 189, 191, 195
Raciology, 8–9
Racism, 1–17; racial discourse, 147, 157–
    58; and racial hierarchy, 41–42, 58; and
    racial minorities, 159–60. *See also* White
    supremacy
Radio Berlin, 9
Radio Tokyo, 9
Ramírez, Lorenzo, 102
Reagan administration, 181
Redistricting, 120–31, 136–39; and racial
    discrimination, 132–35
Refugee (immigration status), 199n.10
Reid, Whitelaw, 27, 36
Reno, Janet, 205n.46
*Reports of the Immigration Commission*, 67
Republicanism, 10
Republican Party, 125, 129, 185, 187, 192,
    200n.17
Richter, John, 192–93
*Rising Tide of Color, The*, 48
Rockefeller, Nelson, 84
Rodríguez, Raymond, 12
Romero, Gloria, 131

University of California, Berkeley, 62–63, 66, 68, 194
University of California, Los Angeles, 178
University of Southern California, 42, 81
Urciuoli, Bonnie, 24
U.S. Army, 150–51
U.S. imperialism. *See* Imperialism (U.S.)
U.S. nationalism. *See* Nationalism (U.S.)
*Utah Nippo*, 98

Vietnam, 7, 19n.33, 152. *See also* Southeast Asia
*Village Voice*, 125
Visayans, 33. *See also* Filipinos
Voting Rights Act (1965), 120, 121, 127, 128

Wake Island, 6
Wald, Gayle, 158, 162–163
Wall Street, 122
Wang, Jessica, 207n.70
Wang, Ling-Chi, 194
War on Terrorism, 16
Warren, Earl, 104
Washington Heights (New York), 155
*Washington Post*, 170, 174
Watergate scandal, 181
Waxman, Al S., 82–83
Wen Ho Lee Defense Fund, 190. *See also* Lee, Wen Ho
West Whittier (Los Angeles), 85
White nationalism, 1, 5, 18n.13. *See also* Nationalism (U.S.)
Whiteness, 1–5, 15–17, 33, 104, 164–67; and Elián González case, 186; and heterosexual masculinization, 167; legal definitions of, 116–17n.36; and manliness,

26; and U.S. nationalism, 1, 5, 14, 37. *See also* Blackness; White supremacy
Whites, 154–55, 164–67; as "American," 159, 163; as racial group, 137; and redistricting, 126, 130, 131; as voters, 132–33, 136, 138. *See also* Whiteness
White supremacy, 1–17, 36–37, 114, 148
Williams, William Appelman, 2
Wilson, Emmet, 96
Winant, Howard, 41
Wirin, A. L., 98, 107–8, 112–13
Wissler, Clark, 66, 67, 69
Wong, Charles A., 65–74, 86
Woofter, T. J., Jr., 78
Worcester, Dean C., 31–33
*Worcester v. Georgia*, 18n.11
Works Progress Administration (WPA), 66, 71, 86
World War II, 72, 76, 94, 97, 99, 100, 133, 179, 194
Wu, Frank H. , 206n.57

Xenophilia, 13
Xenophobia, 13, 24–25, 199n.9. *See also* Nativism

Yamanaka, Lois-Ann, 206n.58
Yellow, as racial category, 5, 72. *See also* Yellow Peril, discourse of
Yellow Peril, discourse of, 41, 45–46, 47, 52, 54
Yin, Xiao-huang, 194
Yung, Judy, 65

Žižek, Slavoj, 184, 186, 203n.33, 204n.39, 204n.42
Zoot suit riots, 19n.31, 99

Nicholas De Genova is an assistant professor of anthropology and Latino studies at Columbia University.

Library of Congress Cataloging-in-Publication Data
Racial transformations : Latinos and Asians remaking the United States / edited by Nicholas De Genova.
p. cm.
Includes bibliographical references and index.
ISBN 0-8223-3704-5 (cloth : alk. paper)
ISBN 0-8223-3716-9 (pbk. : alk. paper)
1. Hispanic Americans—Politics and government. 2. Asian Americans—Politics and government. 3. Hispanic Americans—Social conditions. 4. Asian Americans—Social conditions. 5. United States—Race relations.
I. De Genova, Nicholas.
E184.S75R33 2006
32.17309—dc22      2005028239